TOMB RAIDER™

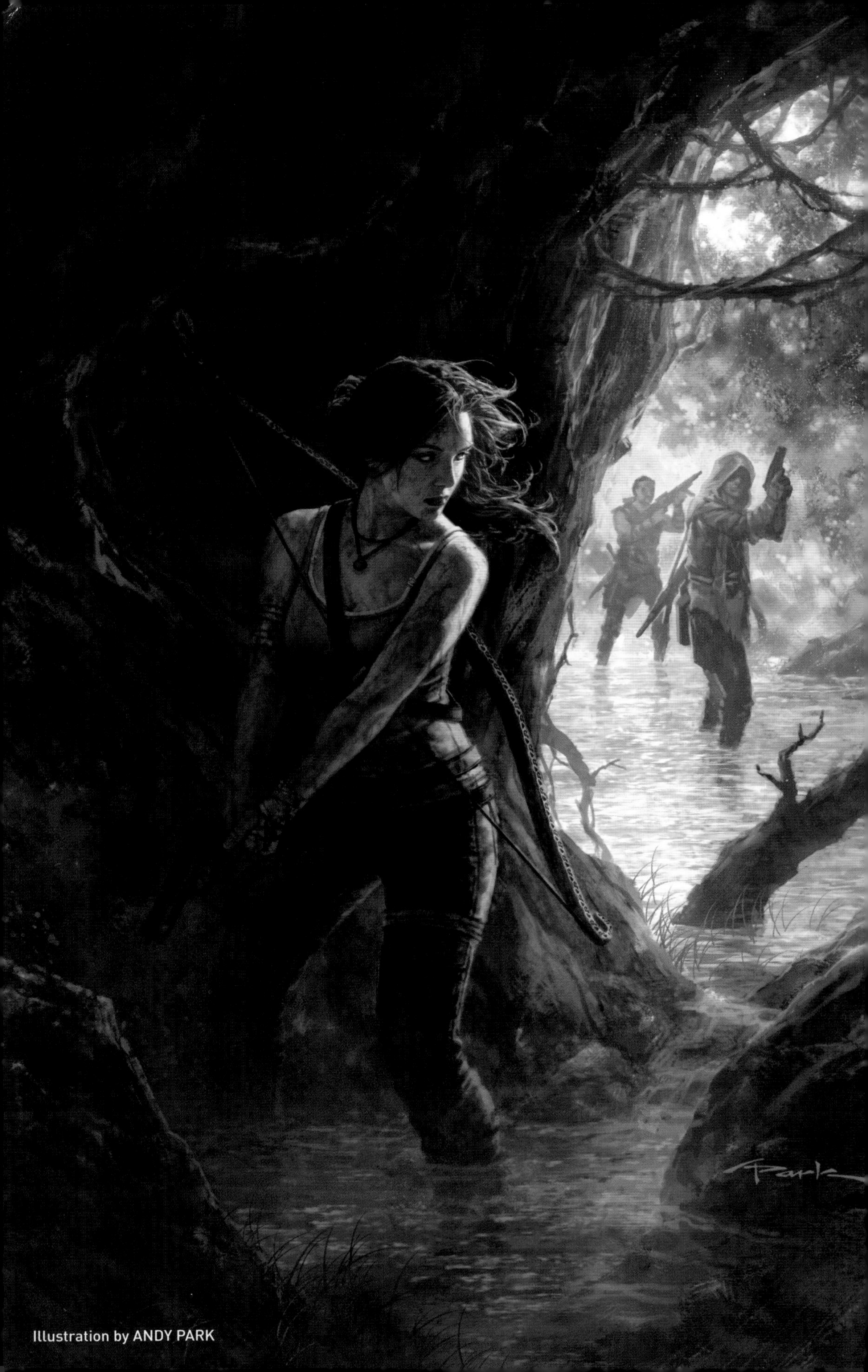

Illustration by ANDY PARK

TOMB RAIDER™

SEASON OF THE WITCH

VOLUME 1

SCRIPT
GAIL SIMONE

PENCILS
NICOLÁS DANIEL SELMA

INKS
JUAN GEDEON

COLORS
MICHAEL ATIYEH

LETTERING
MICHAEL HEISLER

FRONT COVER ART
DAN DOS SANTOS

DARK HORSE BOOKS

PUBLISHER
MIKE RICHARDSON

COLLECTION DESIGNER
SANDY TANAKA

ASSISTANT EDITORS
ROXY POLK
AARON WALKER

EDITOR
DAVE MARSHALL

Special thanks to Crystal Dynamics and Square Enix, including:
Rich Briggs, Brian Horton, and Noah Hughes.

TOMB RAIDER VOLUME 1: SEASON OF THE WITCH

This volume collects issues #1–#6 of the Dark Horse comic-book series *Tomb Raider*.

Published by
Dark Horse Books
A division of
Dark Horse Comics, Inc.
10956 SE Main Street
Milwaukie, OR 97222

DarkHorse.com
TombRaider.com

First trade paperback edition: November 2014
ISBN 978-1-61655-491-0

1 3 5 7 9 10 8 6 4 2
Printed in China

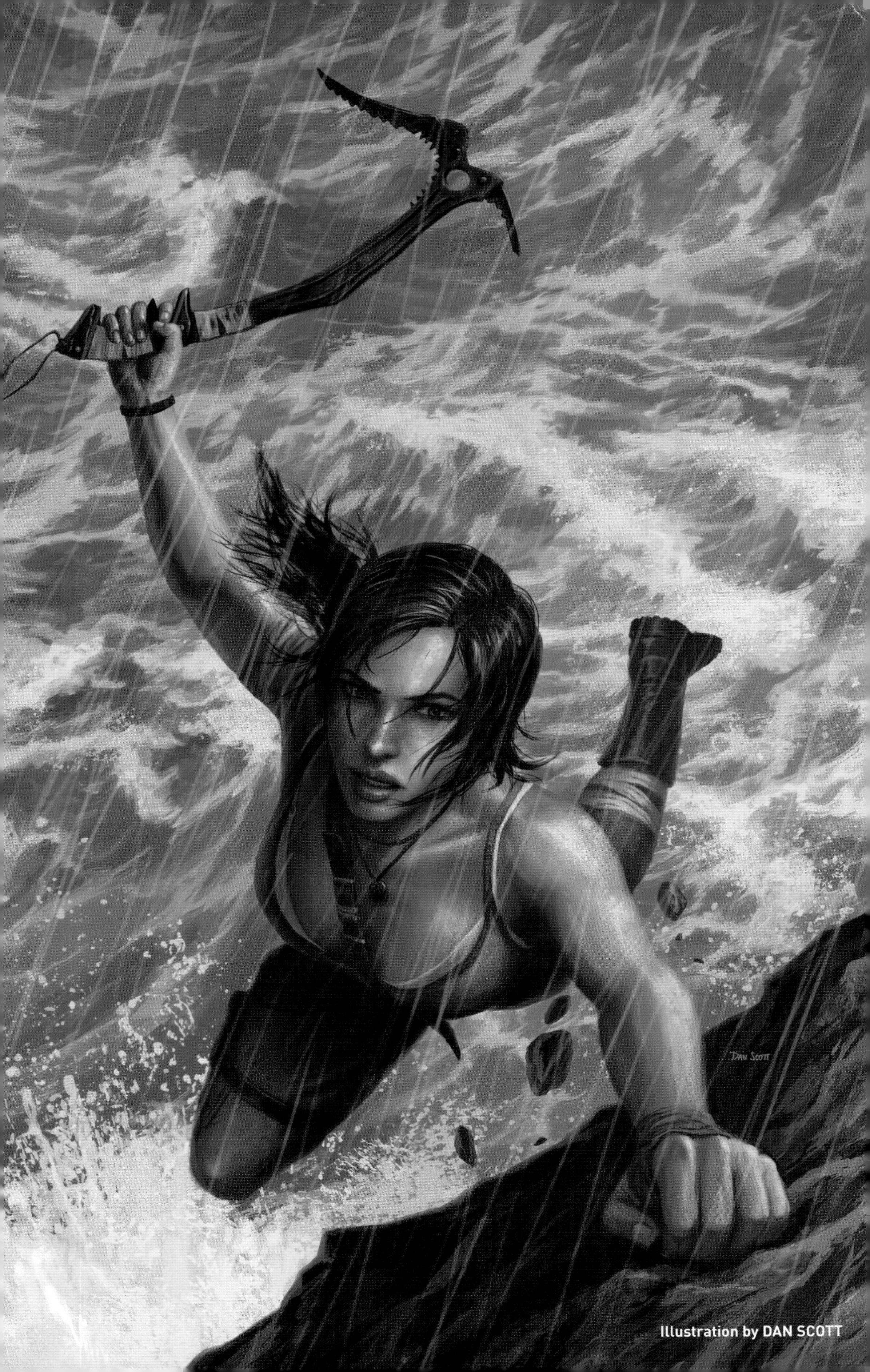
DAN SCOTT

Illustration by DAN SCOTT

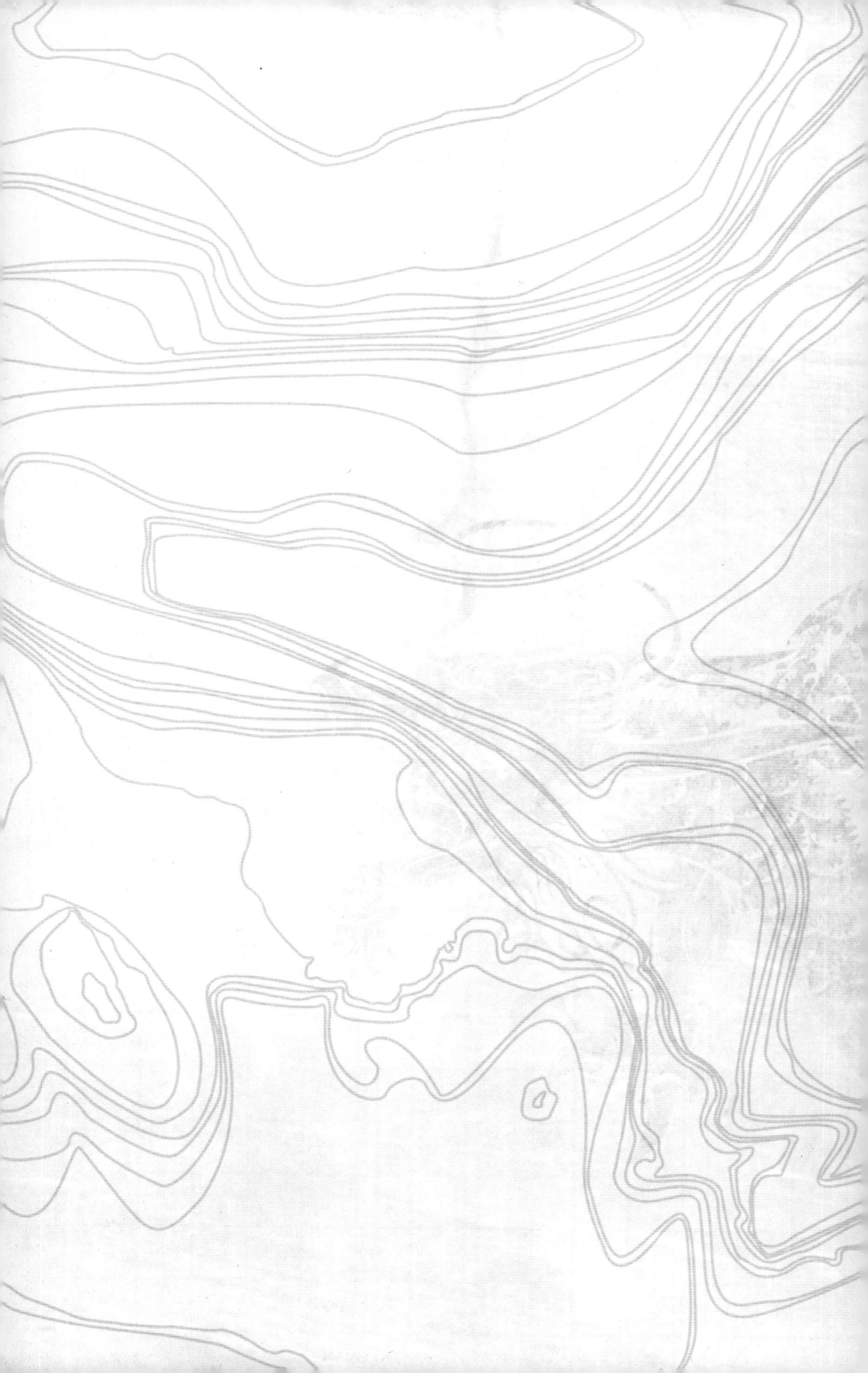

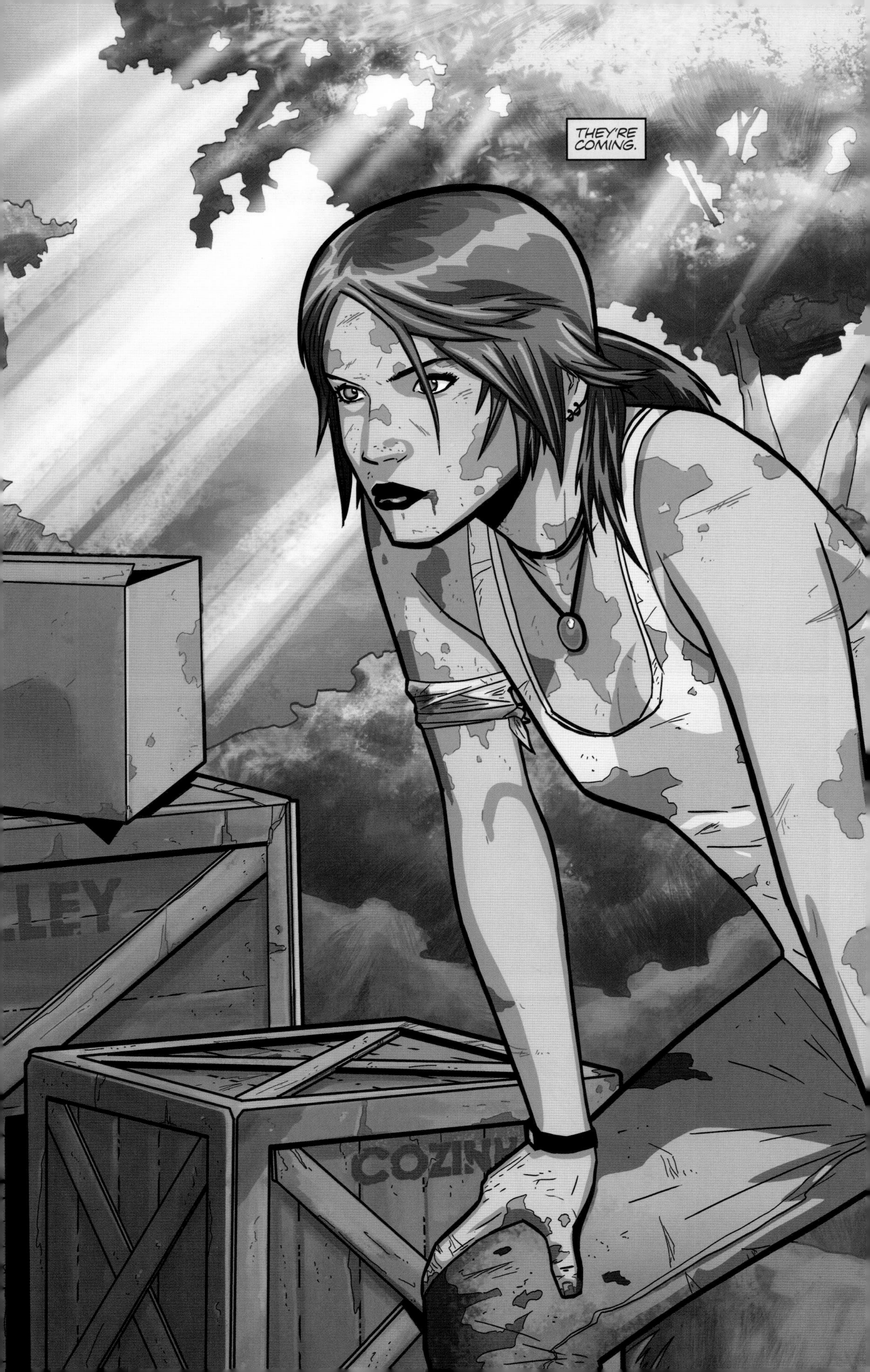
THEY'RE COMING.

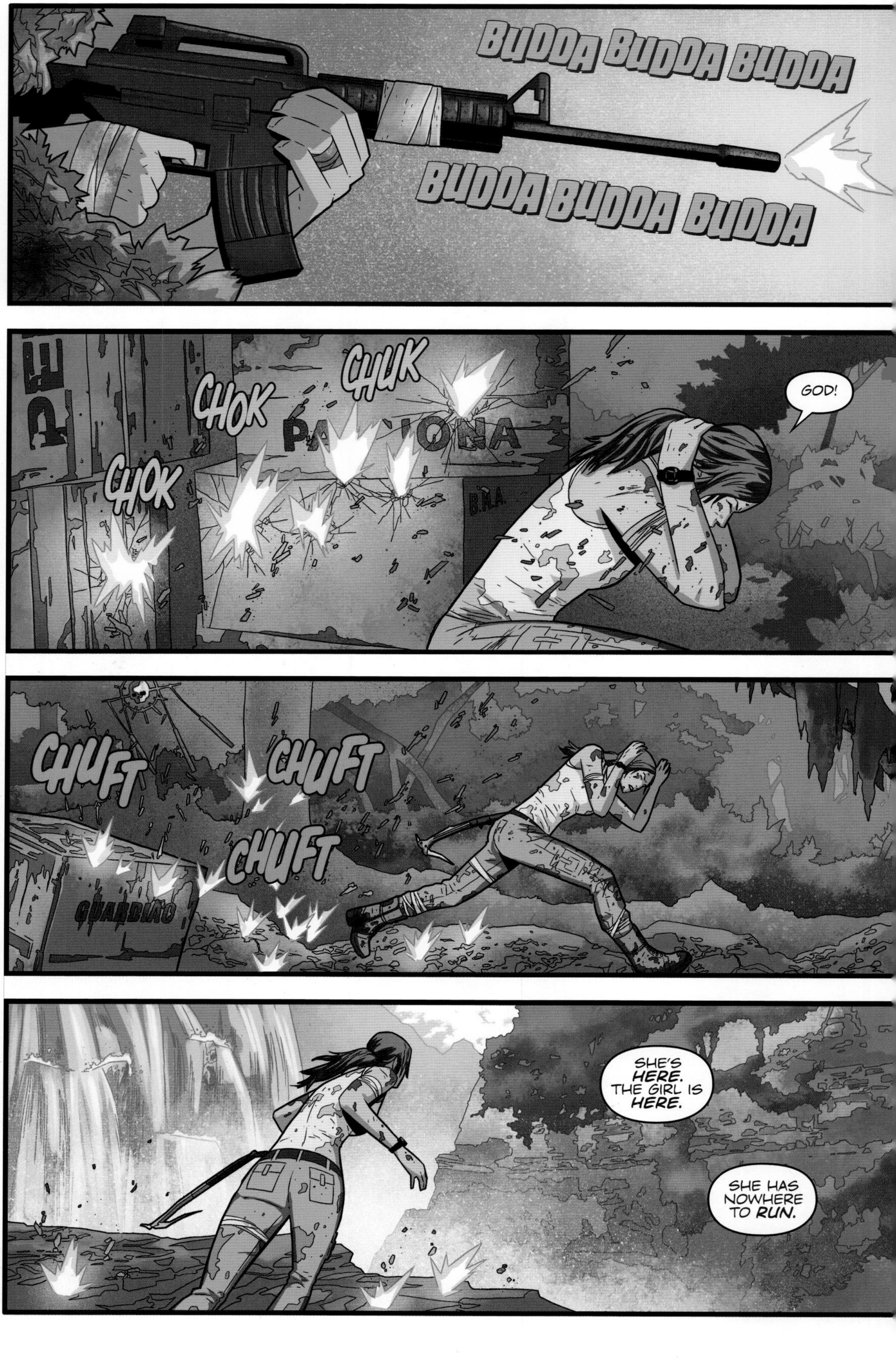
BUDDA BUDDA BUDDA
BUDDA BUDDA BUDDA
CHOK
CHUK
CHOK
GOD!
CHUFT
CHUFT
CHUFT
SHE'S HERE. THE GIRL IS HERE.
SHE HAS NOWHERE TO RUN.

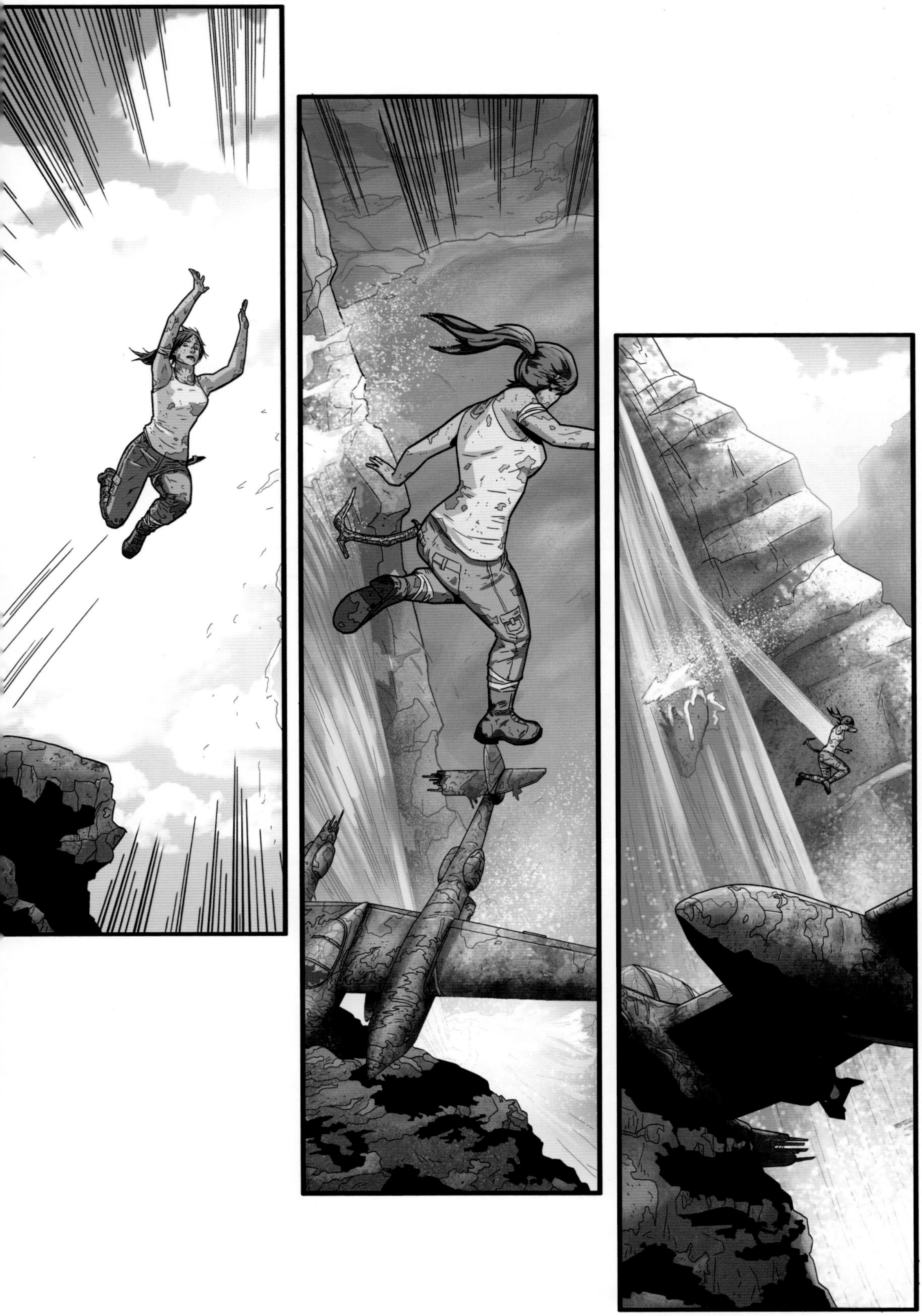

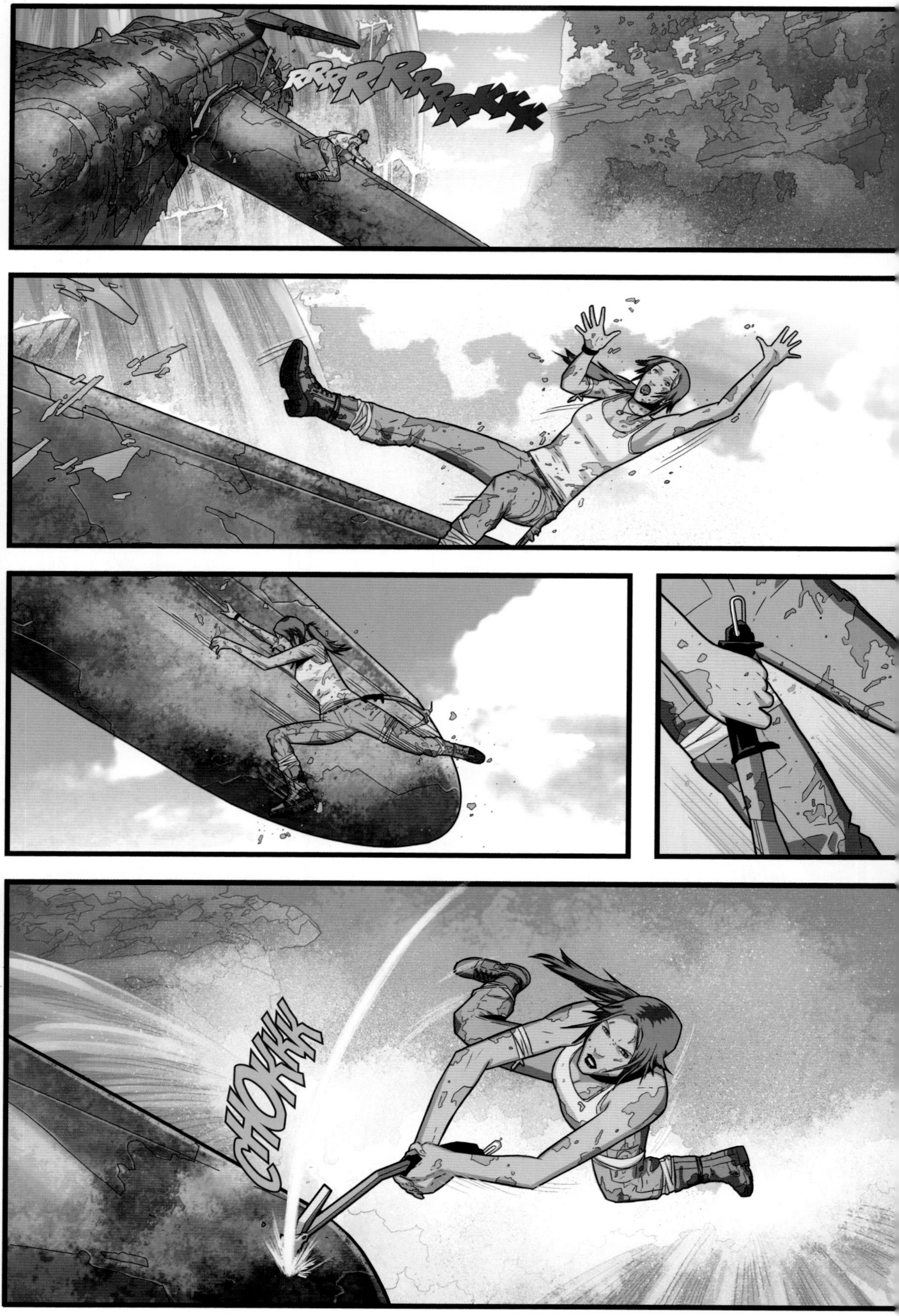
RRRRRRRRRKKK
CHOKKK

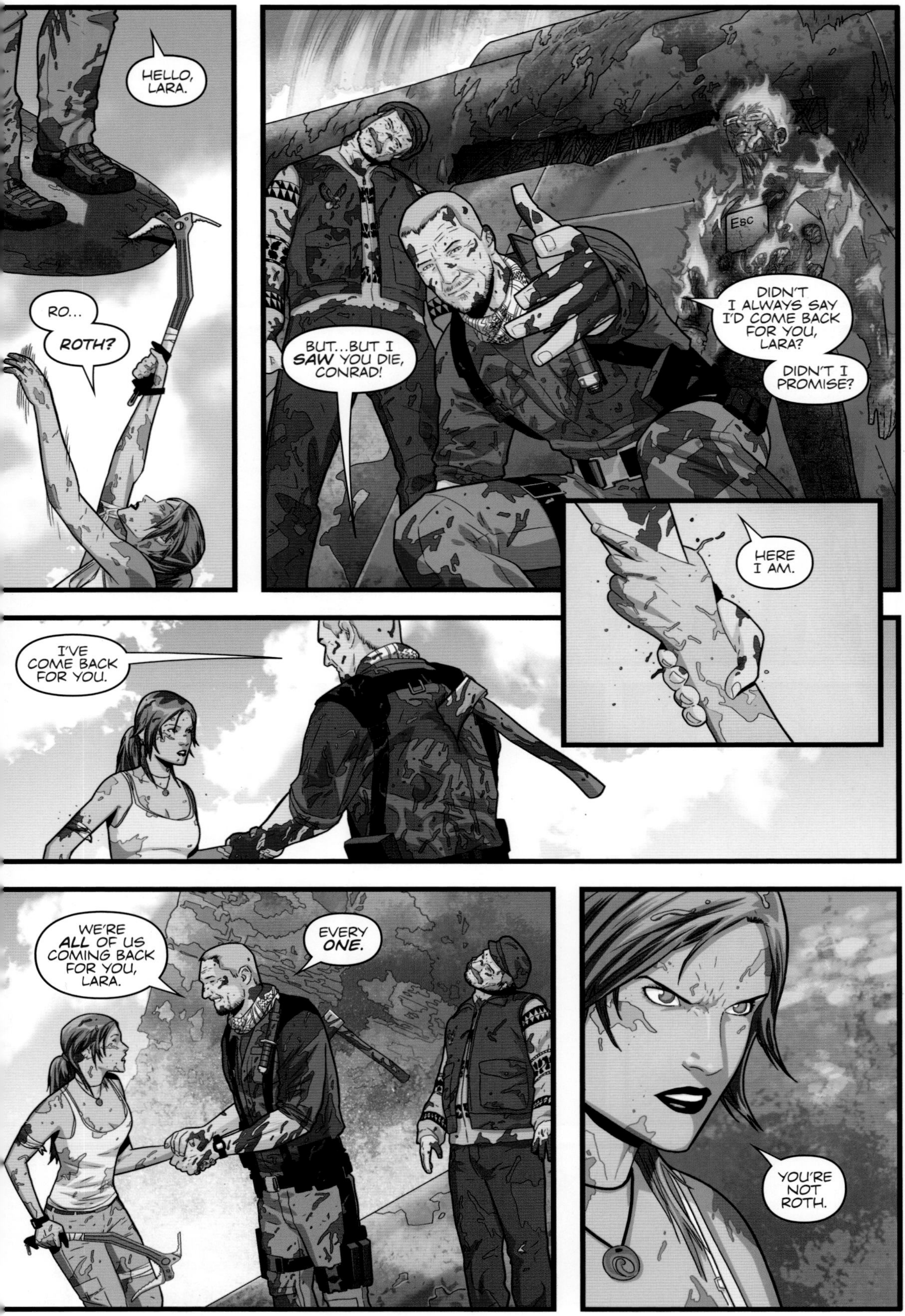
HELLO, LARA.
RO... ROTH?
BUT...BUT I SAW YOU DIE, CONRAD!
DIDN'T I ALWAYS SAY I'D COME BACK FOR YOU, LARA?
DIDN'T I PROMISE?
Esc
HERE I AM.
I'VE COME BACK FOR YOU.
WE'RE ALL OF US COMING BACK FOR YOU, LARA.
EVERY ONE.
YOU'RE NOT ROTH.

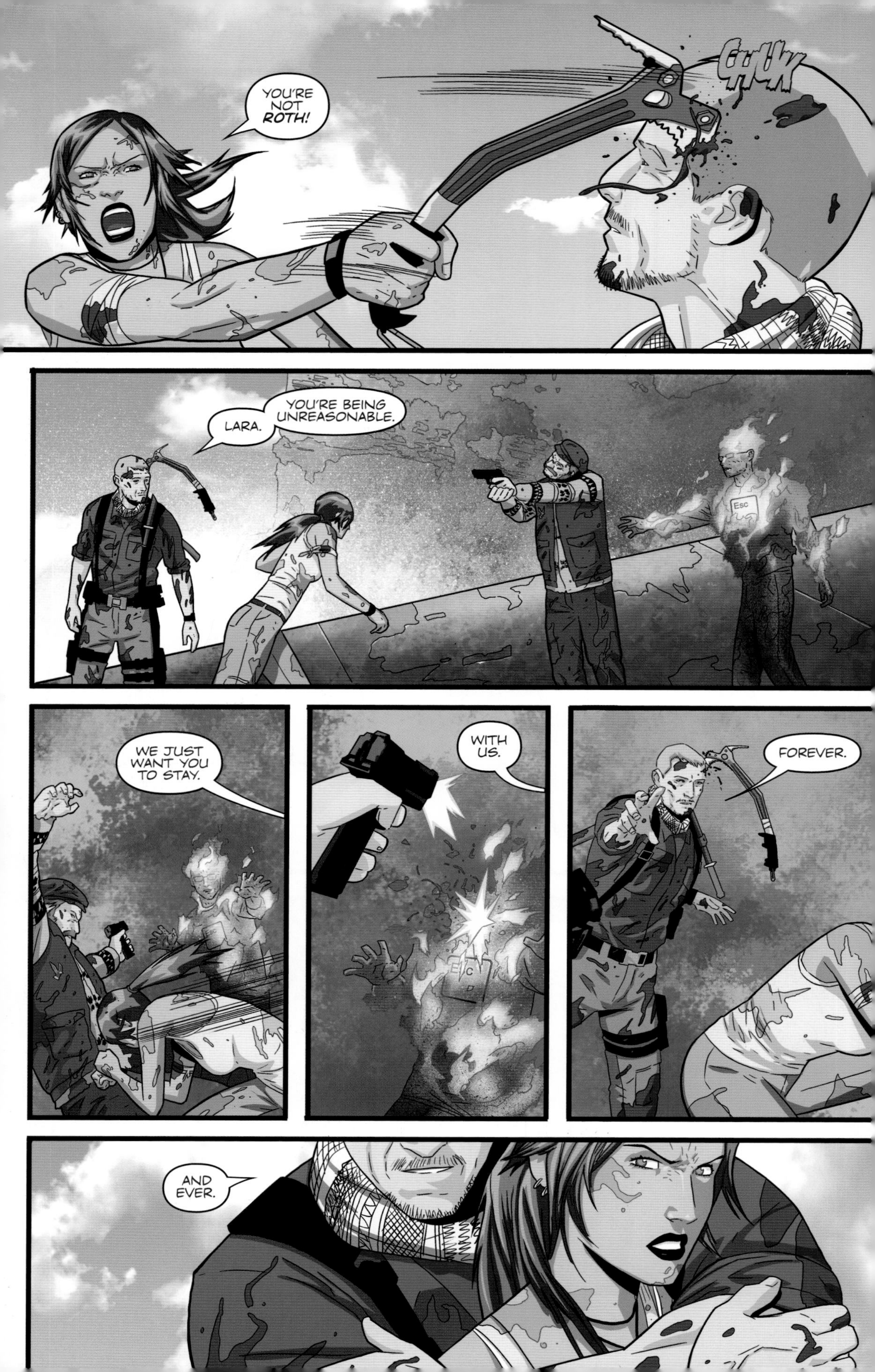
YOU'RE NOT ROTH!
CHUK
LARA.
YOU'RE BEING UNREASONABLE.
Esc
WE JUST WANT YOU TO STAY.
WITH US.
FOREVER.
AND EVER.

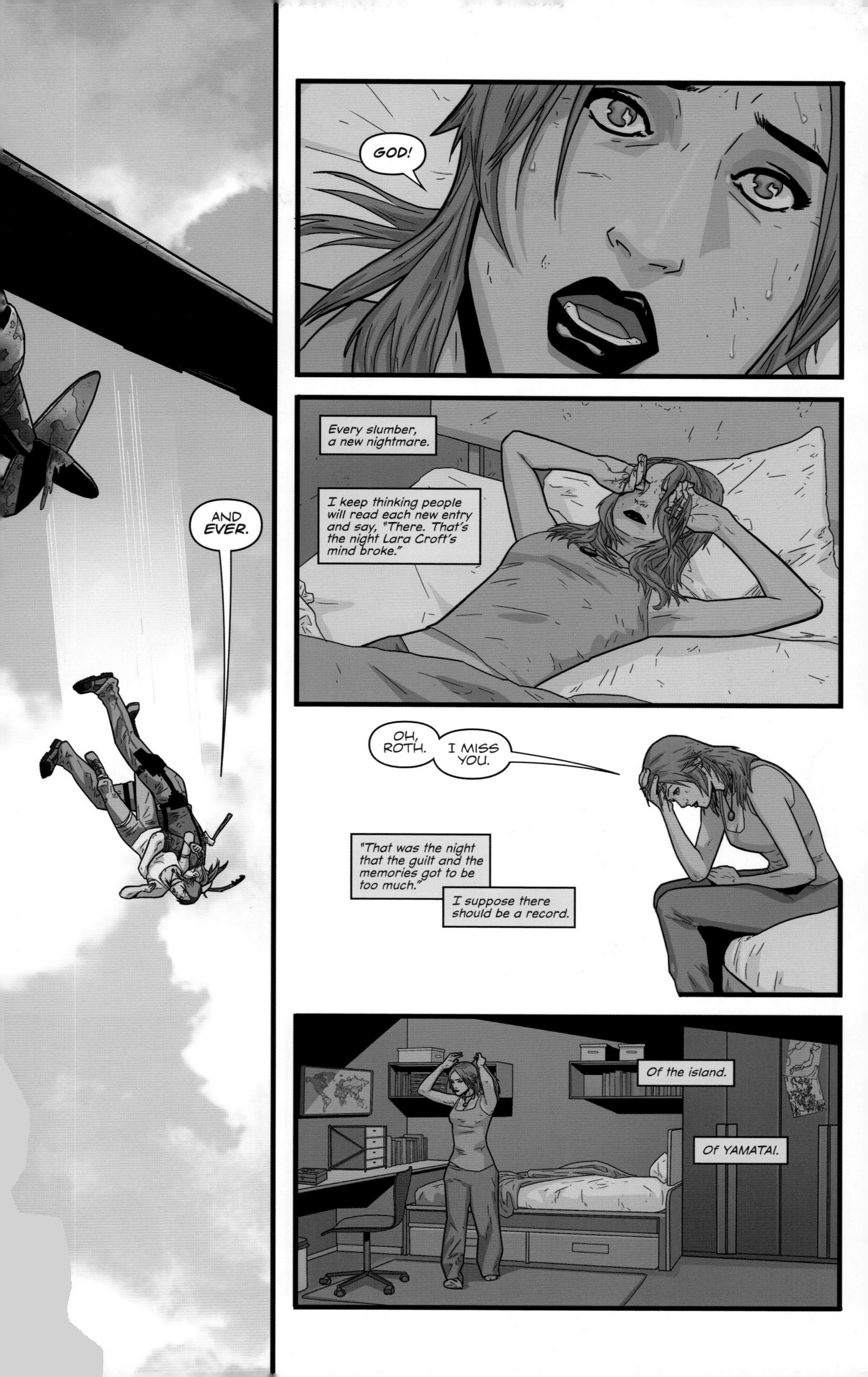
AND EVER.
GOD!
Every slumber, a new nightmare.
I keep thinking people will read each new entry and say, "There. That's the night Lara Croft's mind broke."
OH, ROTH.
I MISS YOU.
"That was the night that the guilt and the memories got to be too much."
I suppose there should be a record.
Of the island.
Of YAMATAI.

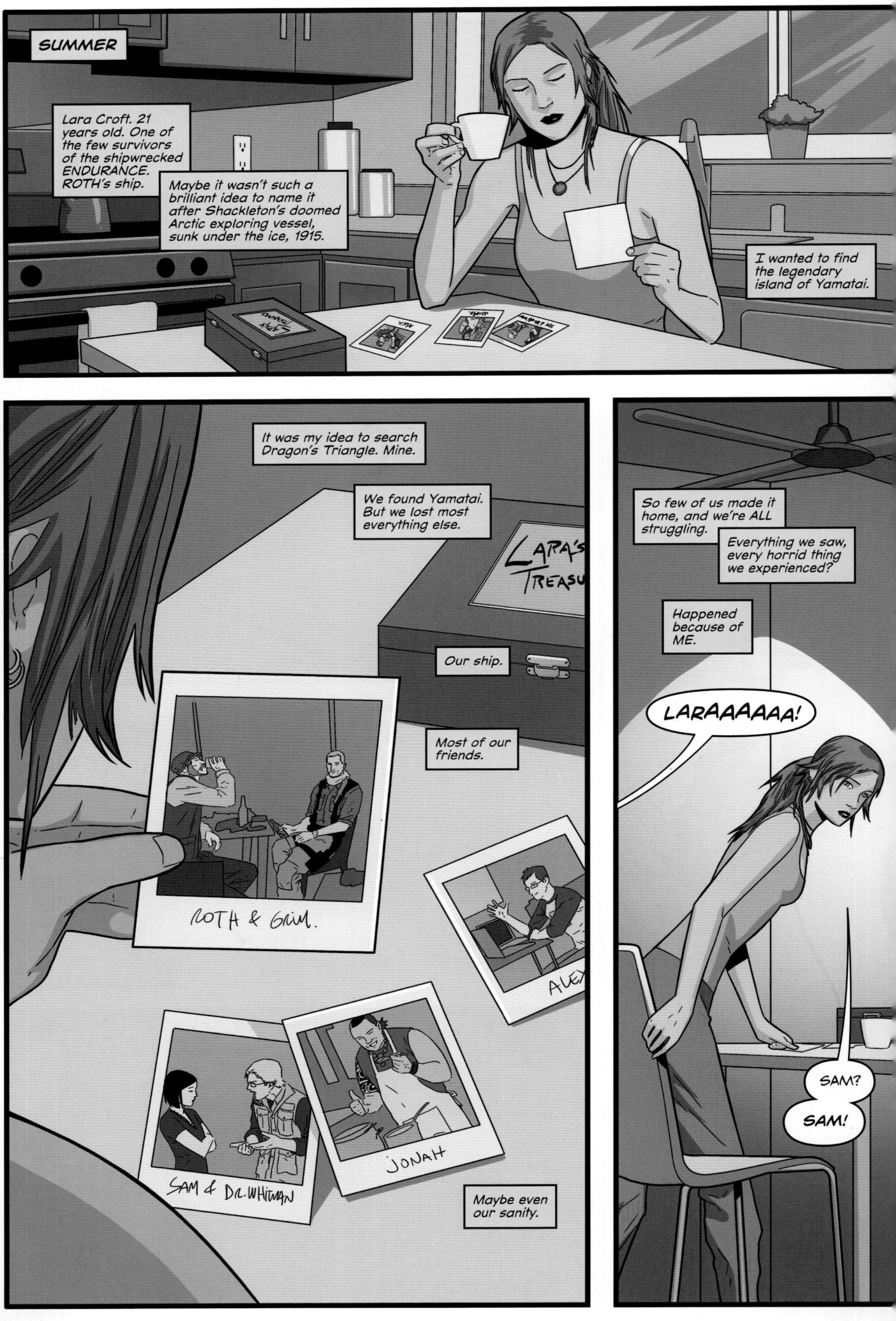
SUMMER
Lara Croft. 21 years old. One of the few survivors of the shipwrecked ENDURANCE. ROTH's ship.
Maybe it wasn't such a brilliant idea to name it after Shackleton's doomed Arctic exploring vessel, sunk under the ice, 1915.
I wanted to find the legendary island of Yamatai.
It was my idea to search Dragon's Triangle. Mine.
We found Yamatai. But we lost most everything else.
LARA'S
TREASU
Our ship.
ROTH & GRIM.
Most of our friends.
ALEX
SAM & DR. WHITMAN
JONAH
Maybe even our sanity.
So few of us made it home, and we're ALL struggling.
Everything we saw, every horrid thing we experienced?
Happened because of ME.
LARAAAAAA!
SAM?
SAM!

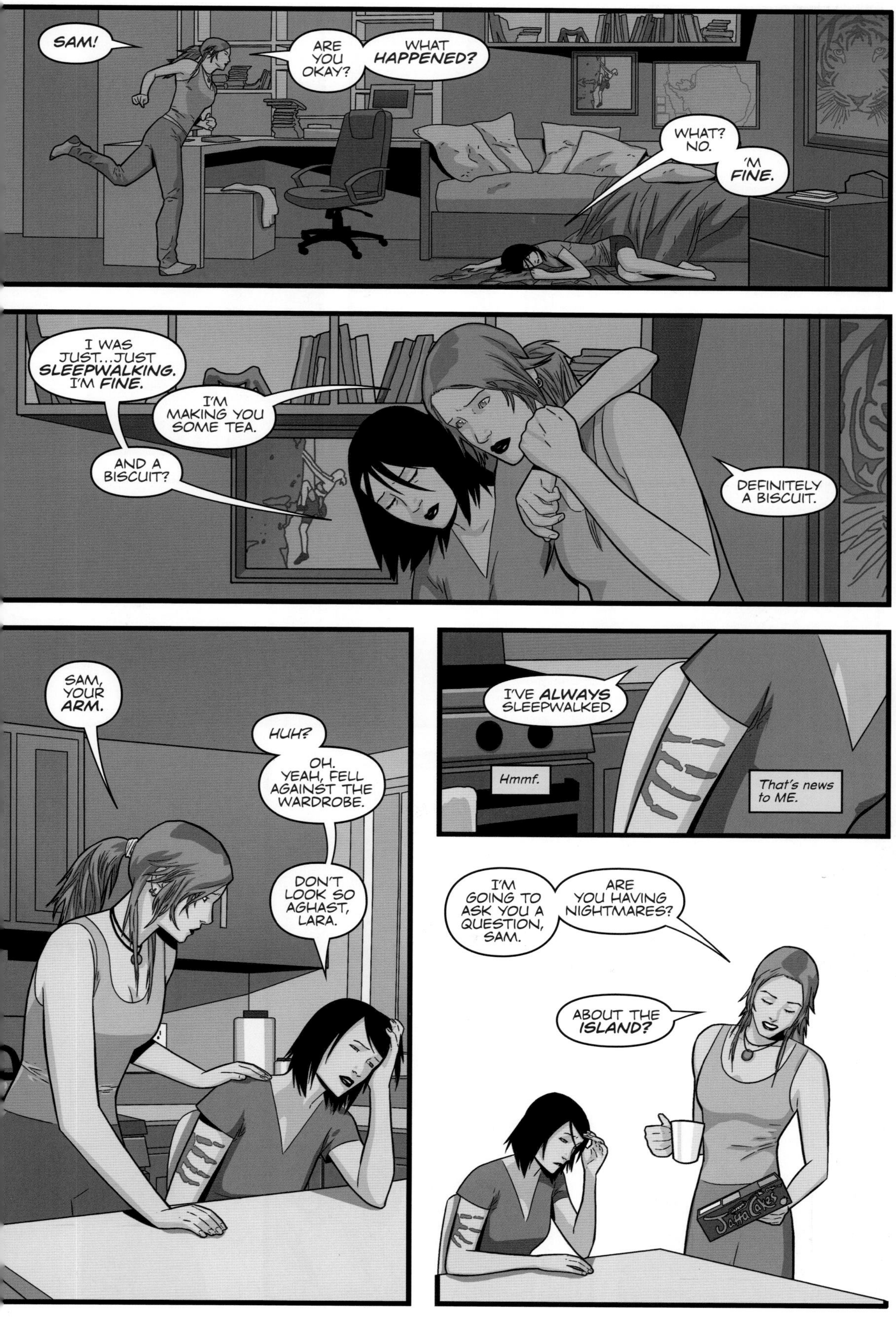
SAM!
ARE YOU OKAY?
WHAT HAPPENED?
WHAT? NO.
'M FINE.
I WAS JUST...JUST SLEEPWALKING. I'M FINE.
I'M MAKING YOU SOME TEA.
AND A BISCUIT?
DEFINITELY A BISCUIT.
SAM, YOUR ARM.
HUH?
OH. YEAH, FELL AGAINST THE WARDROBE.
DON'T LOOK SO AGHAST, LARA.
I'VE ALWAYS SLEEPWALKED.
Hmmf.
That's news to ME.
I'M GOING TO ASK YOU A QUESTION, SAM.
ARE YOU HAVING NIGHTMARES?
ABOUT THE ISLAND?
Jaffa Cakes

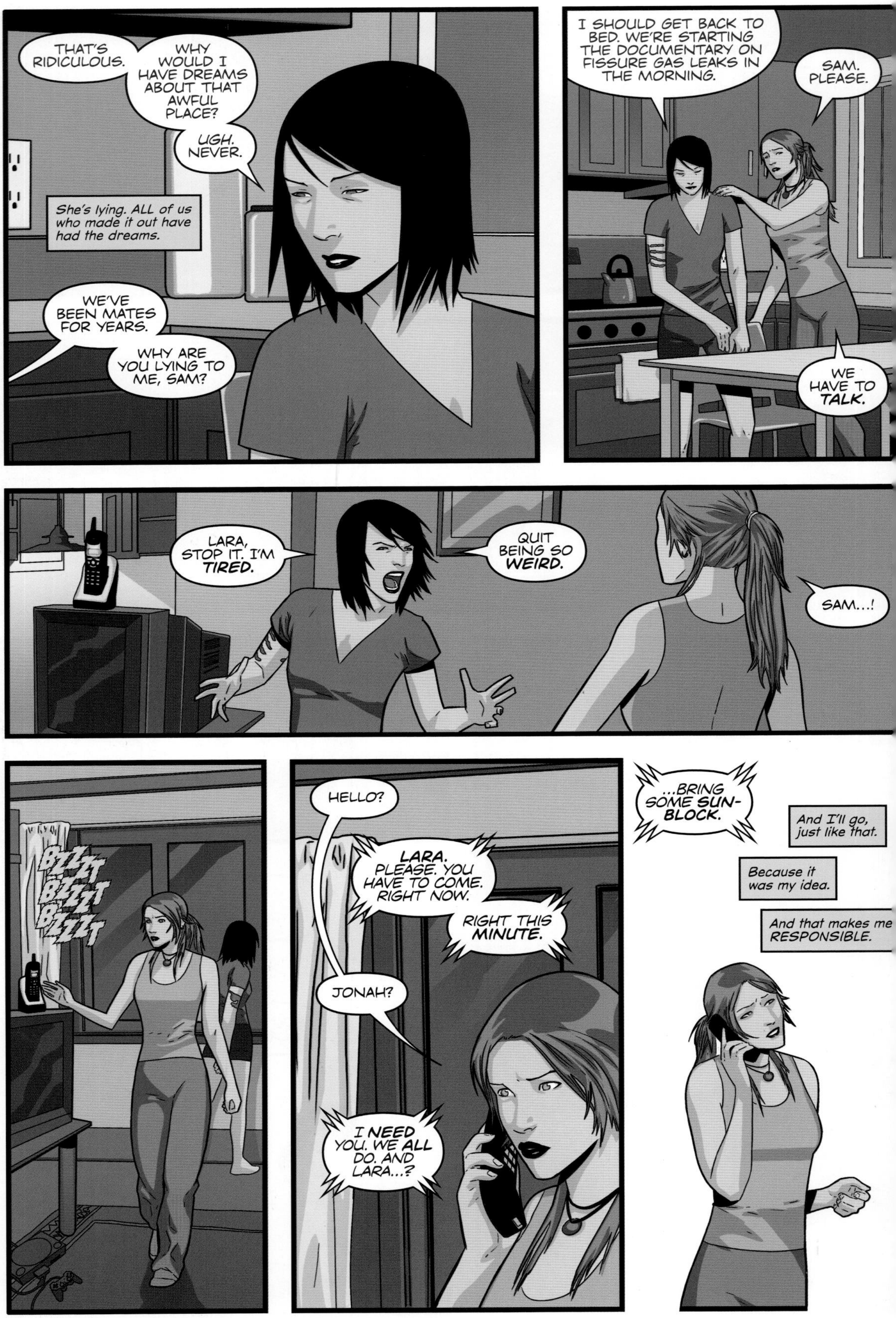

THAT'S RIDICULOUS.
WHY WOULD I HAVE DREAMS ABOUT THAT AWFUL PLACE?
UGH. NEVER.
She's lying. ALL of us who made it out have had the dreams.
WE'VE BEEN MATES FOR YEARS.
WHY ARE YOU LYING TO ME, SAM?
I SHOULD GET BACK TO BED. WE'RE STARTING THE DOCUMENTARY ON FISSURE GAS LEAKS IN THE MORNING.
SAM. PLEASE.
WE HAVE TO **TALK.**
LARA, STOP IT. I'M **TIRED.**
QUIT BEING SO **WEIRD.**
SAM...!
BZZZT BZZZT BZZZT
HELLO?
LARA. PLEASE. YOU HAVE TO COME. RIGHT NOW.
RIGHT THIS **MINUTE.**
JONAH?
I **NEED** YOU. WE **ALL** DO. AND LARA...?
...BRING SOME **SUN-BLOCK.**
And I'll go, just like that.
Because it was my idea.
And that makes me RESPONSIBLE.

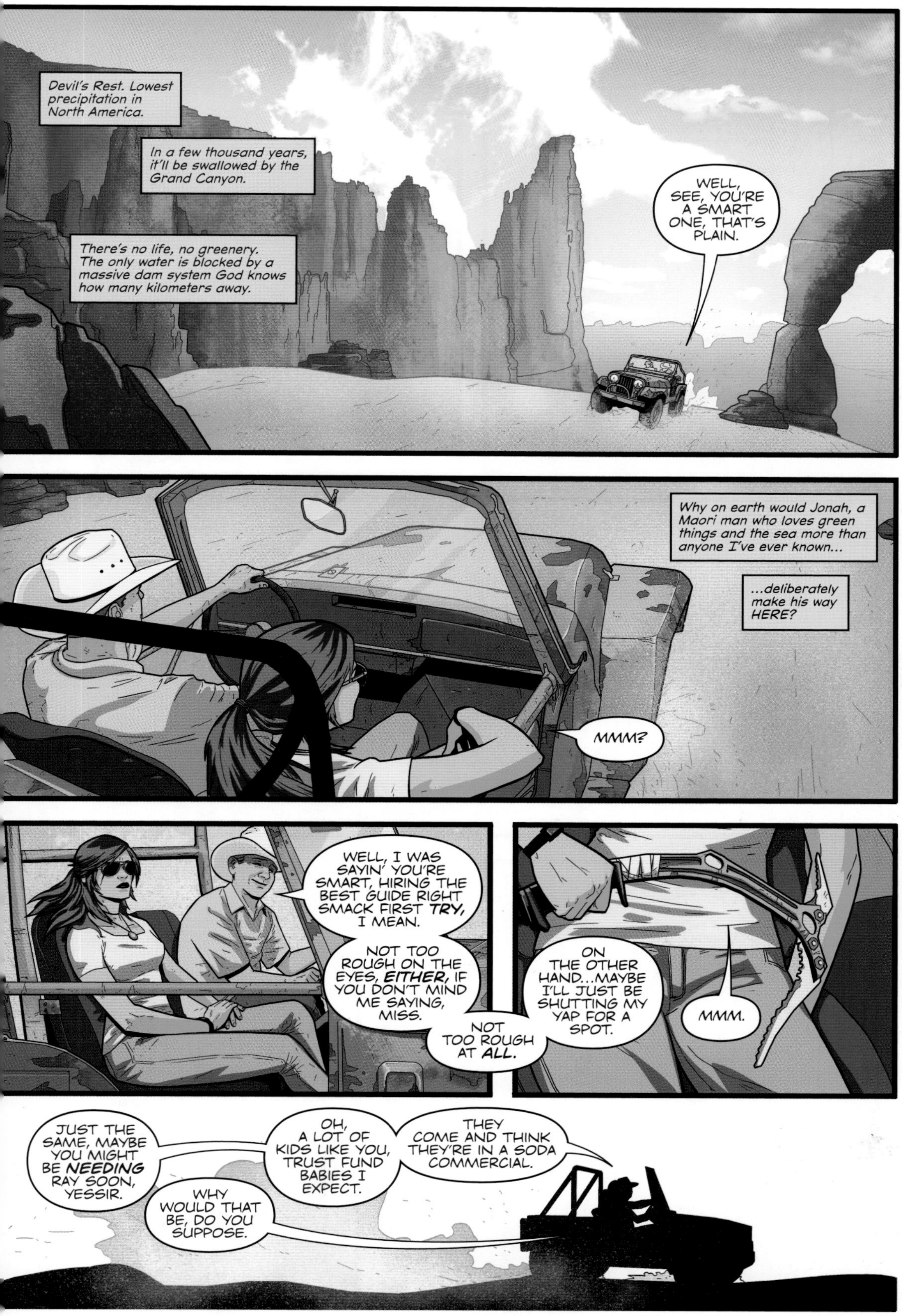

Devil's Rest. Lowest precipitation in North America.
In a few thousand years, it'll be swallowed by the Grand Canyon.
There's no life, no greenery. The only water is blocked by a massive dam system God knows how many kilometers away.
WELL, SEE, YOU'RE A SMART ONE, THAT'S PLAIN.
Why on earth would Jonah, a Maori man who loves green things and the sea more than anyone I've ever known...
...deliberately make his way HERE?
MMM?
WELL, I WAS SAYIN' YOU'RE SMART, HIRING THE BEST GUIDE RIGHT SMACK FIRST TRY, I MEAN.
NOT TOO ROUGH ON THE EYES, EITHER, IF YOU DON'T MIND ME SAYING, MISS.
NOT TOO ROUGH AT ALL.
ON THE OTHER HAND...MAYBE I'LL JUST BE SHUTTING MY YAP FOR A SPOT.
MMM.
THEY COME AND THINK THEY'RE IN A SODA COMMERCIAL.
OH, A LOT OF KIDS LIKE YOU, TRUST FUND BABIES I EXPECT.
JUST THE SAME, MAYBE YOU MIGHT BE NEEDING RAY SOON, YESSIR.
WHY WOULD THAT BE, DO YOU SUPPOSE.

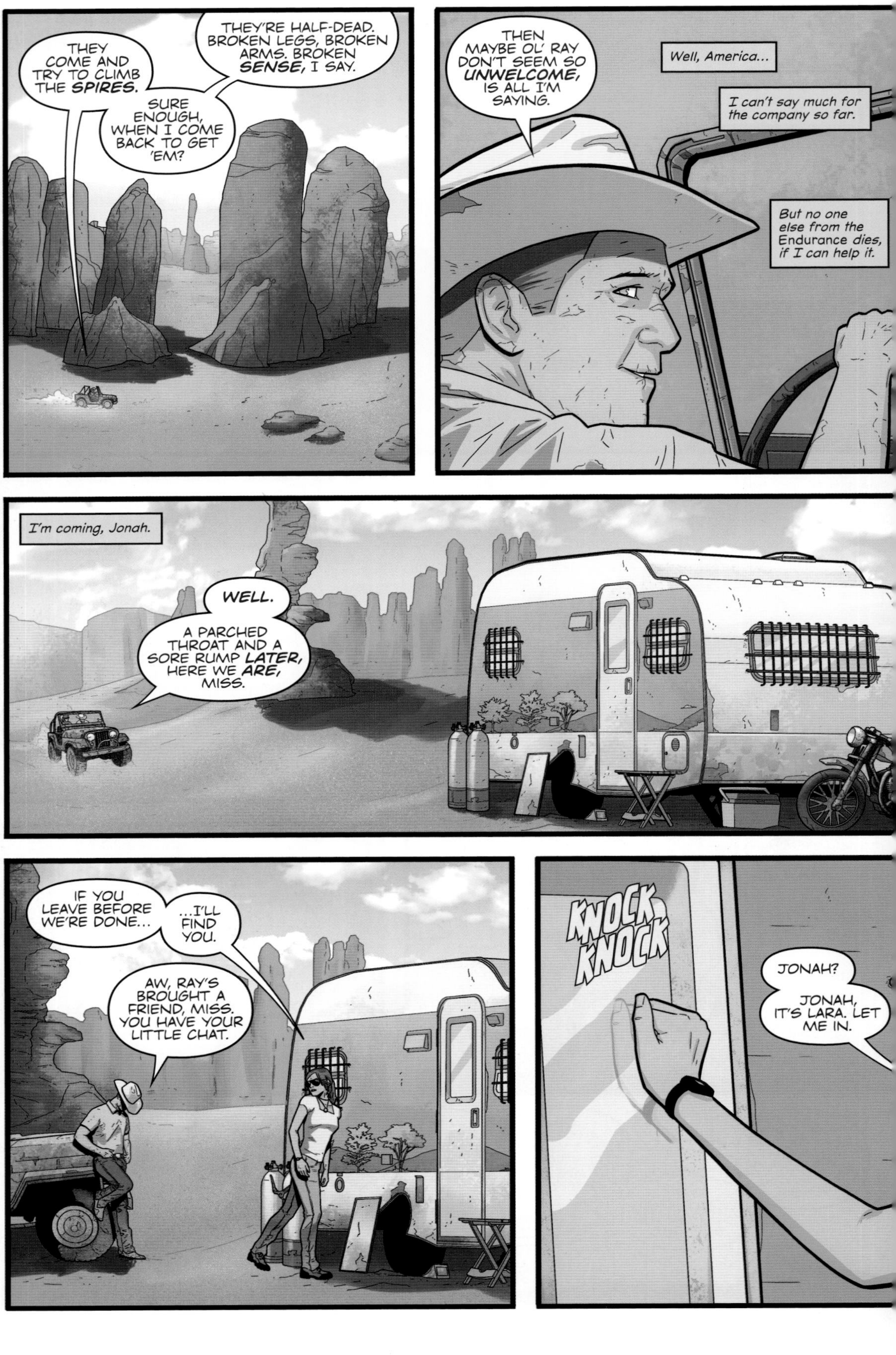
THEY COME AND TRY TO CLIMB THE SPIRES.
THEY'RE HALF-DEAD. BROKEN LEGS, BROKEN ARMS. BROKEN SENSE, I SAY.
SURE ENOUGH, WHEN I COME BACK TO GET 'EM?
THEN MAYBE OL' RAY DON'T SEEM SO UNWELCOME, IS ALL I'M SAYING.
Well, America...
I can't say much for the company so far.
But no one else from the Endurance dies, if I can help it.
I'm coming, Jonah.
WELL.
A PARCHED THROAT AND A SORE RUMP LATER, HERE WE ARE, MISS.
IF YOU LEAVE BEFORE WE'RE DONE...
...I'LL FIND YOU.
AW, RAY'S BROUGHT A FRIEND, MISS. YOU HAVE YOUR LITTLE CHAT.
KNOCK KNOCK
JONAH?
JONAH, IT'S LARA. LET ME IN.

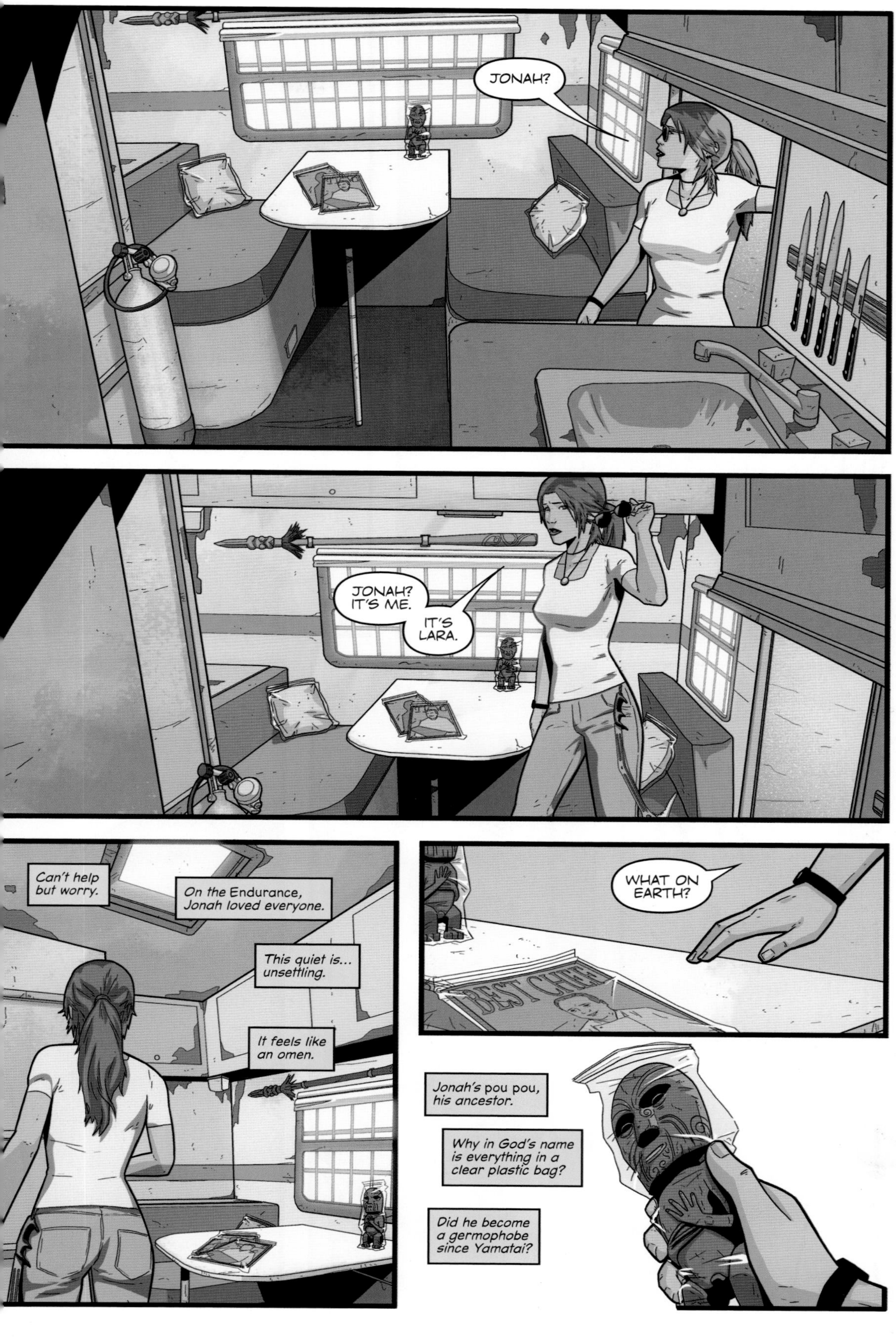
JONAH?
JONAH? IT'S ME.
IT'S LARA.
Can't help but worry.
On the Endurance, Jonah loved everyone.
This quiet is... unsettling.
It feels like an omen.
WHAT ON EARTH?
BEST CHEF
Jonah's pou pou, his ancestor.
Why in God's name is everything in a clear plastic bag?
Did he become a germophobe since Yamatai?

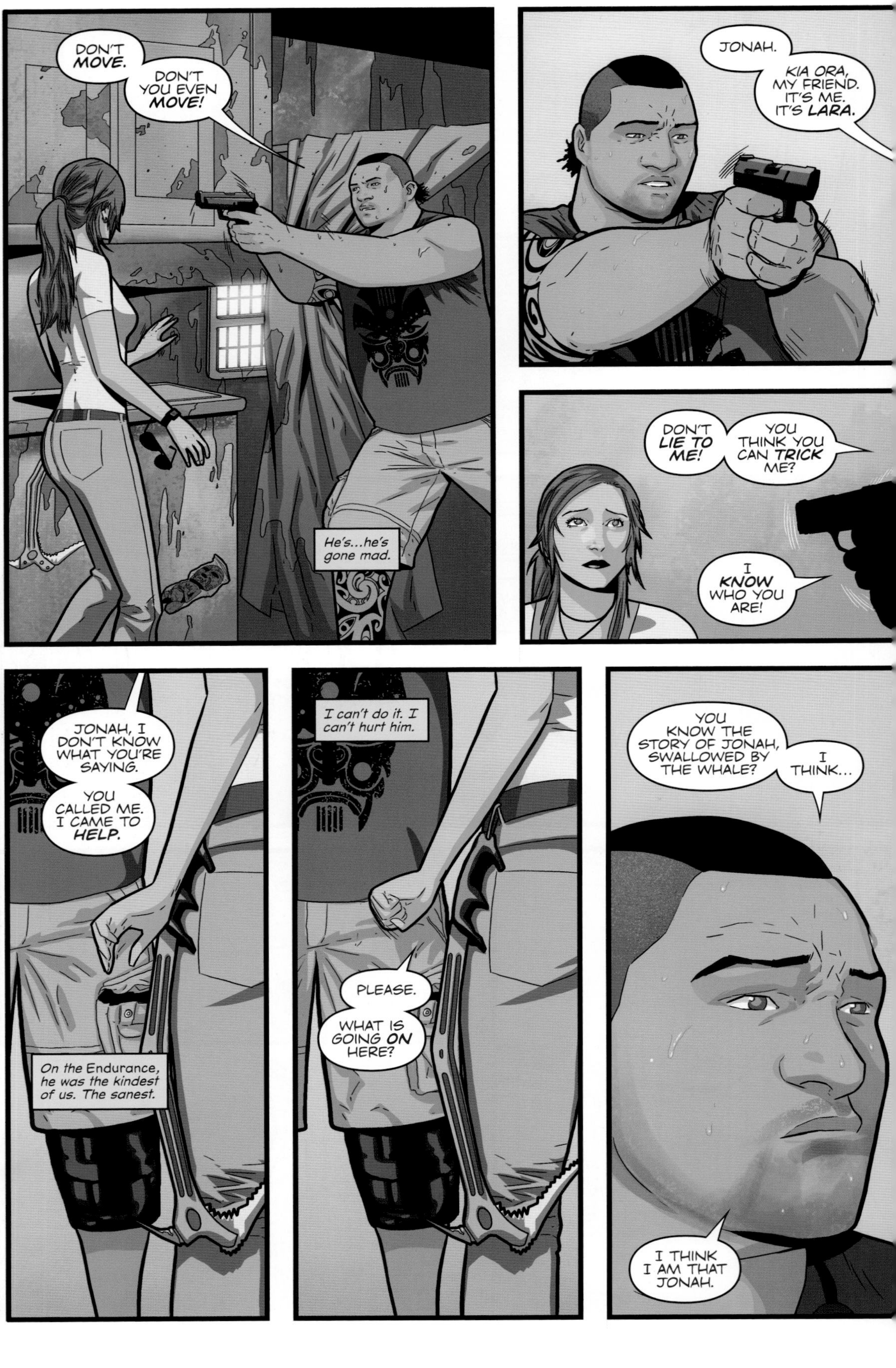
DON'T MOVE.
DON'T YOU EVEN MOVE!
He's...he's gone mad.
JONAH.
KIA ORA, MY FRIEND. IT'S ME. IT'S LARA.
DON'T LIE TO ME!
YOU THINK YOU CAN TRICK ME?
I KNOW WHO YOU ARE!
JONAH, I DON'T KNOW WHAT YOU'RE SAYING.
YOU CALLED ME. I CAME TO HELP.
On the Endurance, he was the kindest of us. The sanest.
I can't do it. I can't hurt him.
PLEASE.
WHAT IS GOING ON HERE?
YOU KNOW THE STORY OF JONAH, SWALLOWED BY THE WHALE?
I THINK...
I THINK I AM THAT JONAH.

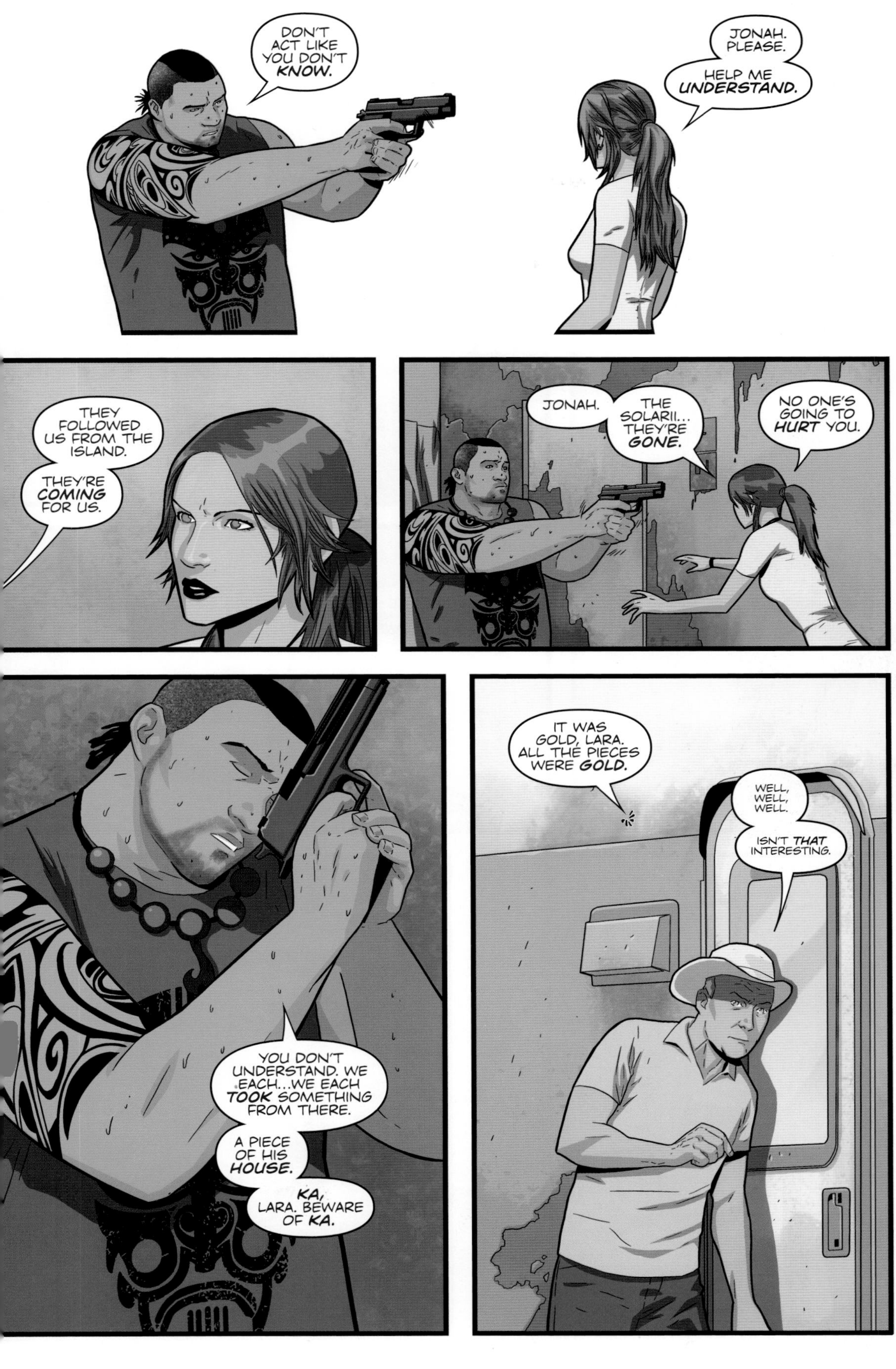

DON'T ACT LIKE YOU DON'T KNOW.
JONAH. PLEASE.
HELP ME UNDERSTAND.
THEY FOLLOWED US FROM THE ISLAND.
THEY'RE COMING FOR US.
JONAH.
THE SOLARII... THEY'RE GONE.
NO ONE'S GOING TO HURT YOU.
YOU DON'T UNDERSTAND. WE EACH...WE EACH TOOK SOMETHING FROM THERE.
A PIECE OF HIS HOUSE.
KA, LARA. BEWARE OF KA.
IT WAS GOLD, LARA. ALL THE PIECES WERE GOLD.
WELL, WELL, WELL.
ISN'T THAT INTERESTING.

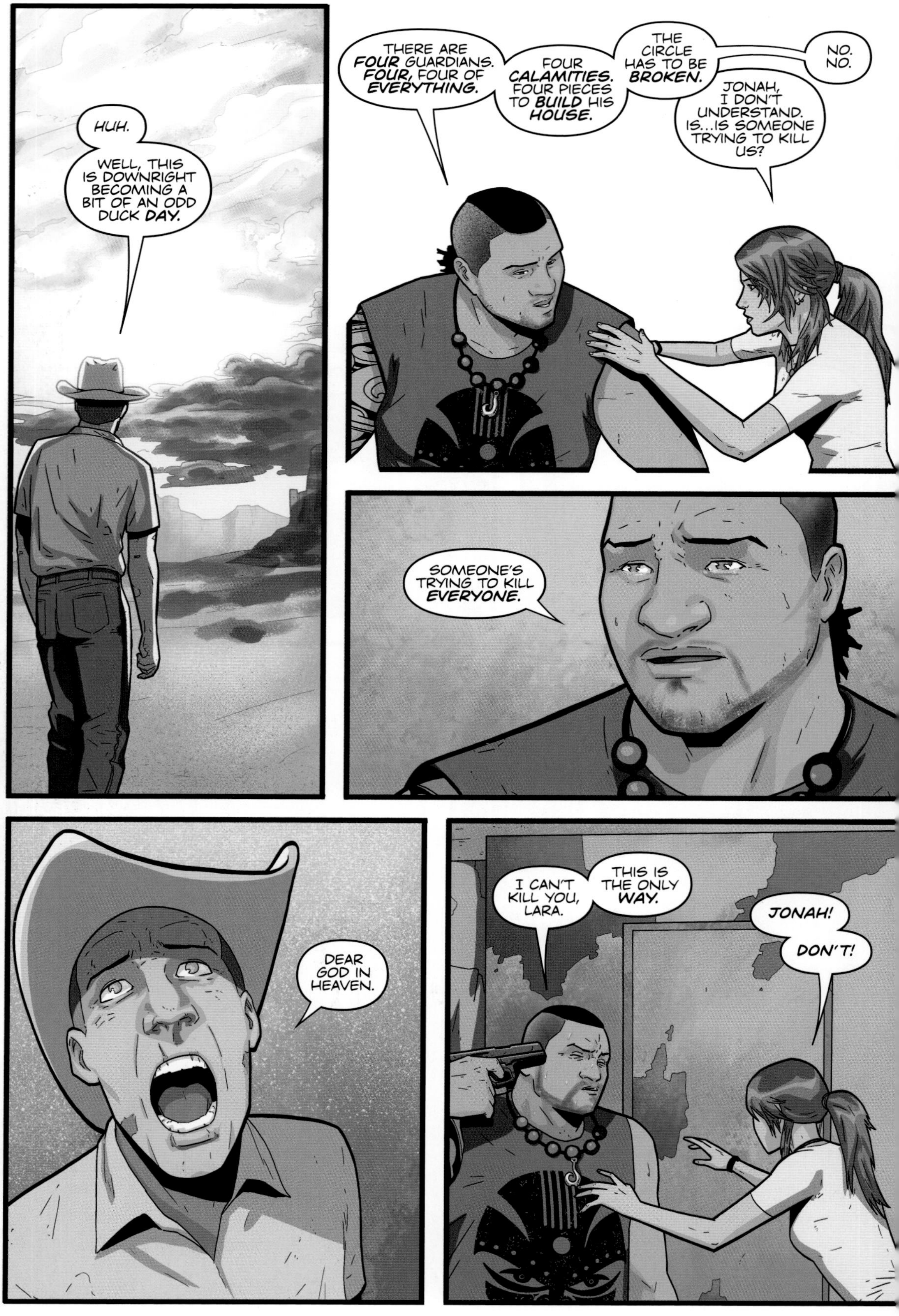
HUH.
WELL, THIS IS DOWNRIGHT BECOMING A BIT OF AN ODD DUCK **DAY.**
THERE ARE **FOUR** GUARDIANS. **FOUR,** FOUR OF **EVERYTHING.**
FOUR **CALAMITIES.** FOUR PIECES TO **BUILD** HIS **HOUSE.**
THE CIRCLE HAS TO BE **BROKEN.**
NO. NO.
JONAH, I DON'T UNDERSTAND. IS...IS SOMEONE TRYING TO KILL US?
SOMEONE'S TRYING TO KILL **EVERYONE.**
DEAR GOD IN HEAVEN.
I CAN'T KILL YOU, LARA.
THIS IS THE ONLY **WAY.**
JONAH!
DON'T!

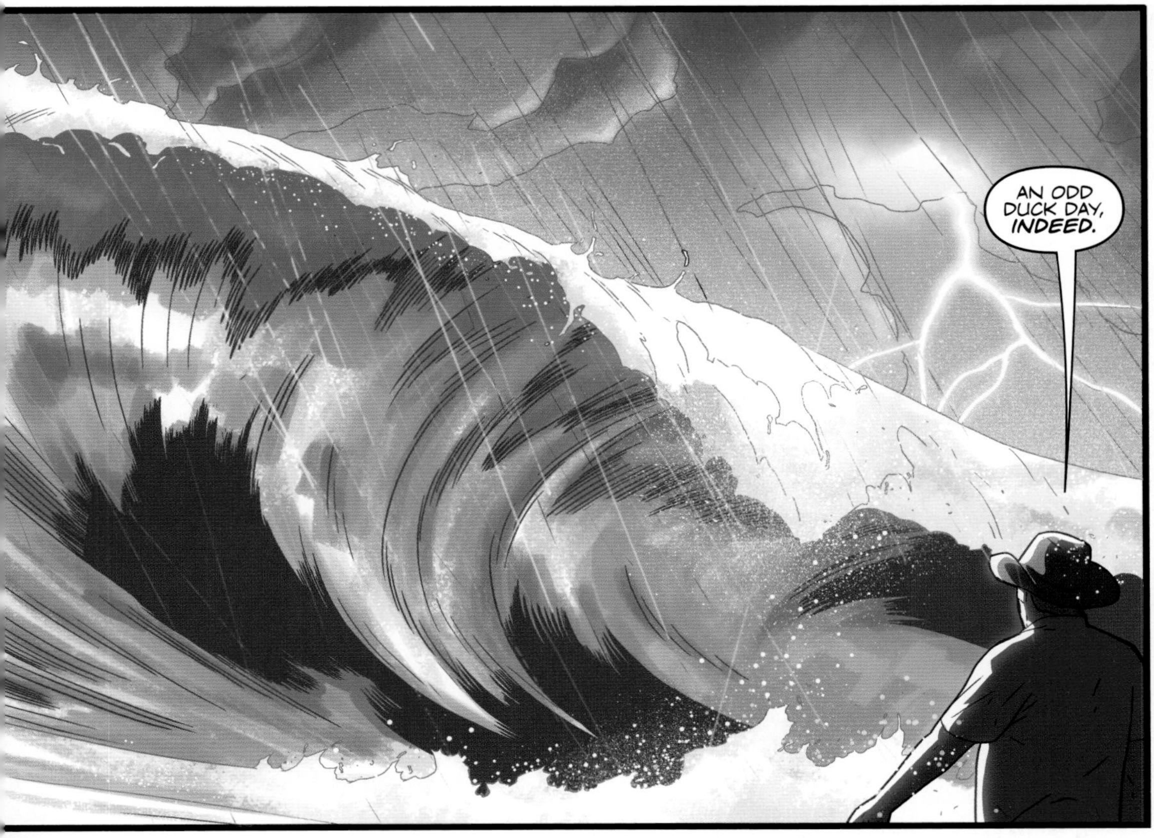
AN ODD DUCK DAY, INDEED.

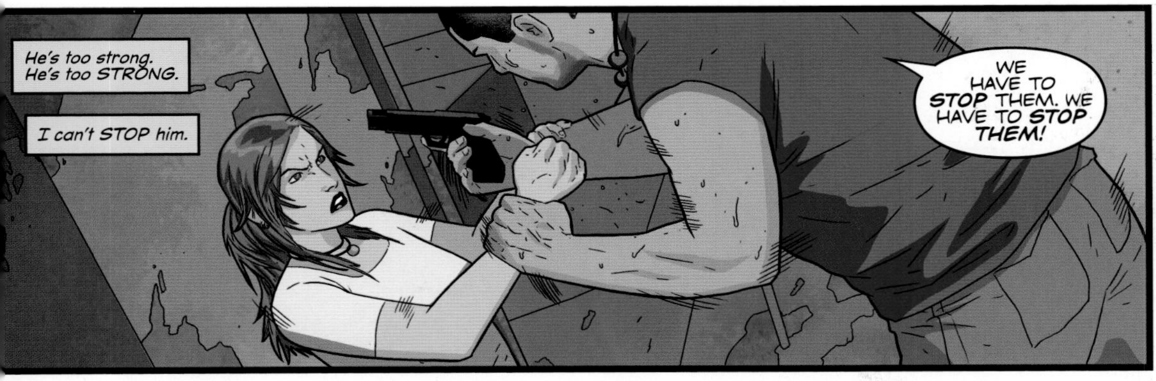
He's too strong. He's too STRONG.
I can't STOP him.
WE HAVE TO STOP THEM. WE HAVE TO STOP THEM!

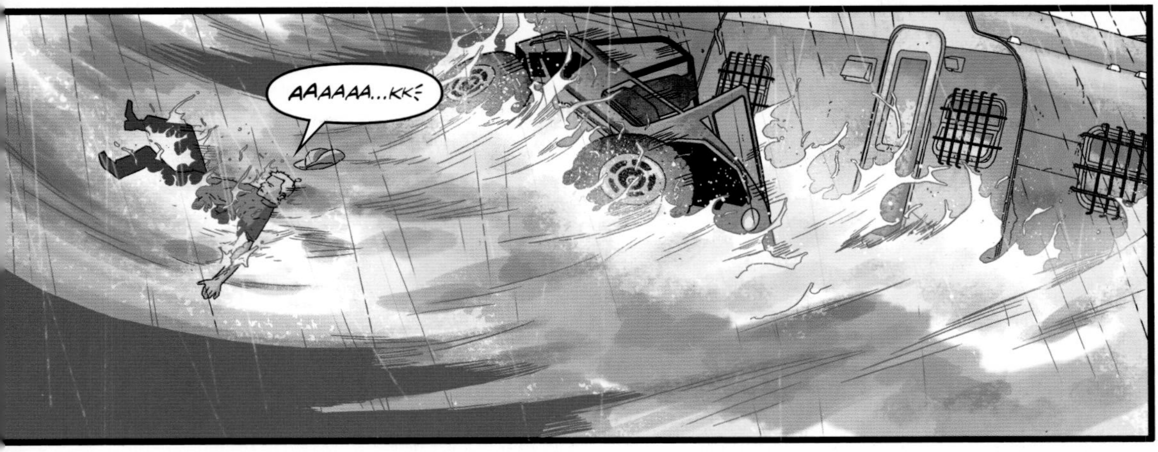
AAAAAA...KK!

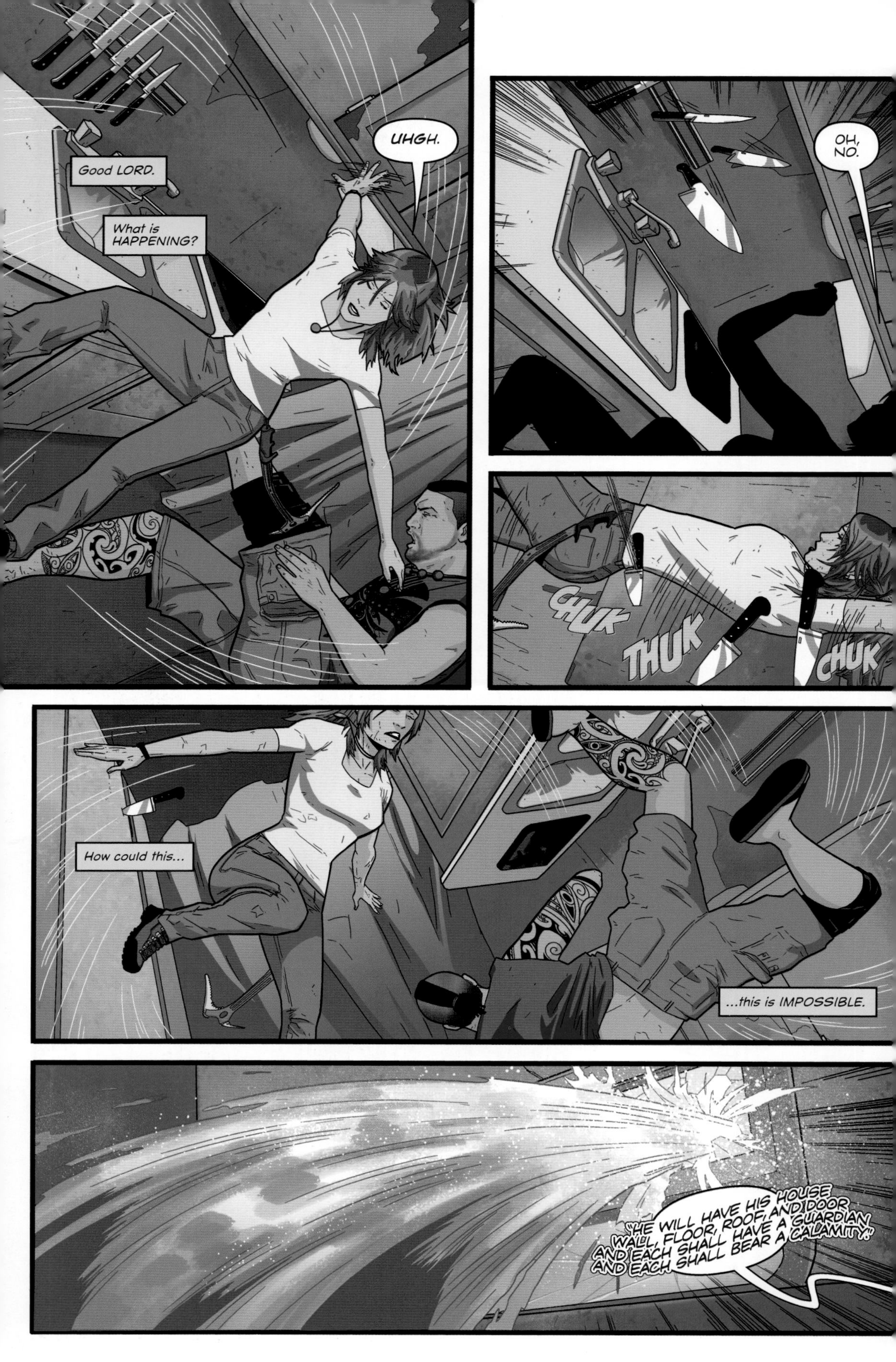
Good LORD.
What is HAPPENING?
UHGH.
OH, NO.
CHUK
THUK
CHUK
How could this...
...this is IMPOSSIBLE.
"HE WILL HAVE HIS HOUSE WALL, FLOOR, ROOF, AND DOOR AND EACH SHALL HAVE A GUARDIAN AND EACH SHALL BEAR A CALAMITY."

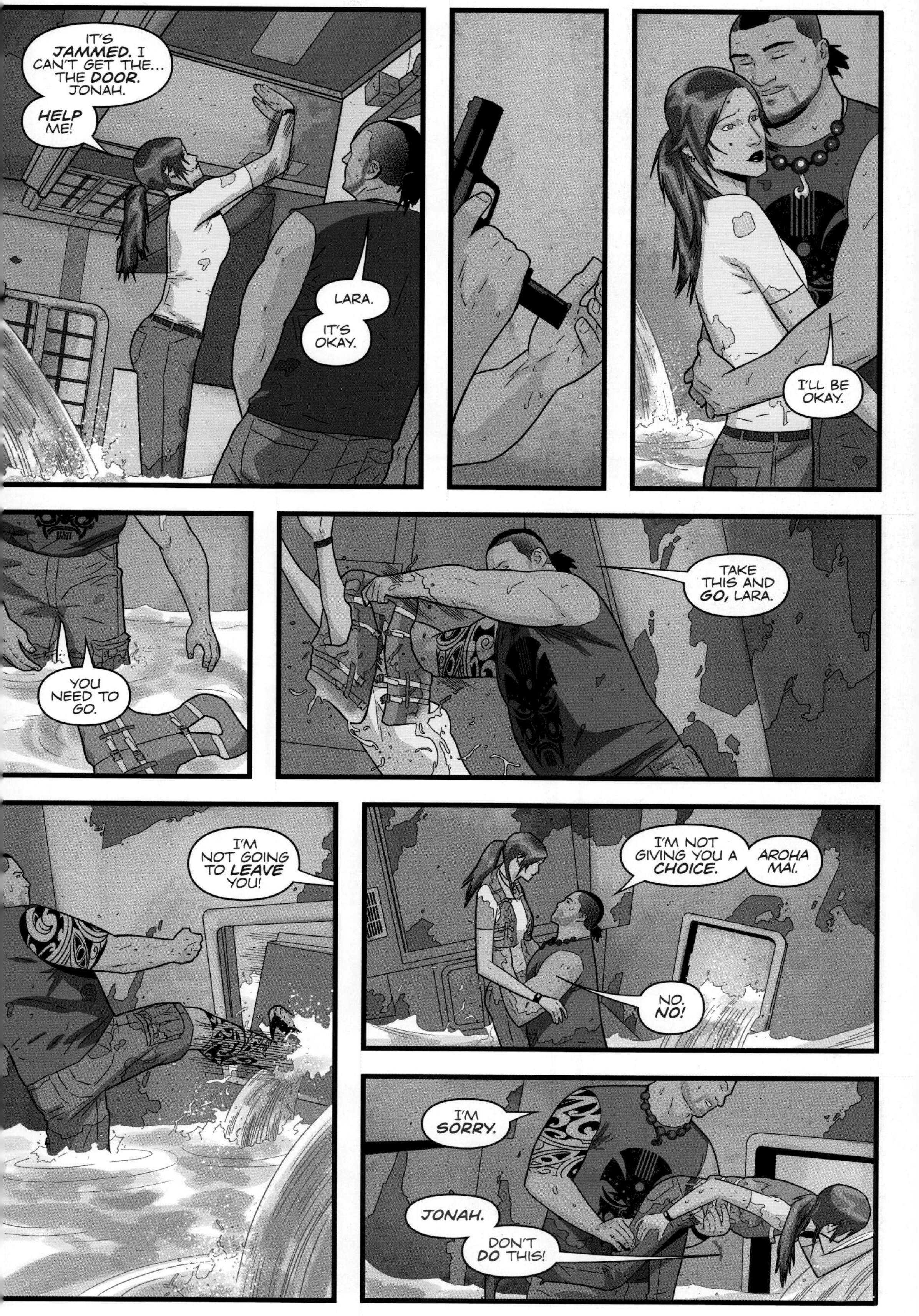
IT'S JAMMED. I CAN'T GET THE... THE DOOR. JONAH.
HELP ME!
LARA.
IT'S OKAY.
I'LL BE OKAY.
YOU NEED TO GO.
TAKE THIS AND GO, LARA.
I'M NOT GOING TO LEAVE YOU!
I'M NOT GIVING YOU A CHOICE.
AROHA MAI.
NO. NO!
I'M SORRY.
JONAH.
DON'T DO THIS!

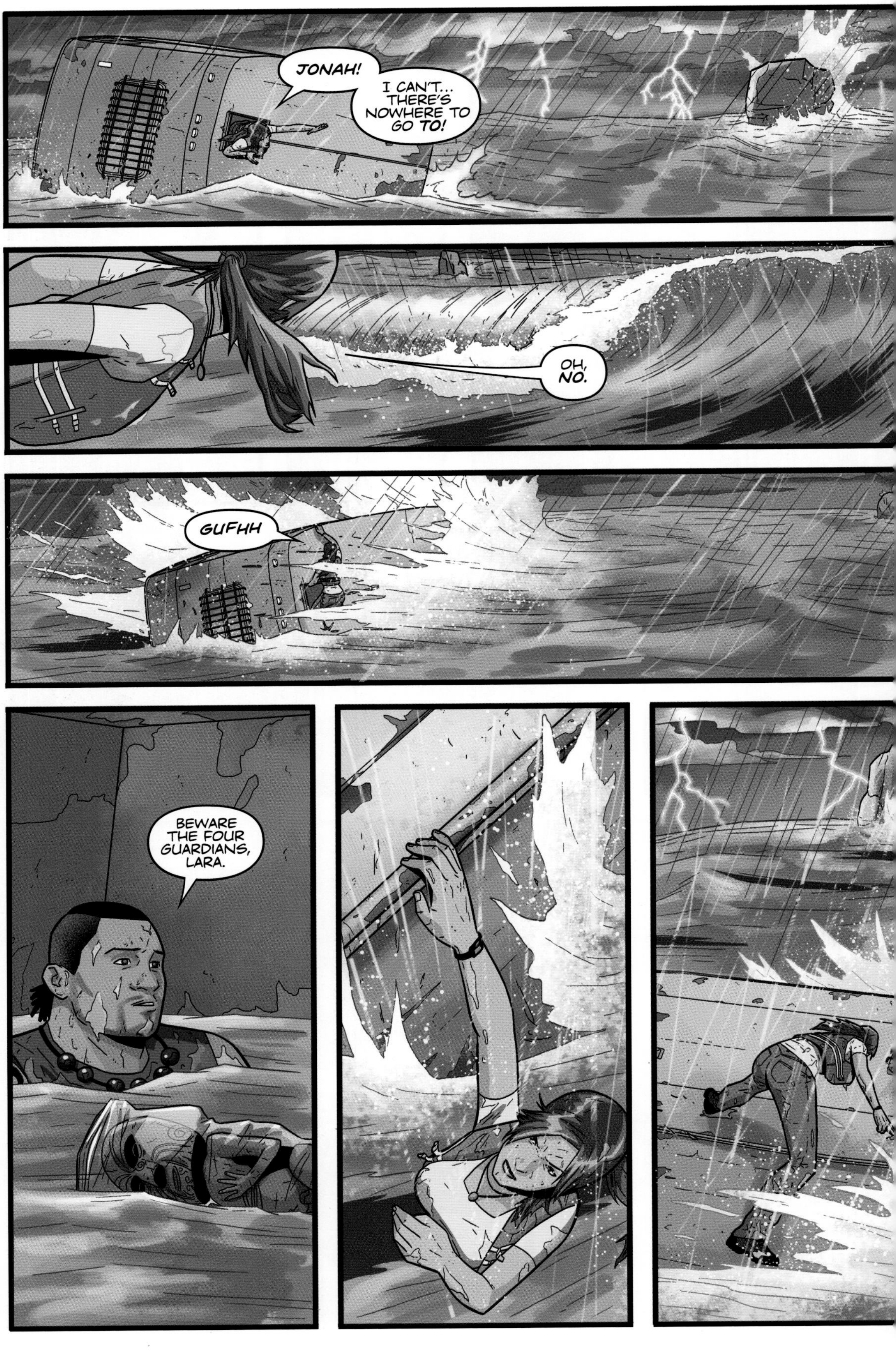
JONAH!
I CAN'T... THERE'S NOWHERE TO GO TO!
OH, NO.
GUFHH
BEWARE THE FOUR GUARDIANS, LARA.

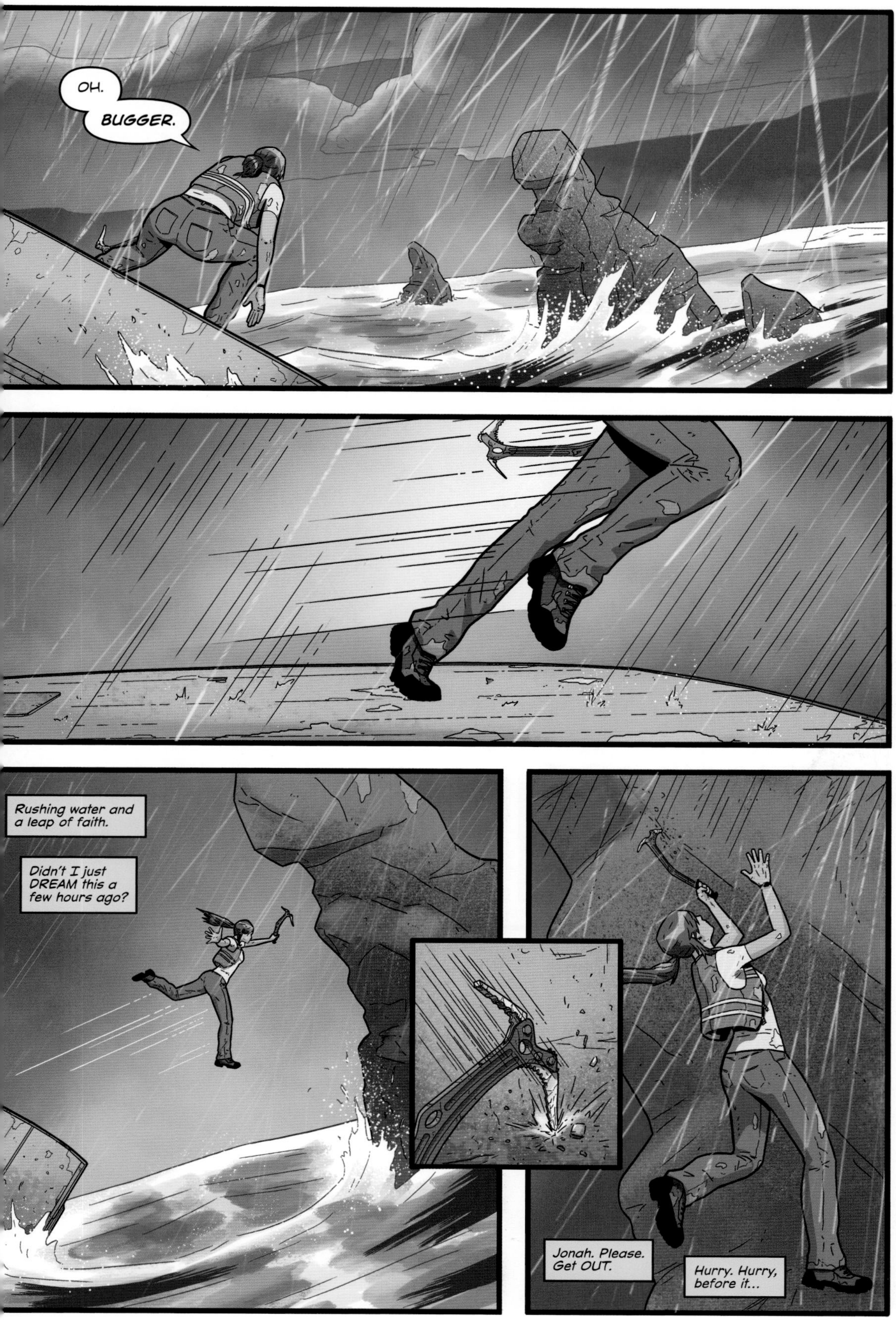
OH.
BUGGER.
Rushing water and a leap of faith.
Didn't I just DREAM this a few hours ago?
Jonah. Please. Get OUT.
Hurry. Hurry, before it...

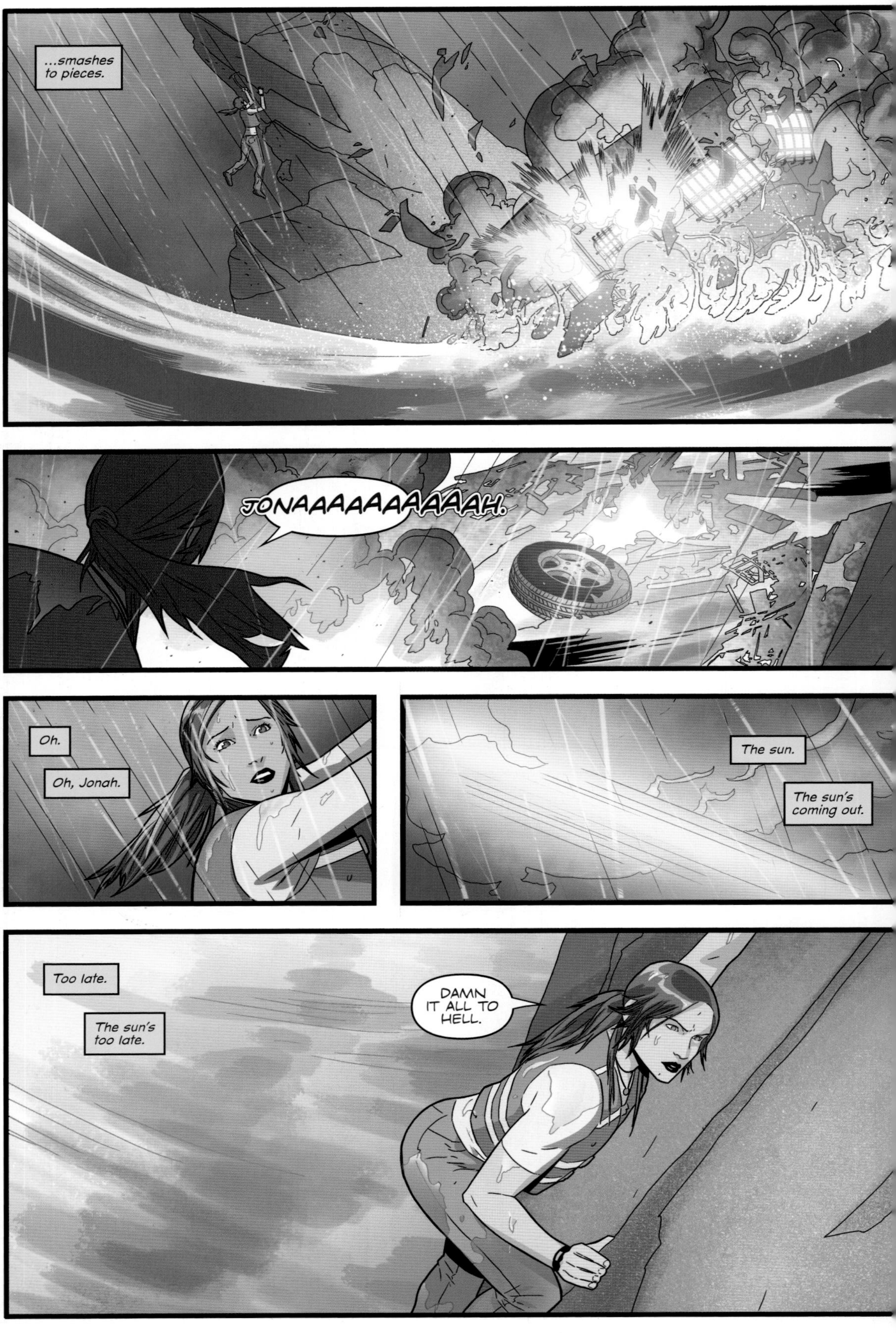
...smashes to pieces.
JONAAAAAAAAAAH.
Oh.
Oh, Jonah.
The sun.
The sun's coming out.
Too late.
The sun's too late.
DAMN IT ALL TO HELL.

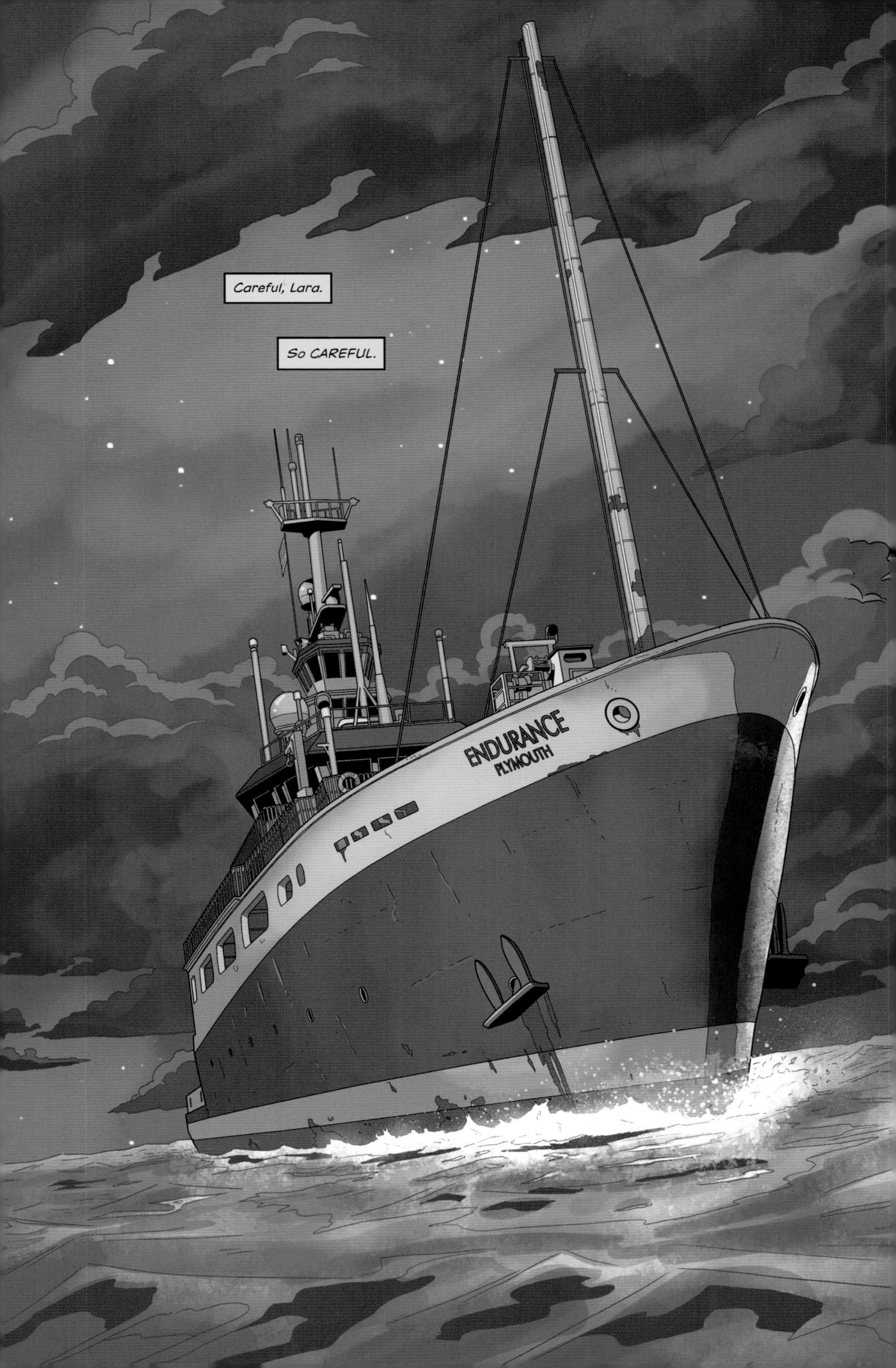
Careful, Lara.
So CAREFUL.
ENDURANCE
PLYMOUTH

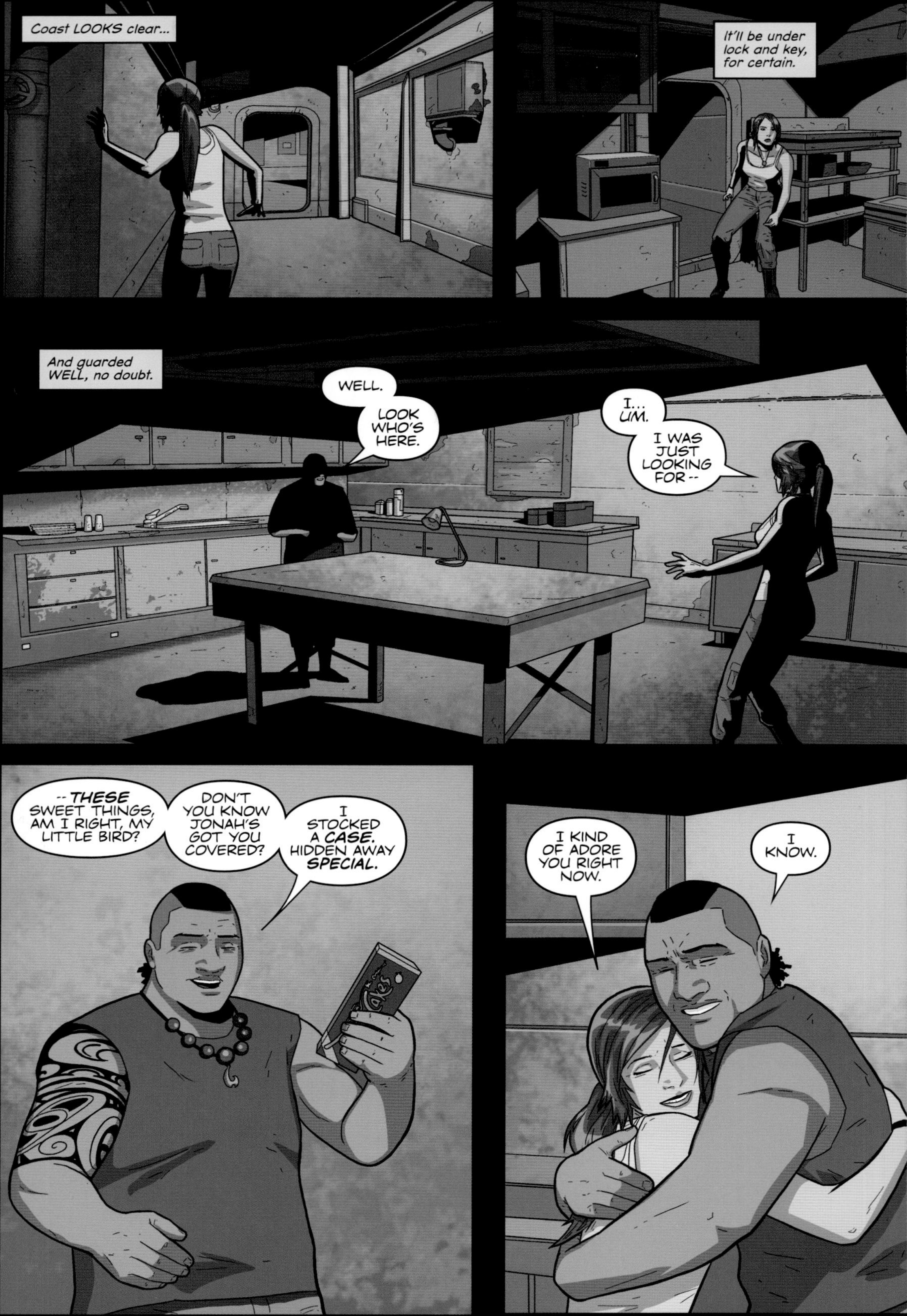
Coast LOOKS clear...
It'll be under lock and key, for certain.
And guarded WELL, no doubt.
WELL.
LOOK WHO'S HERE.
I... UM.
I WAS JUST LOOKING FOR --
-- THESE SWEET THINGS, AM I RIGHT, MY LITTLE BIRD?
DON'T YOU KNOW JONAH'S GOT YOU COVERED?
I STOCKED A CASE. HIDDEN AWAY SPECIAL.
I KIND OF ADORE YOU RIGHT NOW.
I KNOW.

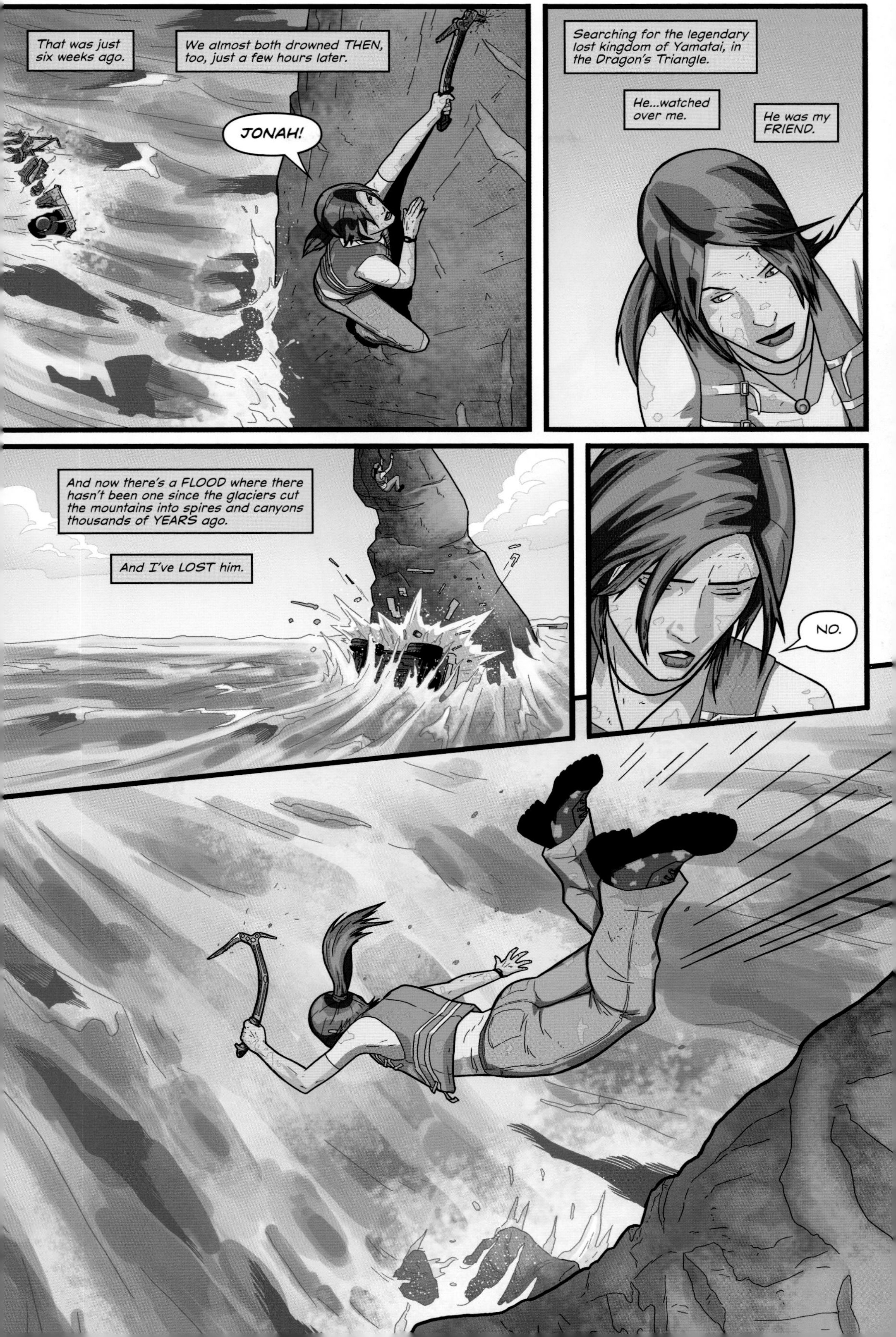
That was just six weeks ago.
We almost both drowned THEN, too, just a few hours later.
JONAH!
Searching for the legendary lost kingdom of Yamatai, in the Dragon's Triangle.
He...watched over me.
He was my FRIEND.
And now there's a FLOOD where there hasn't been one since the glaciers cut the mountains into spires and canyons thousands of YEARS ago.
And I've LOST him.
NO.

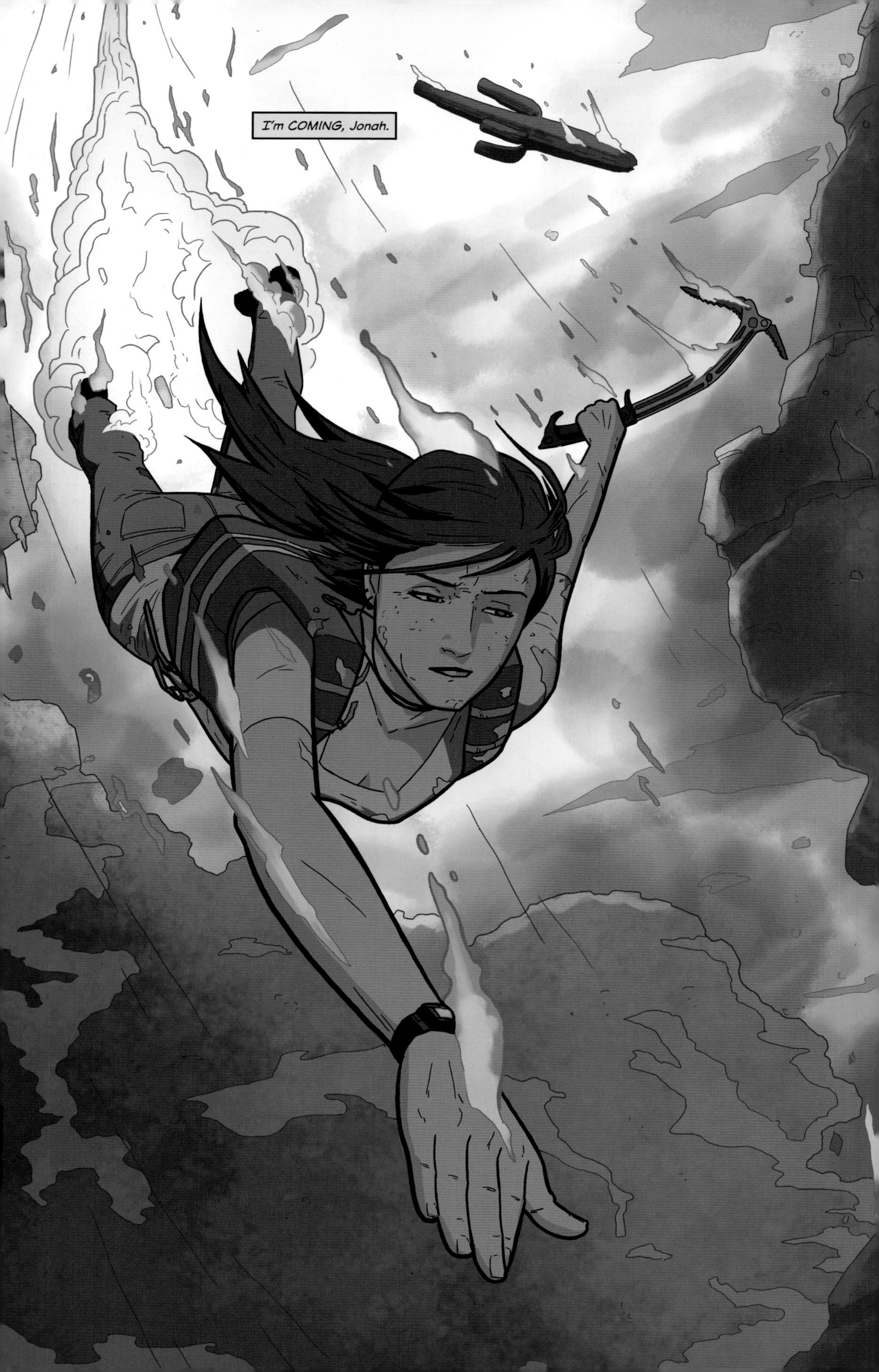
I'm COMING, Jonah.

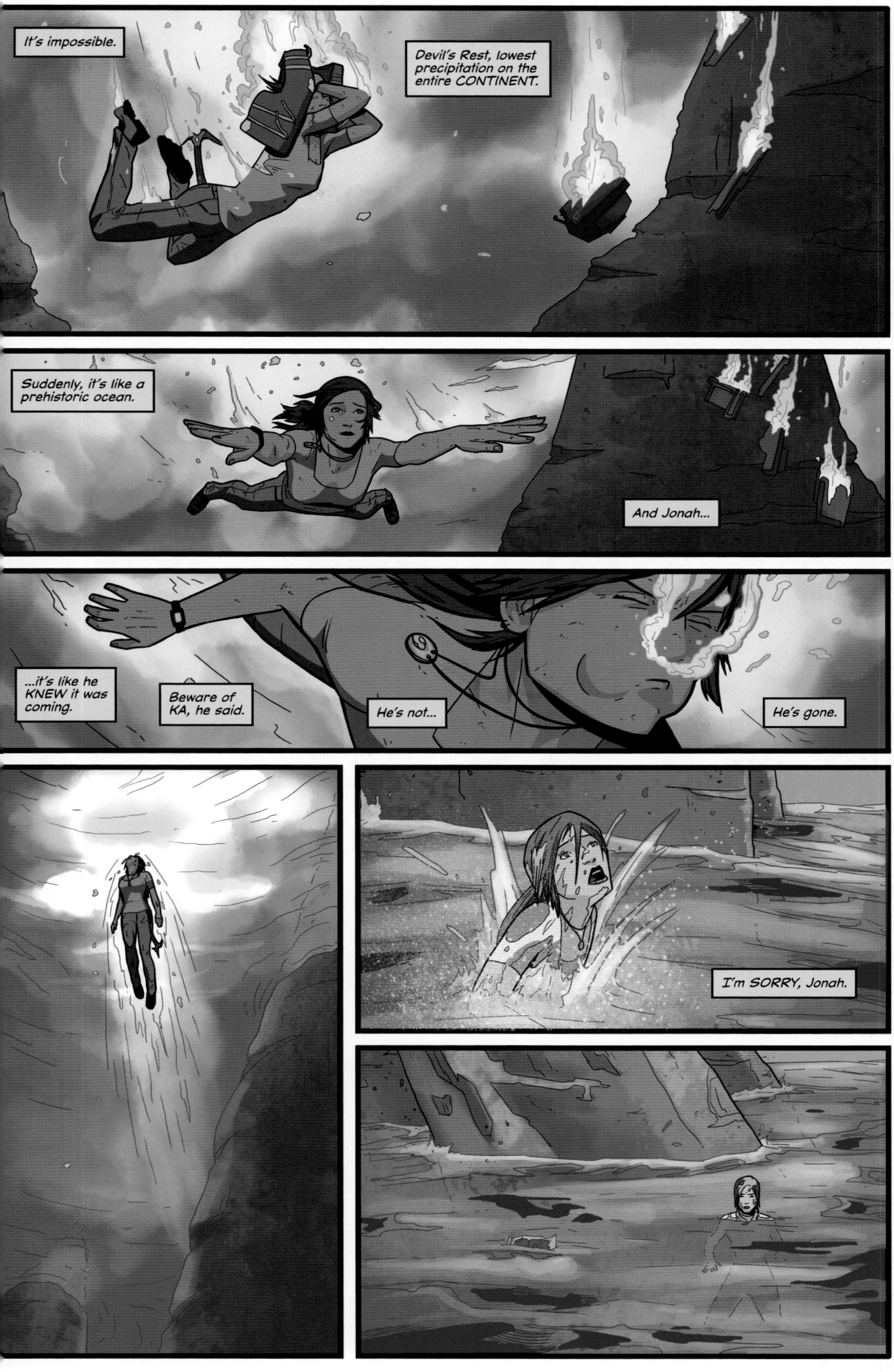

It's impossible.
Devil's Rest, lowest precipitation on the entire CONTINENT.
Suddenly, it's like a prehistoric ocean.
And Jonah...
...it's like he KNEW it was coming.
Beware of KA, he said.
He's not...
He's gone.
I'm SORRY, Jonah.

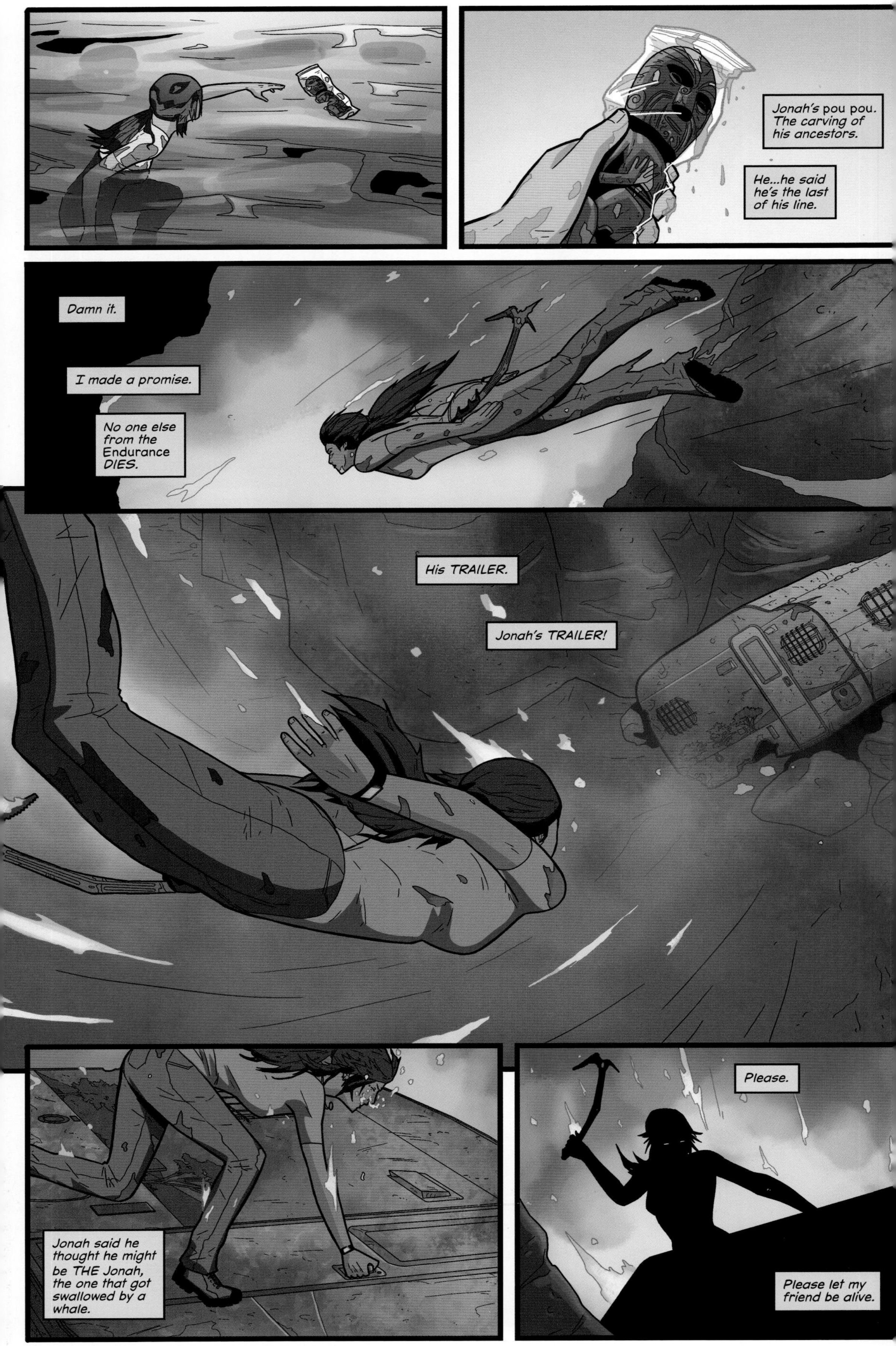
Jonah's pou pou. The carving of his ancestors.
He...he said he's the last of his line.
Damn it.
I made a promise.
No one else from the Endurance DIES.
His TRAILER.
Jonah's TRAILER!
Jonah said he thought he might be THE Jonah, the one that got swallowed by a whale.
Please.
Please let my friend be alive.

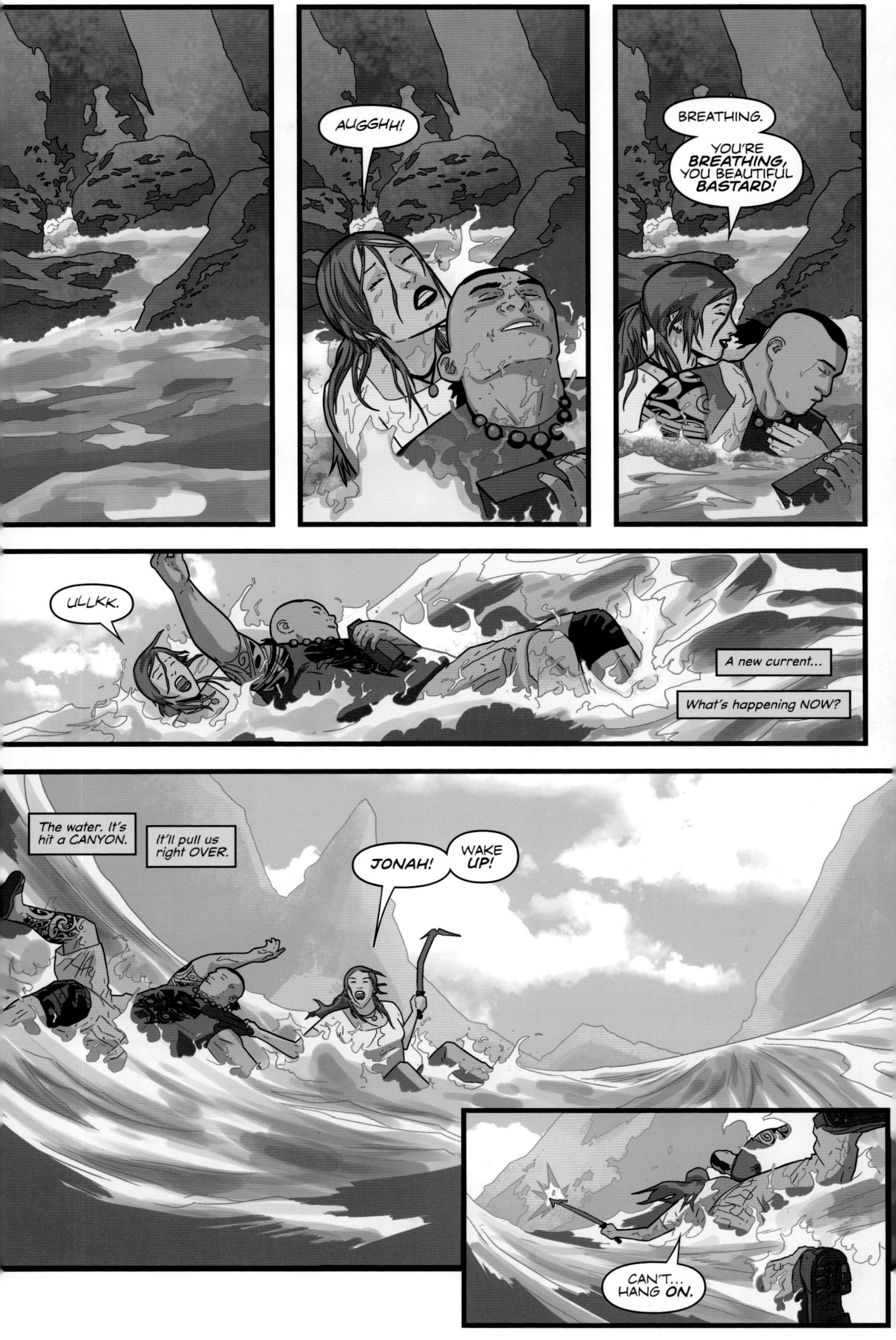
AUGGHH!
BREATHING.
YOU'RE BREATHING, YOU BEAUTIFUL BASTARD!
ULLKK.
A new current...
What's happening NOW?
The water. It's hit a CANYON.
It'll pull us right OVER.
JONAH!
WAKE UP!
CAN'T... HANG ON.

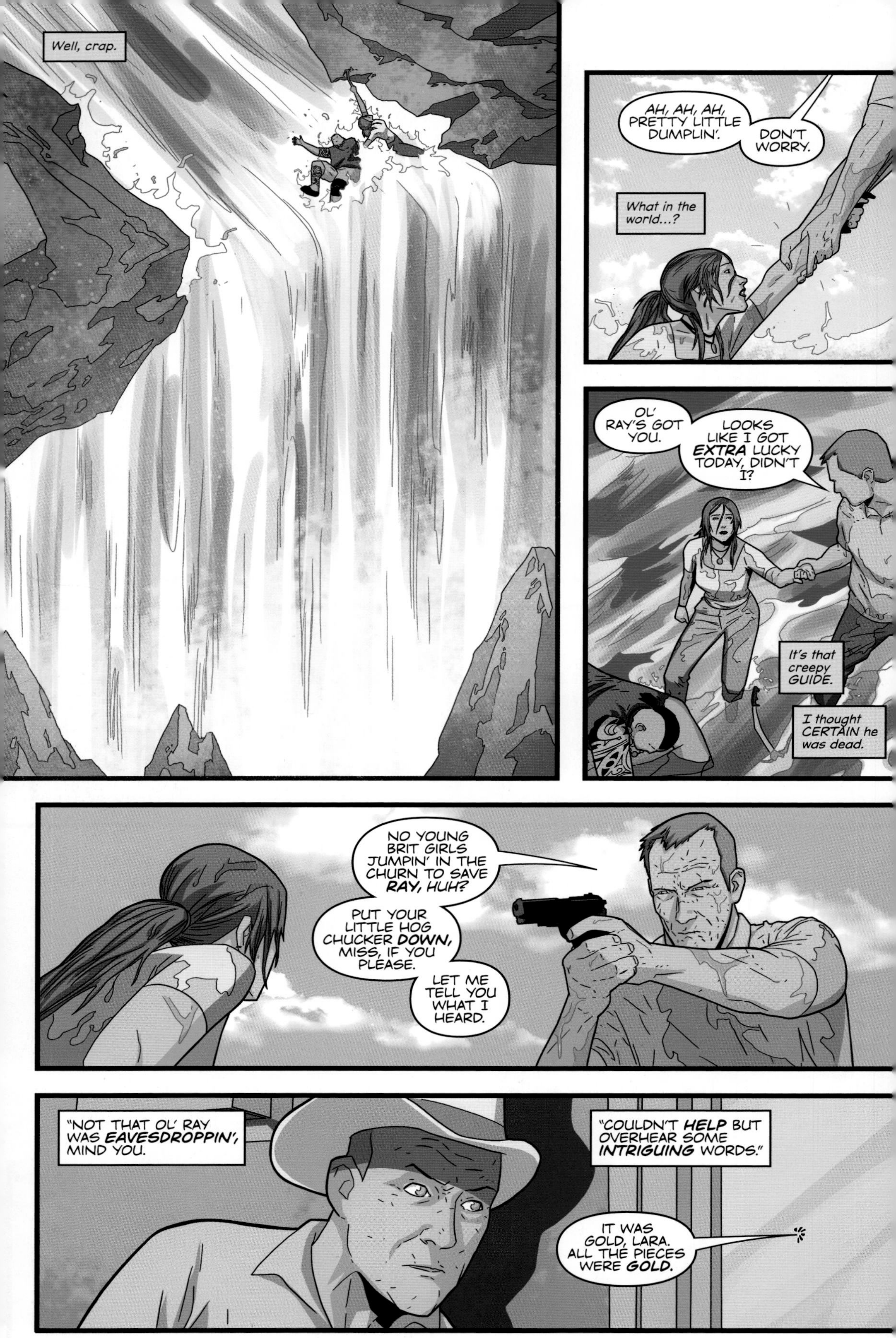
Well, crap.
AH, AH, AH, PRETTY LITTLE DUMPLIN'.
DON'T WORRY.
What in the world...?
OL' RAY'S GOT YOU.
LOOKS LIKE I GOT EXTRA LUCKY TODAY, DIDN'T I?
It's that creepy GUIDE.
I thought CERTAIN he was dead.
NO YOUNG BRIT GIRLS JUMPIN' IN THE CHURN TO SAVE RAY, HUH?
PUT YOUR LITTLE HOG CHUCKER DOWN, MISS, IF YOU PLEASE.
LET ME TELL YOU WHAT I HEARD.
"NOT THAT OL' RAY WAS EAVESDROPPIN', MIND YOU.
"COULDN'T HELP BUT OVERHEAR SOME INTRIGUING WORDS."
IT WAS GOLD, LARA. ALL THE PIECES WERE GOLD.

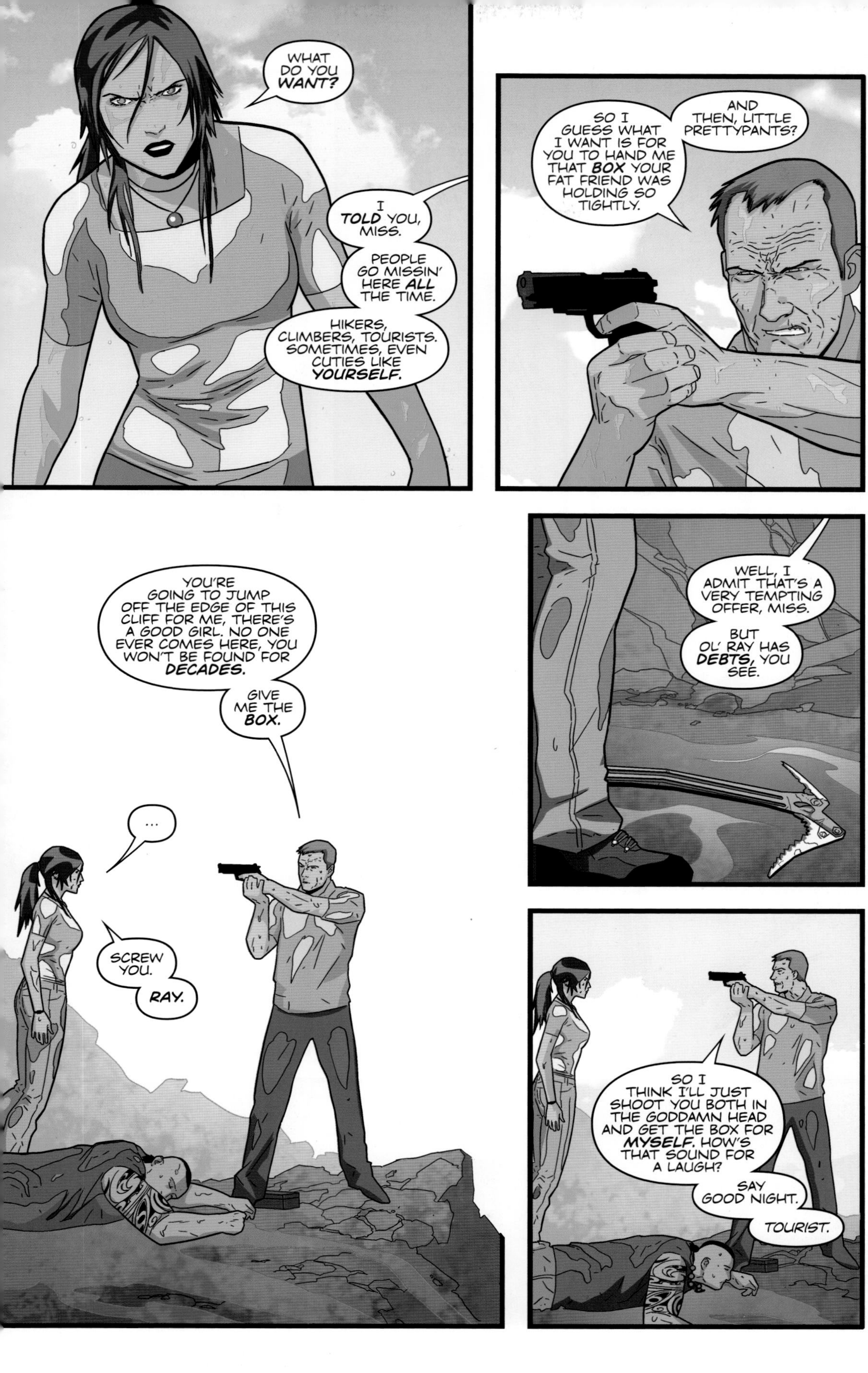
WHAT DO YOU WANT?
I TOLD YOU, MISS.
PEOPLE GO MISSIN' HERE ALL THE TIME.
HIKERS, CLIMBERS, TOURISTS. SOMETIMES, EVEN CUTIES LIKE YOURSELF.
SO I GUESS WHAT I WANT IS FOR YOU TO HAND ME THAT BOX YOUR FAT FRIEND WAS HOLDING SO TIGHTLY.
AND THEN, LITTLE PRETTYPANTS?
YOU'RE GOING TO JUMP OFF THE EDGE OF THIS CLIFF FOR ME, THERE'S A GOOD GIRL. NO ONE EVER COMES HERE, YOU WON'T BE FOUND FOR DECADES.
GIVE ME THE BOX.
...
SCREW YOU.
RAY.
WELL, I ADMIT THAT'S A VERY TEMPTING OFFER, MISS.
BUT OL' RAY HAS DEBTS, YOU SEE.
SO I THINK I'LL JUST SHOOT YOU BOTH IN THE GODDAMN HEAD AND GET THE BOX FOR MYSELF. HOW'S THAT SOUND FOR A LAUGH?
SAY GOOD NIGHT.
TOURIST.

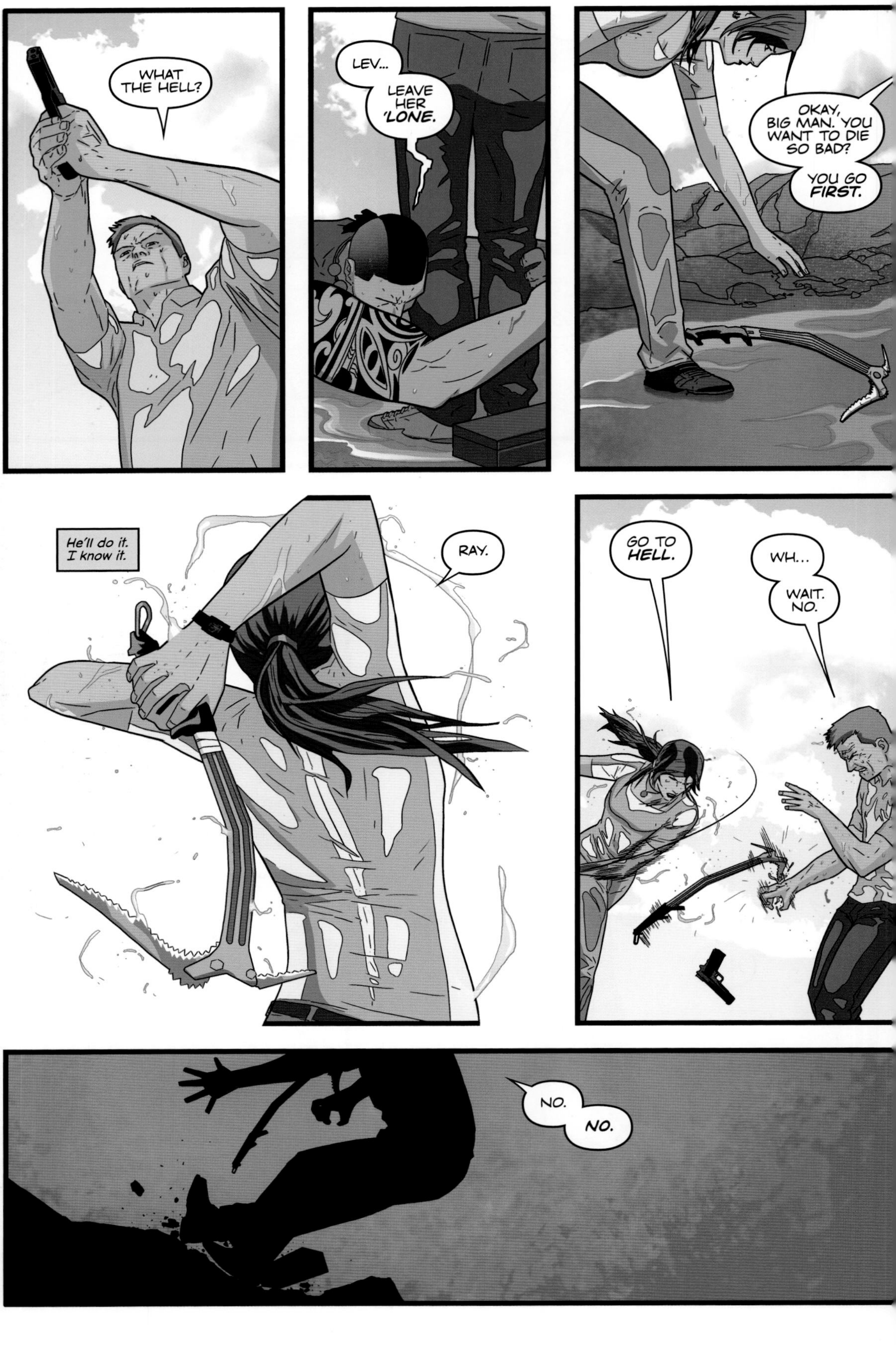
WHAT THE HELL?
LEV... LEAVE HER 'LONE.
OKAY, BIG MAN. YOU WANT TO DIE SO BAD?
YOU GO FIRST.
He'll do it. I know it.
RAY.
GO TO HELL.
WH... WAIT. NO.
NO.
NO.

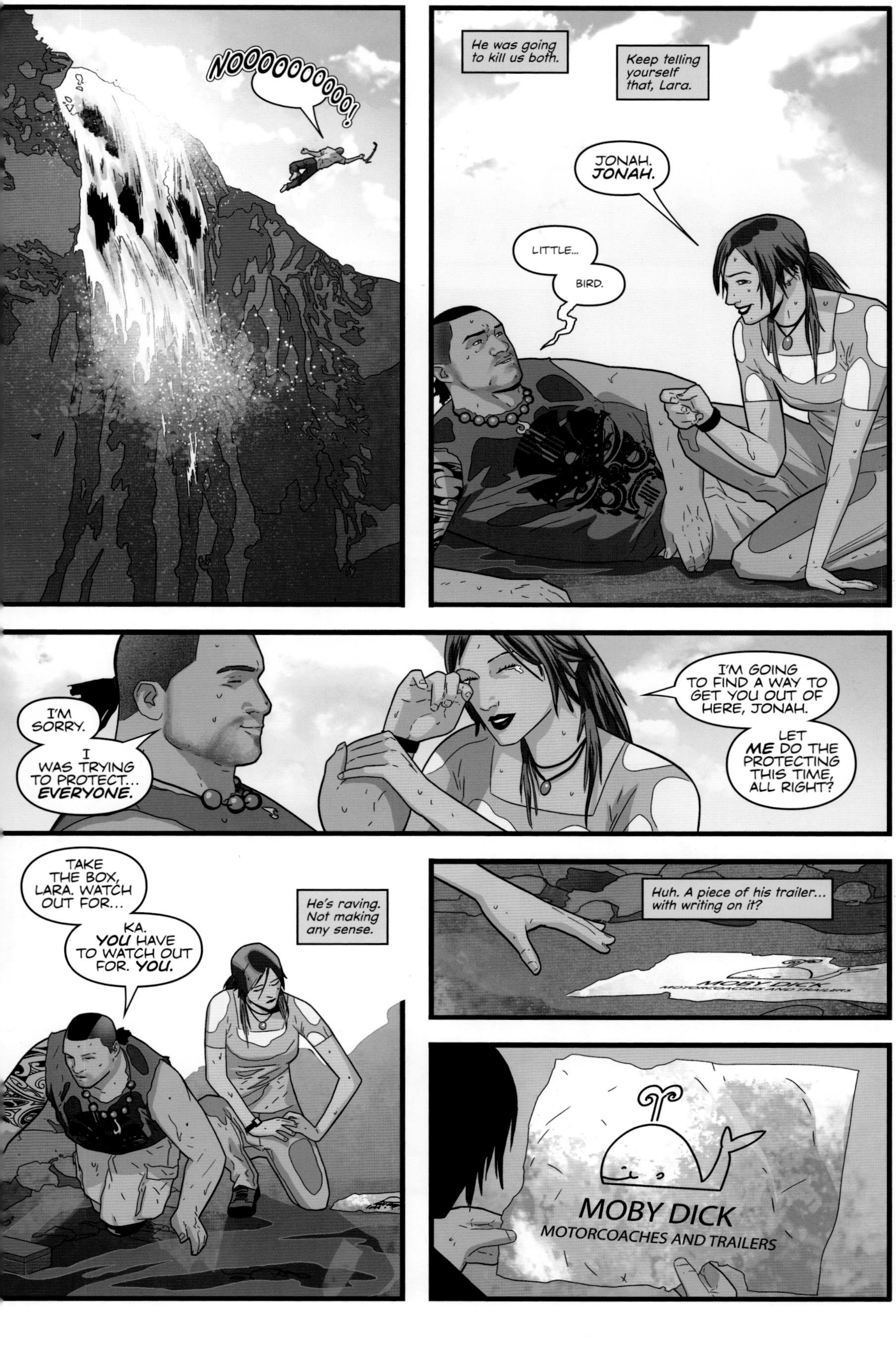
NOOOOOOOOOO!
He was going to kill us both.
Keep telling yourself that, Lara.
JONAH. JONAH.
LITTLE...
BIRD.
I'M SORRY.
I WAS TRYING TO PROTECT... EVERYONE.
I'M GOING TO FIND A WAY TO GET YOU OUT OF HERE, JONAH.
LET ME DO THE PROTECTING THIS TIME, ALL RIGHT?
TAKE THE BOX, LARA. WATCH OUT FOR...
KA. YOU HAVE TO WATCH OUT FOR. YOU.
He's raving. Not making any sense.
Huh. A piece of his trailer... with writing on it?
MOBY DICK
MOTORCOACHES AND TRAILERS
MOBY DICK
MOTORCOACHES AND TRAILERS

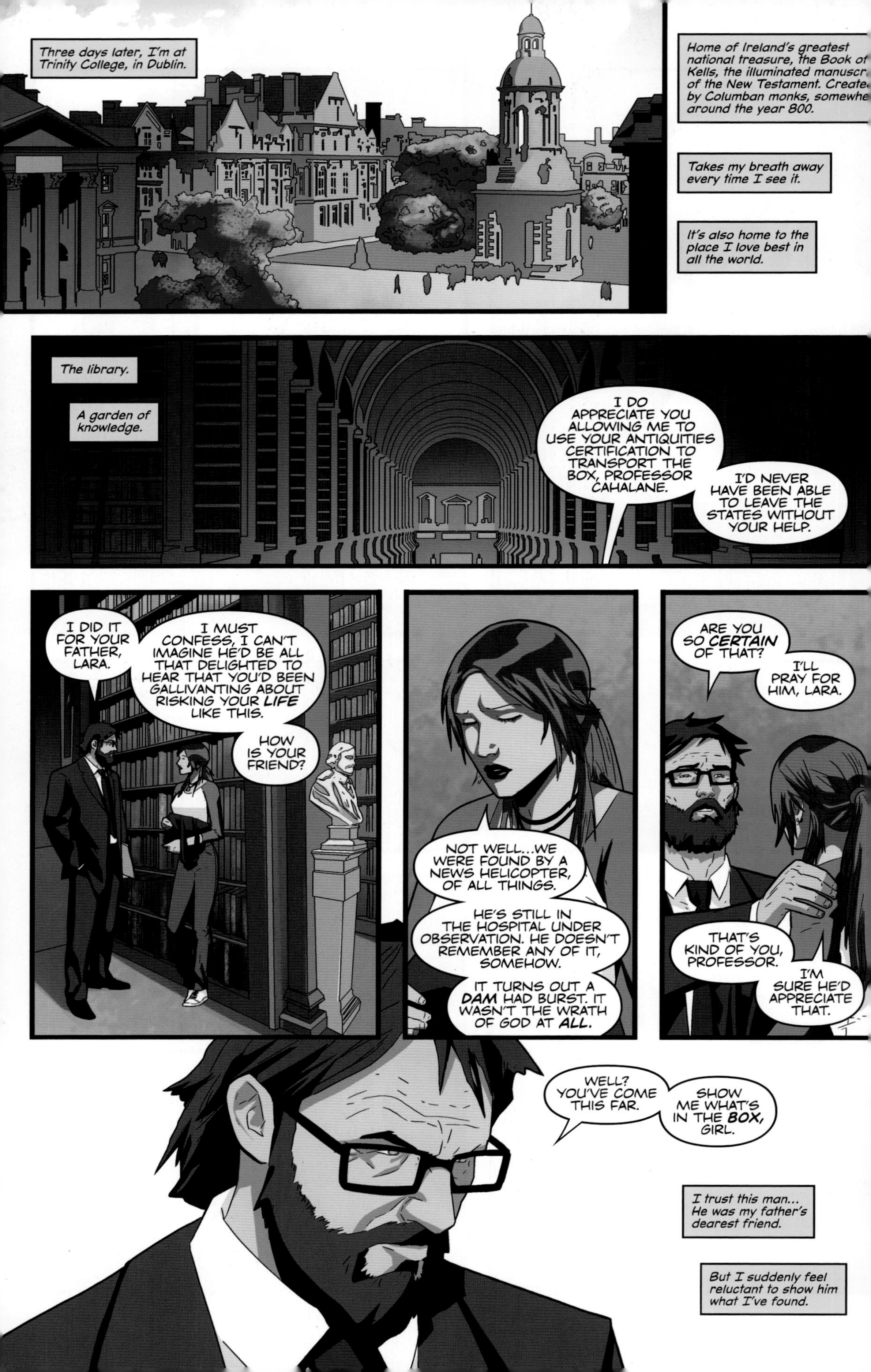
Three days later, I'm at Trinity College, in Dublin.
Home of Ireland's greatest national treasure, the Book of Kells, the illuminated manuscr of the New Testament. Create by Columban monks, somewhe around the year 800.
Takes my breath away every time I see it.
It's also home to the place I love best in all the world.
The library.
A garden of knowledge.
I DO APPRECIATE YOU ALLOWING ME TO USE YOUR ANTIQUITIES CERTIFICATION TO TRANSPORT THE BOX, PROFESSOR CAHALANE.
I'D NEVER HAVE BEEN ABLE TO LEAVE THE STATES WITHOUT YOUR HELP.
I DID IT FOR YOUR FATHER, LARA.
I MUST CONFESS, I CAN'T IMAGINE HE'D BE ALL THAT DELIGHTED TO HEAR THAT YOU'D BEEN GALLIVANTING ABOUT RISKING YOUR ***LIFE*** LIKE THIS.
HOW IS YOUR FRIEND?
NOT WELL...WE WERE FOUND BY A NEWS HELICOPTER, OF ALL THINGS.
HE'S STILL IN THE HOSPITAL UNDER OBSERVATION. HE DOESN'T REMEMBER ANY OF IT, SOMEHOW.
IT TURNS OUT A ***DAM*** HAD BURST. IT WASN'T THE WRATH OF GOD AT ***ALL.***
ARE YOU SO ***CERTAIN*** OF THAT?
I'LL PRAY FOR HIM, LARA.
THAT'S KIND OF YOU, PROFESSOR.
I'M SURE HE'D APPRECIATE THAT.
WELL? YOU'VE COME THIS FAR.
SHOW ME WHAT'S IN THE ***BOX,*** GIRL.
I trust this man... He was my father's dearest friend.
But I suddenly feel reluctant to show him what I've found.

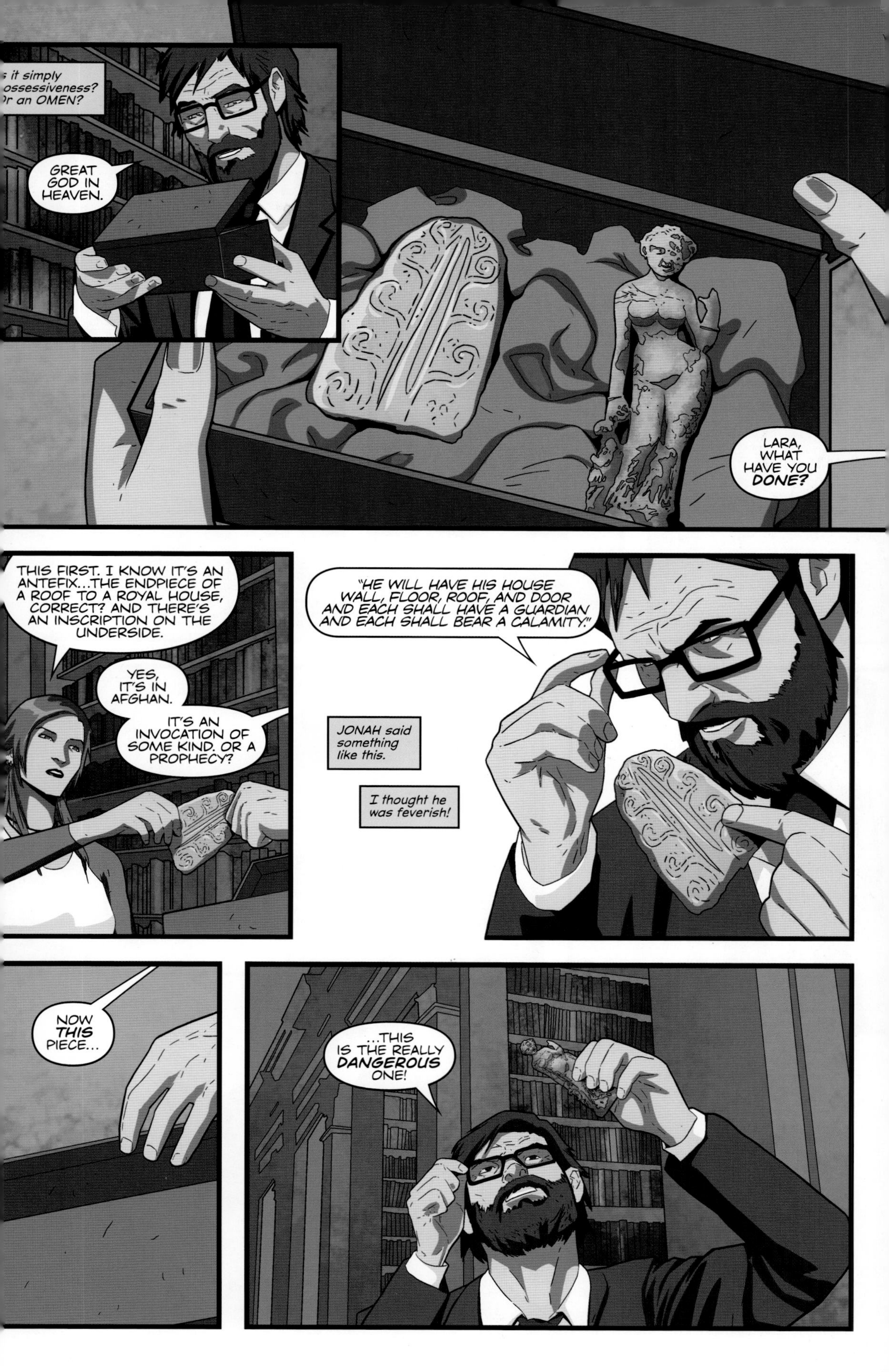

s it simply
ossessiveness?
Or an OMEN?
GREAT GOD IN HEAVEN.
LARA, WHAT HAVE YOU DONE?
THIS FIRST. I KNOW IT'S AN ANTEFIX...THE ENDPIECE OF A ROOF TO A ROYAL HOUSE, CORRECT? AND THERE'S AN INSCRIPTION ON THE UNDERSIDE.
YES, IT'S IN AFGHAN.
IT'S AN INVOCATION OF SOME KIND. OR A PROPHECY?
"HE WILL HAVE HIS HOUSE WALL, FLOOR, ROOF, AND DOOR AND EACH SHALL HAVE A GUARDIAN AND EACH SHALL BEAR A CALAMITY."
JONAH said something like this.
I thought he was feverish!
NOW THIS PIECE...
...THIS IS THE REALLY DANGEROUS ONE!

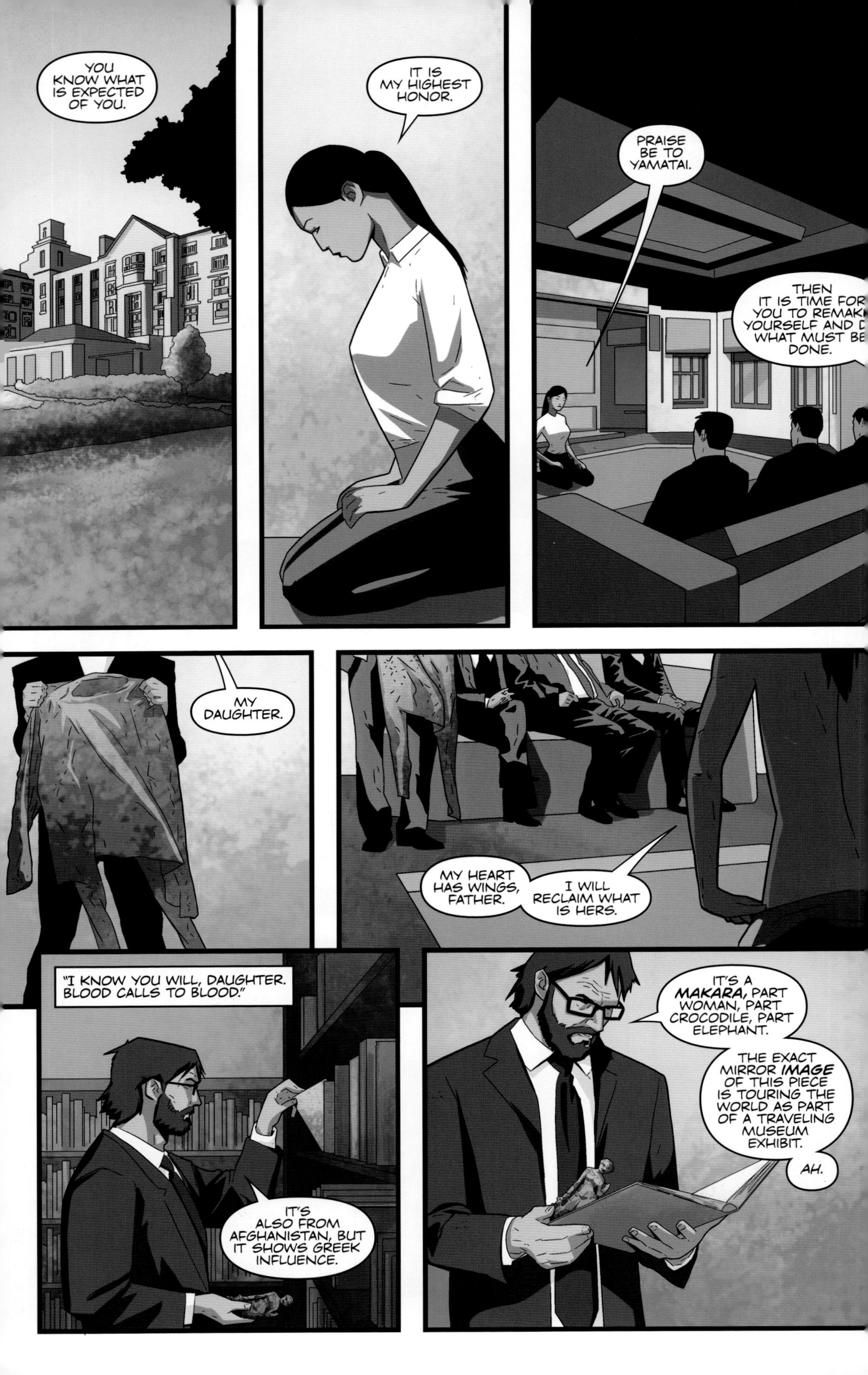
YOU KNOW WHAT IS EXPECTED OF YOU.
IT IS MY HIGHEST HONOR.
PRAISE BE TO YAMATAI.
THEN IT IS TIME FOR YOU TO REMAK YOURSELF AND D WHAT MUST BE DONE.
MY DAUGHTER.
MY HEART HAS WINGS, FATHER.
I WILL RECLAIM WHAT IS HERS.
"I KNOW YOU WILL, DAUGHTER. BLOOD CALLS TO BLOOD."
IT'S ALSO FROM AFGHANISTAN, BUT IT SHOWS GREEK INFLUENCE.
IT'S A MAKARA, PART WOMAN, PART CROCODILE, PART ELEPHANT.
THE EXACT MIRROR IMAGE OF THIS PIECE IS TOURING THE WORLD AS PART OF A TRAVELING MUSEUM EXHIBIT.
AH.

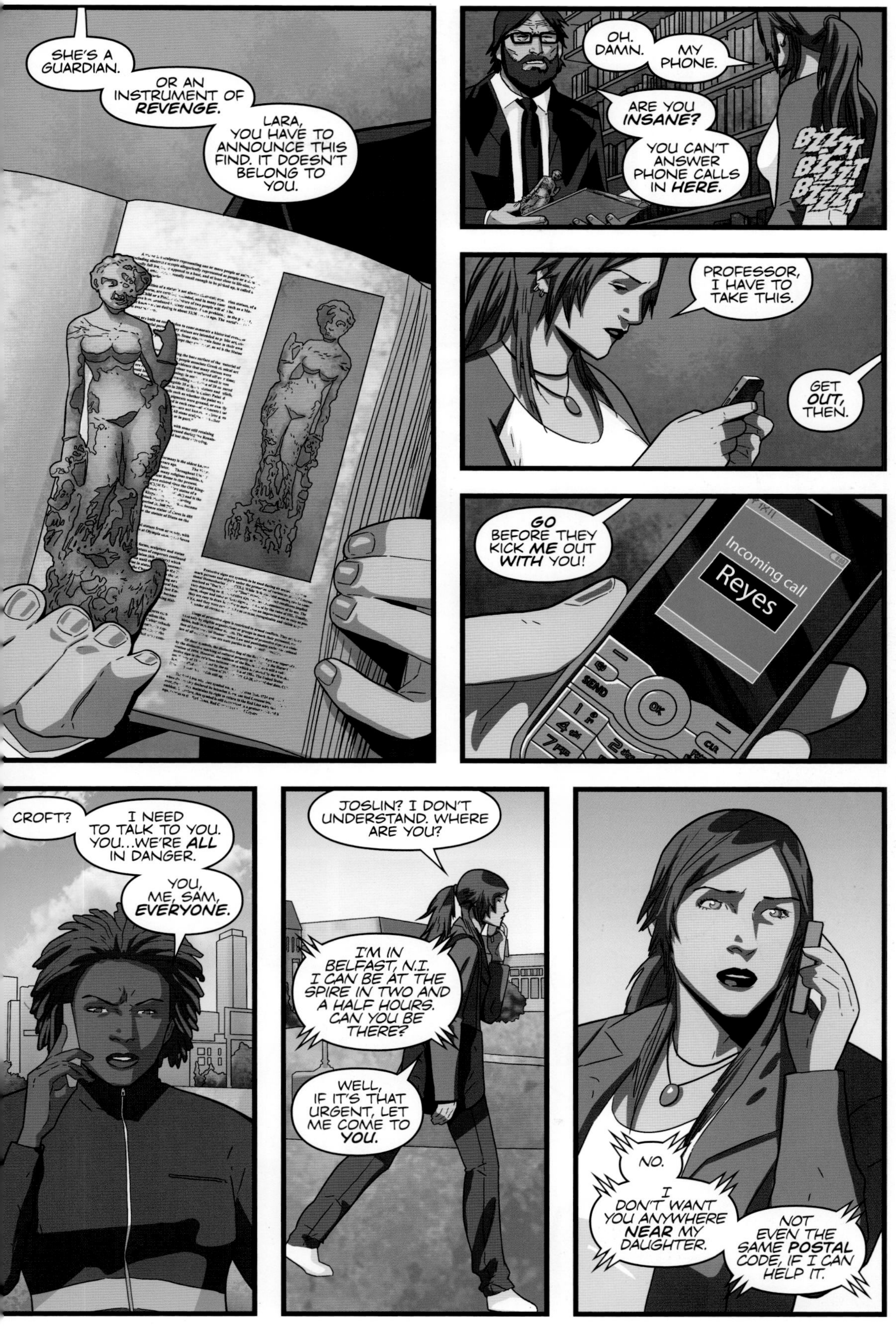

SHE'S A GUARDIAN.
OR AN INSTRUMENT OF **REVENGE**.
LARA, YOU HAVE TO ANNOUNCE THIS FIND. IT DOESN'T BELONG TO YOU.
OH. DAMN.
MY PHONE.
ARE YOU **INSANE?**
YOU CAN'T ANSWER PHONE CALLS IN **HERE**.
BZZZT BZZZT BZZZT
PROFESSOR, I HAVE TO TAKE THIS.
GET **OUT**, THEN.
GO BEFORE THEY KICK **ME** OUT **WITH** YOU!
Incoming call
Reyes
CROFT?
I NEED TO TALK TO YOU. YOU...WE'RE **ALL** IN DANGER.
YOU, ME, SAM, **EVERYONE**.
JOSLIN? I DON'T UNDERSTAND. WHERE ARE YOU?
I'M IN BELFAST, N.I. I CAN BE AT THE SPIRE IN TWO AND A HALF HOURS. CAN YOU BE THERE?
WELL, IF IT'S THAT URGENT, LET ME COME TO **YOU**.
NO.
I DON'T WANT YOU ANYWHERE **NEAR** MY DAUGHTER.
NOT EVEN THE SAME **POSTAL** CODE, IF I CAN HELP IT.

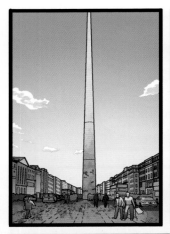

I WASN'T SURE YOU'D COME.

THAT MAKES TWO OF US. FANCY A PINT?

MORE THAN YOU'LL EVER KNOW.

I KNOW WHAT HAPPENED TO JONAH.

HOW --

DO YOU HAVE THE PIECES?

I HAVE THE ANTEFIX, REYES. THE PROFESSOR BEGGED TO STUDY THE MAKARA.

I HAVE TO SHOW YOU SOMETHING, LARA.

I'M DOING THIS TO WARN YOU OFF.

TO SAVE YOUR LIFE. BECAUSE *ROTH* CARED ABOUT YOU, YOU UNDERSTAND?

YOU SEE...

I HAVE AN ARTIFACT, *TOO.*

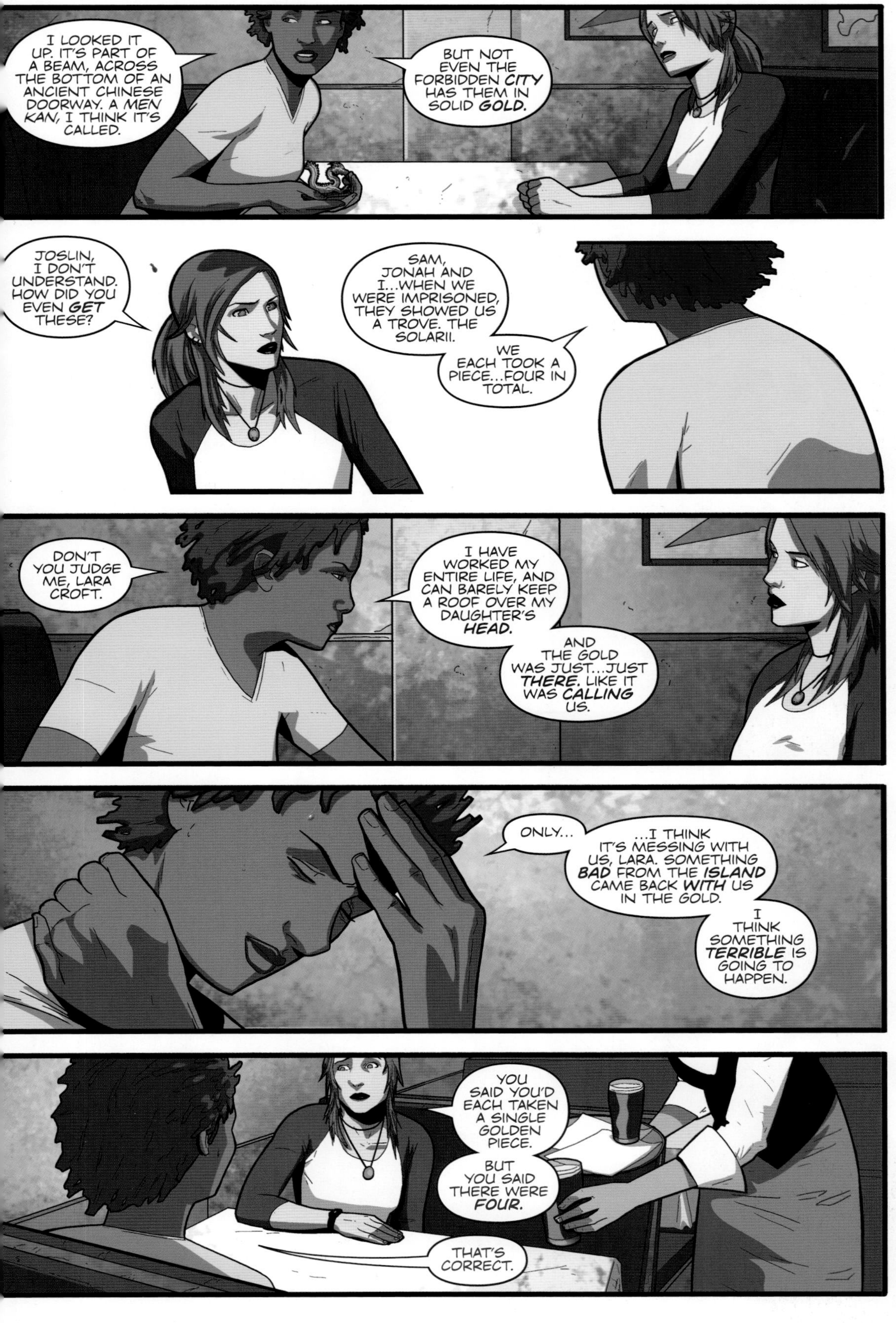
I LOOKED IT UP. IT'S PART OF A BEAM, ACROSS THE BOTTOM OF AN ANCIENT CHINESE DOORWAY. A *MEN KAN*, I THINK IT'S CALLED.
BUT NOT EVEN THE FORBIDDEN **CITY** HAS THEM IN SOLID **GOLD.**
JOSLIN, I DON'T UNDERSTAND. HOW DID YOU EVEN **GET** THESE?
SAM, JONAH AND I...WHEN WE WERE IMPRISONED, THEY SHOWED US A TROVE. THE SOLARII.
WE EACH TOOK A PIECE...FOUR IN TOTAL.
DON'T YOU JUDGE ME, LARA CROFT.
I HAVE WORKED MY ENTIRE LIFE, AND CAN BARELY KEEP A ROOF OVER MY DAUGHTER'S **HEAD.**
AND THE GOLD WAS JUST...JUST **THERE.** LIKE IT WAS **CALLING** US.
ONLY...
...I THINK IT'S MESSING WITH US, LARA. SOMETHING **BAD** FROM THE **ISLAND** CAME BACK **WITH** US IN THE GOLD.
I THINK SOMETHING **TERRIBLE** IS GOING TO HAPPEN.
YOU SAID YOU'D EACH TAKEN A SINGLE GOLDEN PIECE.
BUT YOU SAID THERE WERE **FOUR.**
THAT'S CORRECT.

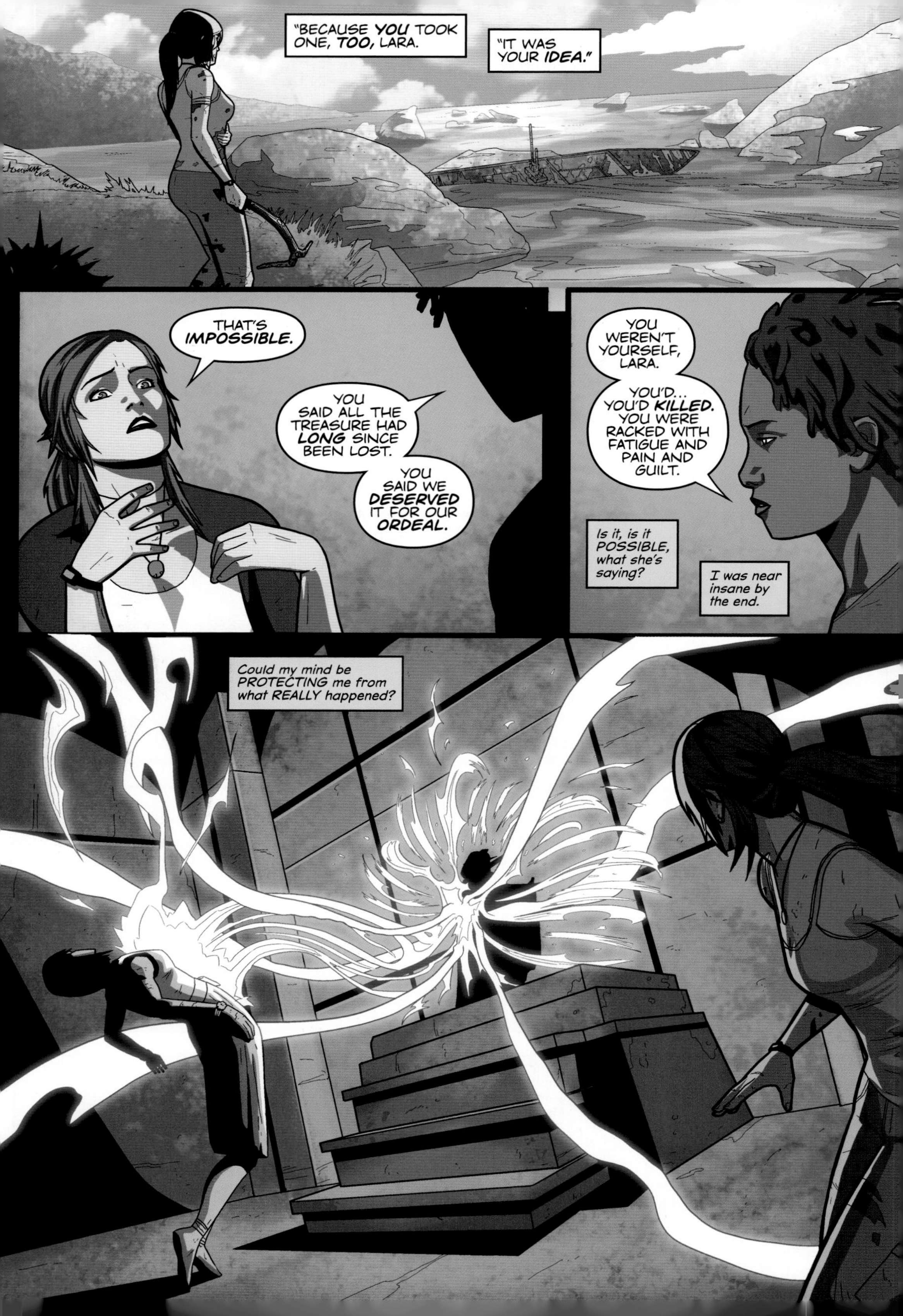
"BECAUSE YOU TOOK ONE, TOO, LARA.
"IT WAS YOUR IDEA."
THAT'S IMPOSSIBLE.
YOU SAID ALL THE TREASURE HAD LONG SINCE BEEN LOST.
YOU SAID WE DESERVED IT FOR OUR ORDEAL.
YOU WEREN'T YOURSELF, LARA.
YOU'D... YOU'D KILLED. YOU WERE RACKED WITH FATIGUE AND PAIN AND GUILT.
Is it, is it POSSIBLE, what she's saying?
I was near insane by the end.
Could my mind be PROTECTING me from what REALLY happened?

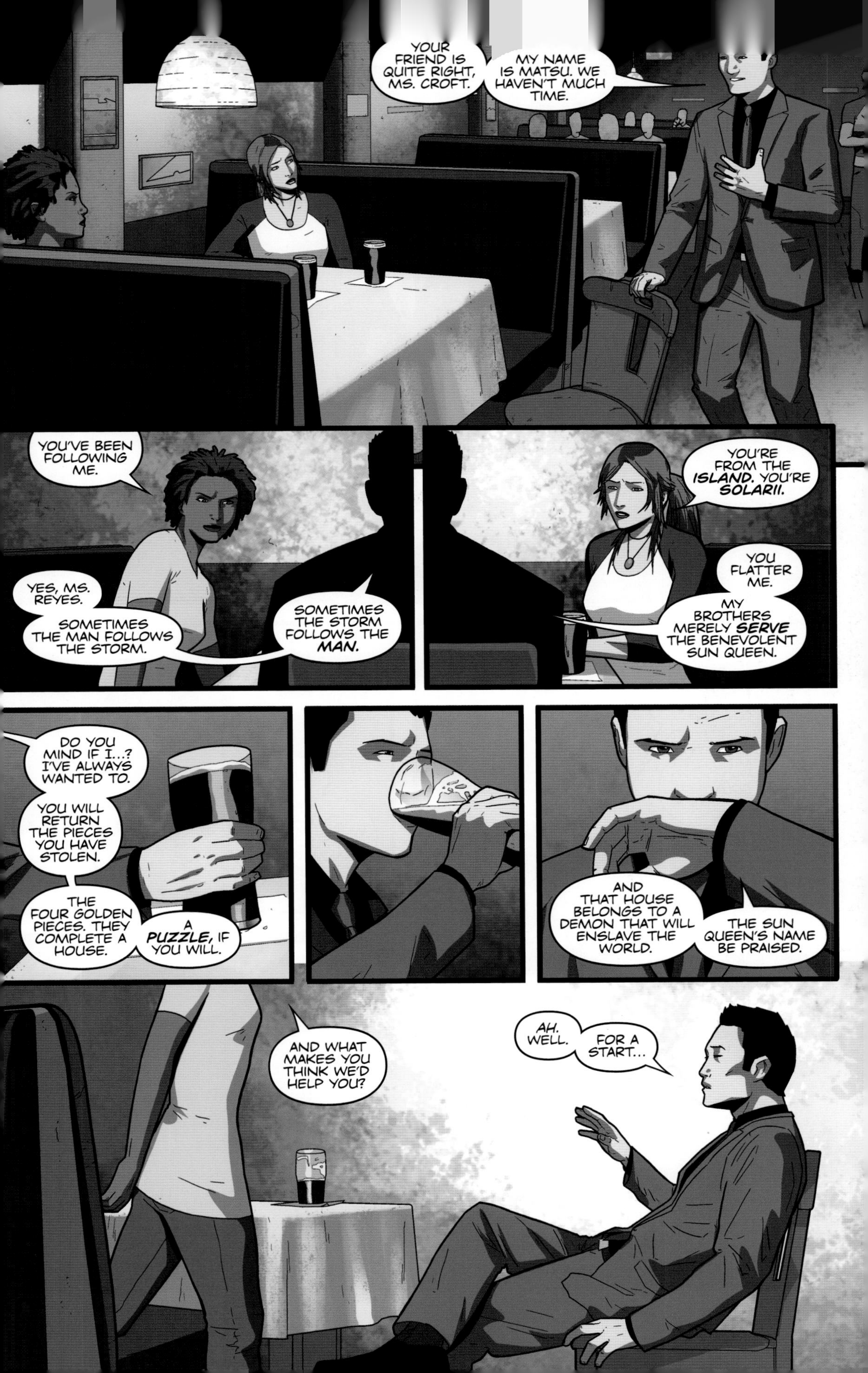
YOUR FRIEND IS QUITE RIGHT, MS. CROFT.
MY NAME IS MATSU. WE HAVEN'T MUCH TIME.
YOU'VE BEEN FOLLOWING ME.
YES, MS. REYES.
SOMETIMES THE MAN FOLLOWS THE STORM.
SOMETIMES THE STORM FOLLOWS THE MAN.
YOU'RE FROM THE ISLAND. YOU'RE SOLARII.
YOU FLATTER ME.
MY BROTHERS MERELY SERVE THE BENEVOLENT SUN QUEEN.
DO YOU MIND IF I...? I'VE ALWAYS WANTED TO.
YOU WILL RETURN THE PIECES YOU HAVE STOLEN.
THE FOUR GOLDEN PIECES. THEY COMPLETE A HOUSE.
A PUZZLE, IF YOU WILL.
AND THAT HOUSE BELONGS TO A DEMON THAT WILL ENSLAVE THE WORLD.
THE SUN QUEEN'S NAME BE PRAISED.
AND WHAT MAKES YOU THINK WE'D HELP YOU?
AH. WELL.
FOR A START...

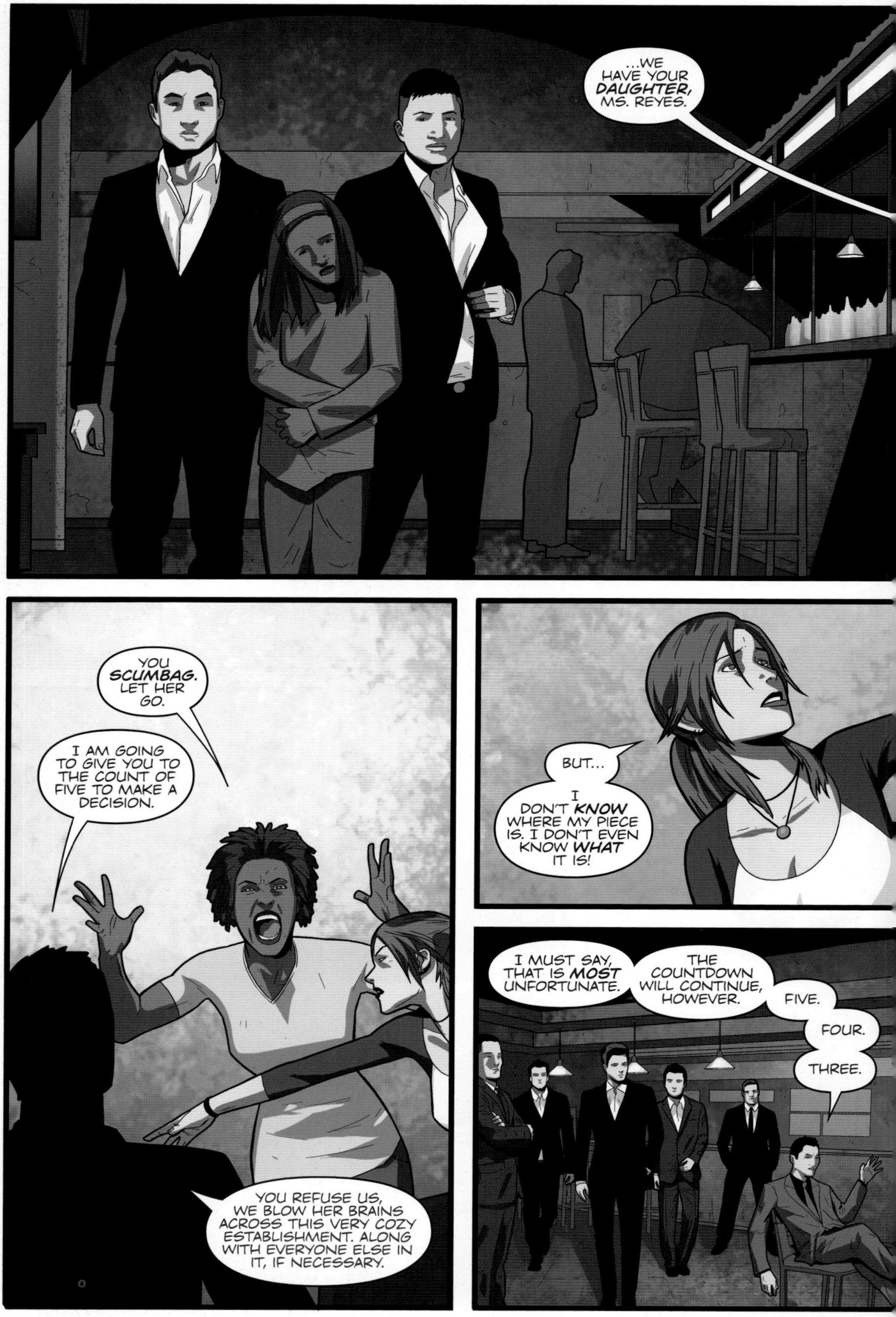
...WE HAVE YOUR DAUGHTER, MS. REYES.
YOU SCUMBAG. LET HER GO.
I AM GOING TO GIVE YOU TO THE COUNT OF FIVE TO MAKE A DECISION.
YOU REFUSE US, WE BLOW HER BRAINS ACROSS THIS VERY COZY ESTABLISHMENT. ALONG WITH EVERYONE ELSE IN IT, IF NECESSARY.
BUT...
I DON'T KNOW WHERE MY PIECE IS. I DON'T EVEN KNOW WHAT IT IS!
I MUST SAY, THAT IS MOST UNFORTUNATE.
THE COUNTDOWN WILL CONTINUE, HOWEVER.
FIVE.
FOUR.
THREE.

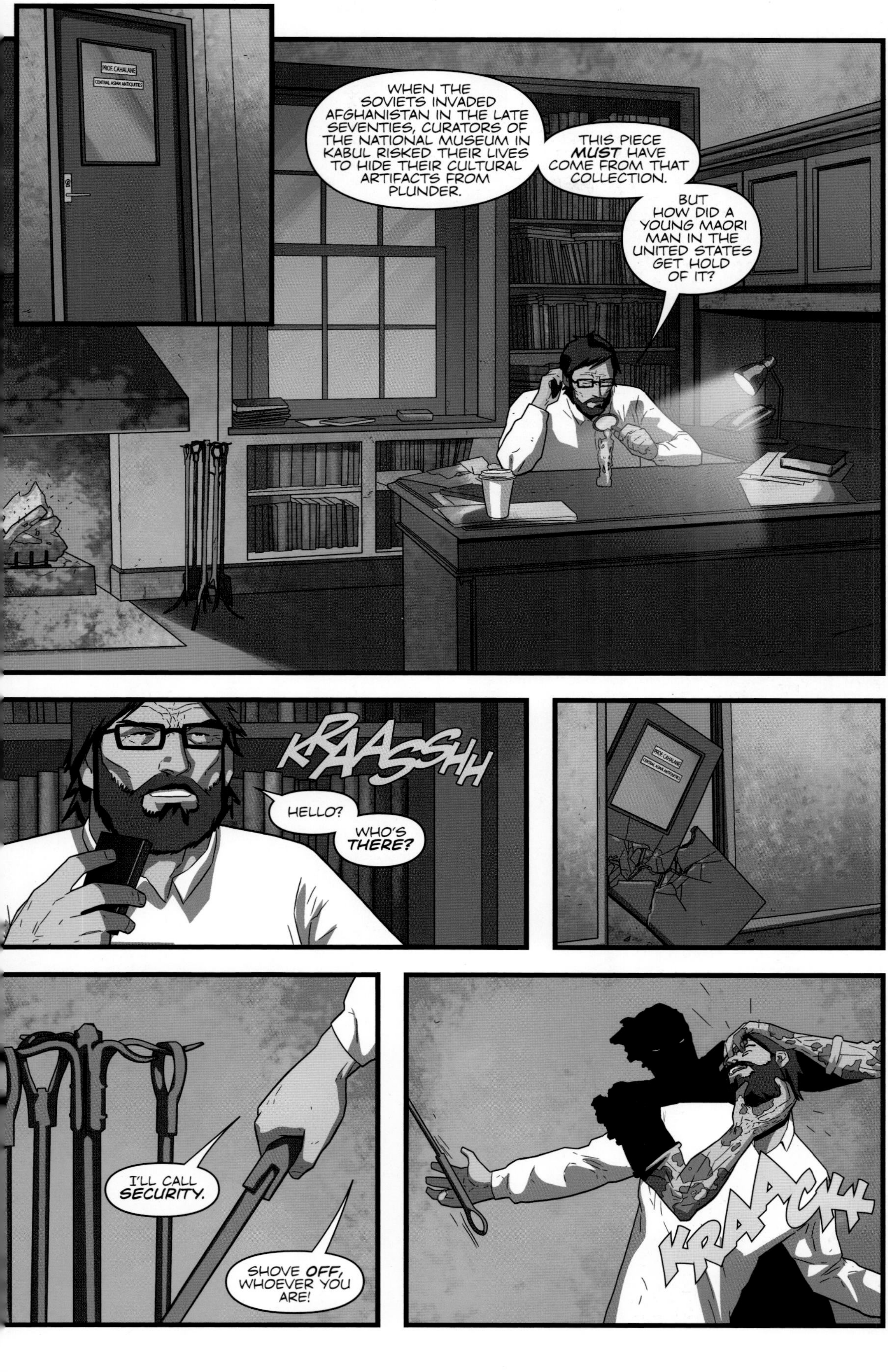
PROF. CAHALANE
CENTRAL ASIAN ANTIQUITIES
WHEN THE SOVIETS INVADED AFGHANISTAN IN THE LATE SEVENTIES, CURATORS OF THE NATIONAL MUSEUM IN KABUL RISKED THEIR LIVES TO HIDE THEIR CULTURAL ARTIFACTS FROM PLUNDER.
THIS PIECE MUST HAVE COME FROM THAT COLLECTION.
BUT HOW DID A YOUNG MAORI MAN IN THE UNITED STATES GET HOLD OF IT?
KRAASSHH
HELLO?
WHO'S THERE?
PROF. CAHALANE
CENTRAL ASIAN ANTIQUITIES
I'LL CALL SECURITY.
SHOVE OFF, WHOEVER YOU ARE!
KRAACKK

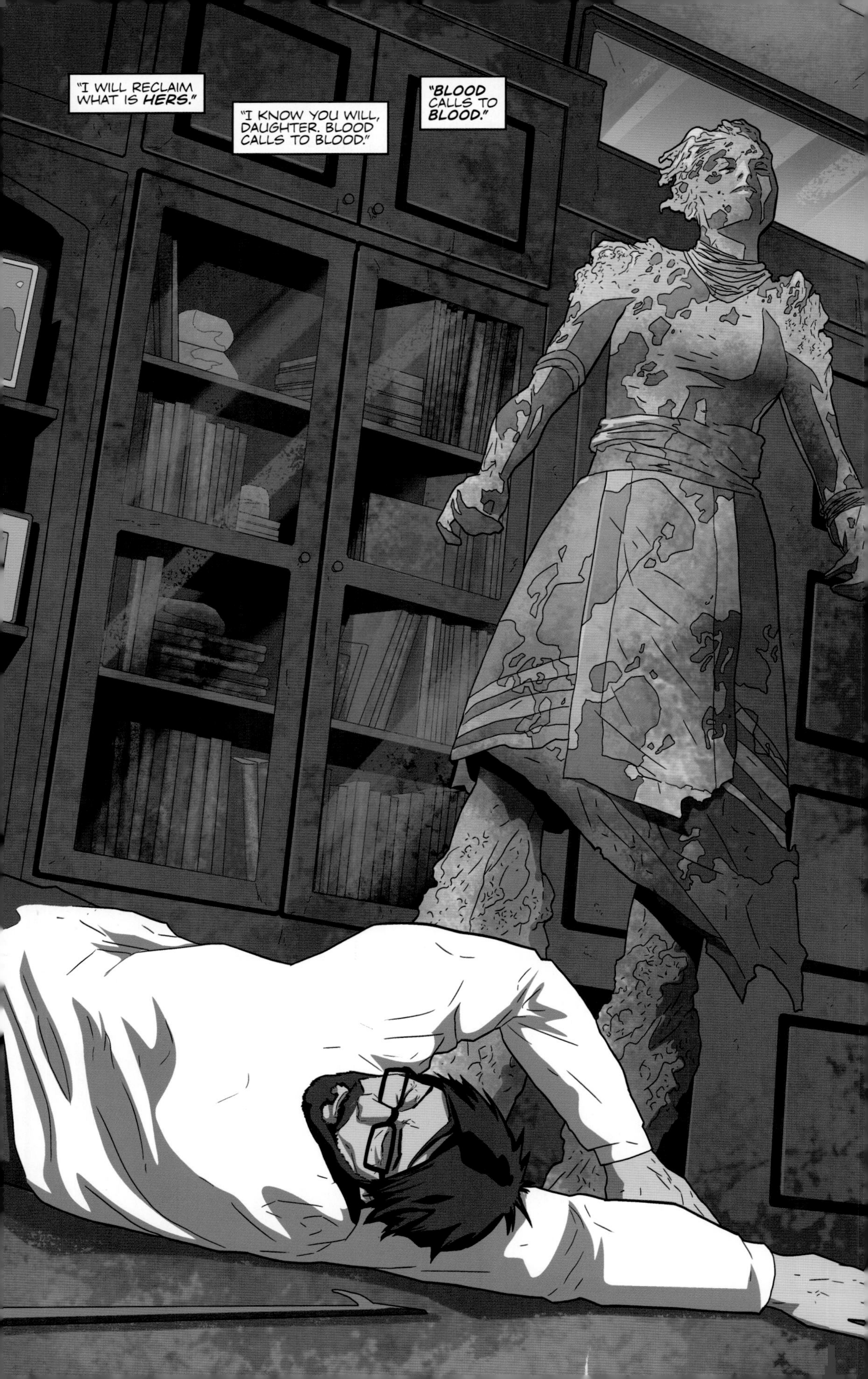
"I WILL RECLAIM WHAT IS **HERS**."
"I KNOW YOU WILL, DAUGHTER. BLOOD CALLS TO BLOOD."
"**BLOOD** CALLS TO **BLOOD**."

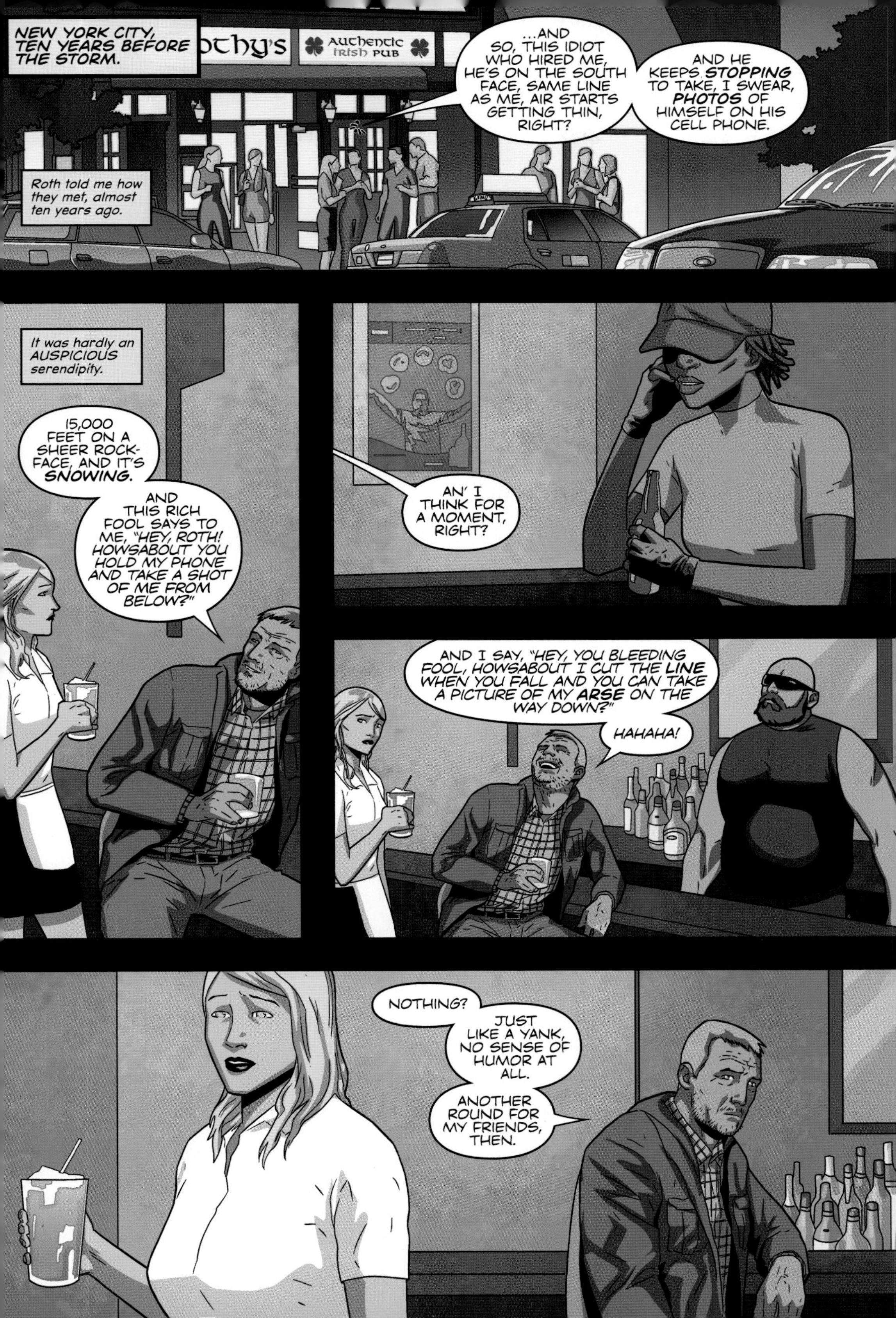
NEW YORK CITY, TEN YEARS BEFORE THE STORM.
...OTHY'S
AUTHENTIC IRISH PUB
Roth told me how they met, almost ten years ago.
...AND SO, THIS IDIOT WHO HIRED ME, HE'S ON THE SOUTH FACE, SAME LINE AS ME, AIR STARTS GETTING THIN, RIGHT?
AND HE KEEPS **STOPPING** TO TAKE, I SWEAR, **PHOTOS** OF HIMSELF ON HIS CELL PHONE.
It was hardly an AUSPICIOUS serendipity.
15,000 FEET ON A SHEER ROCK-FACE, AND IT'S **SNOWING.**
AND THIS RICH FOOL SAYS TO ME, "HEY, ROTH! HOWSABOUT YOU HOLD MY PHONE AND TAKE A SHOT OF ME FROM BELOW?"
AN' I THINK FOR A MOMENT, RIGHT?
AND I SAY, "HEY, YOU BLEEDING FOOL, HOWSABOUT I CUT THE **LINE** WHEN YOU FALL AND YOU CAN TAKE A PICTURE OF MY **ARSE** ON THE WAY DOWN?"
HAHAHA!
NOTHING?
JUST LIKE A YANK, NO SENSE OF HUMOR AT ALL.
ANOTHER ROUND FOR MY FRIENDS, THEN.

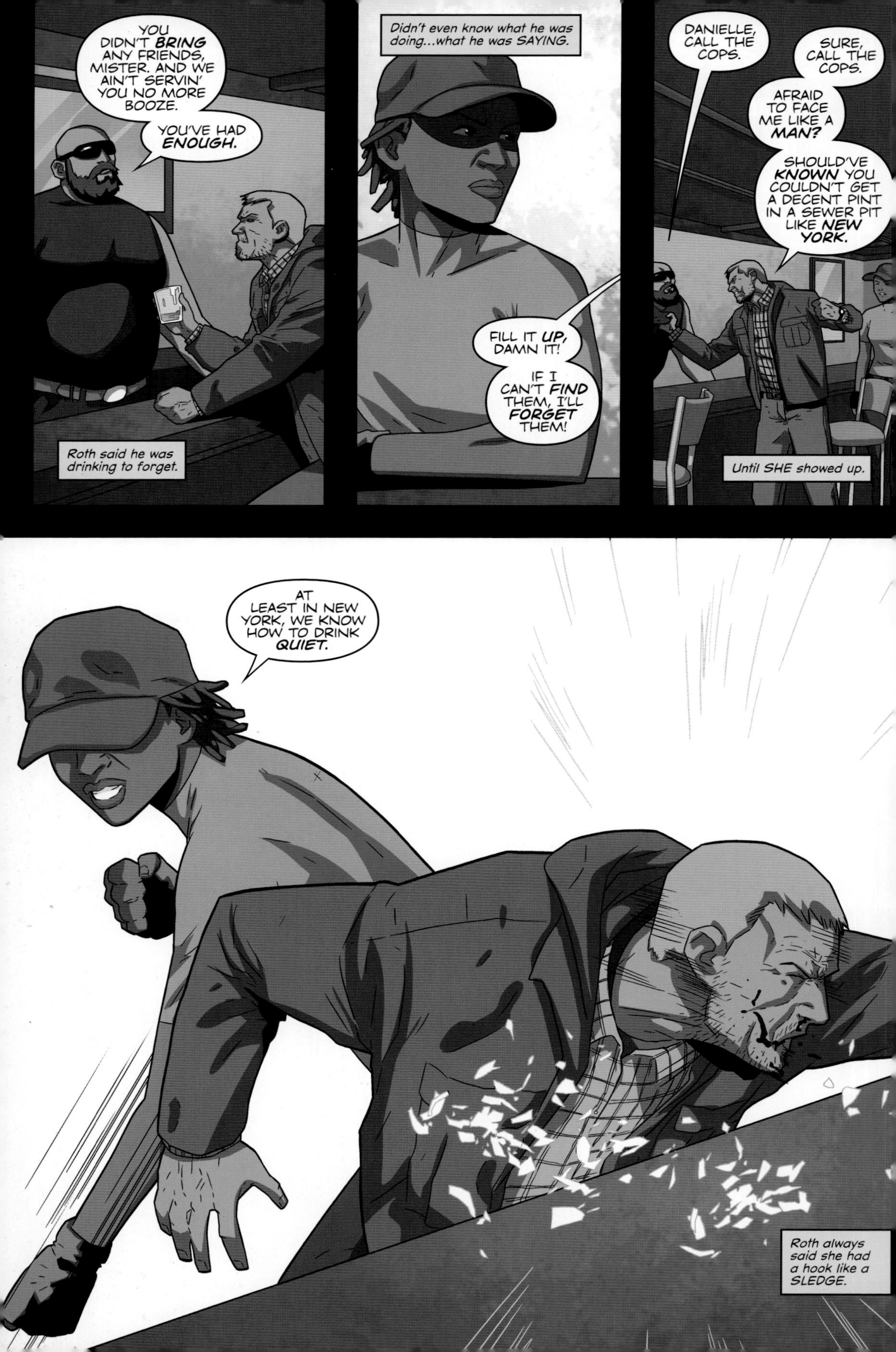
YOU DIDN'T BRING ANY FRIENDS, MISTER. AND WE AIN'T SERVIN' YOU NO MORE BOOZE.
YOU'VE HAD ENOUGH.
Roth said he was drinking to forget.
Didn't even know what he was doing...what he was SAYING.
FILL IT UP, DAMN IT!
IF I CAN'T FIND THEM, I'LL FORGET THEM!
DANIELLE, CALL THE COPS.
SURE, CALL THE COPS.
AFRAID TO FACE ME LIKE A MAN?
SHOULD'VE KNOWN YOU COULDN'T GET A DECENT PINT IN A SEWER PIT LIKE NEW YORK.
Until SHE showed up.
AT LEAST IN NEW YORK, WE KNOW HOW TO DRINK QUIET.
Roth always said she had a hook like a SLEDGE.

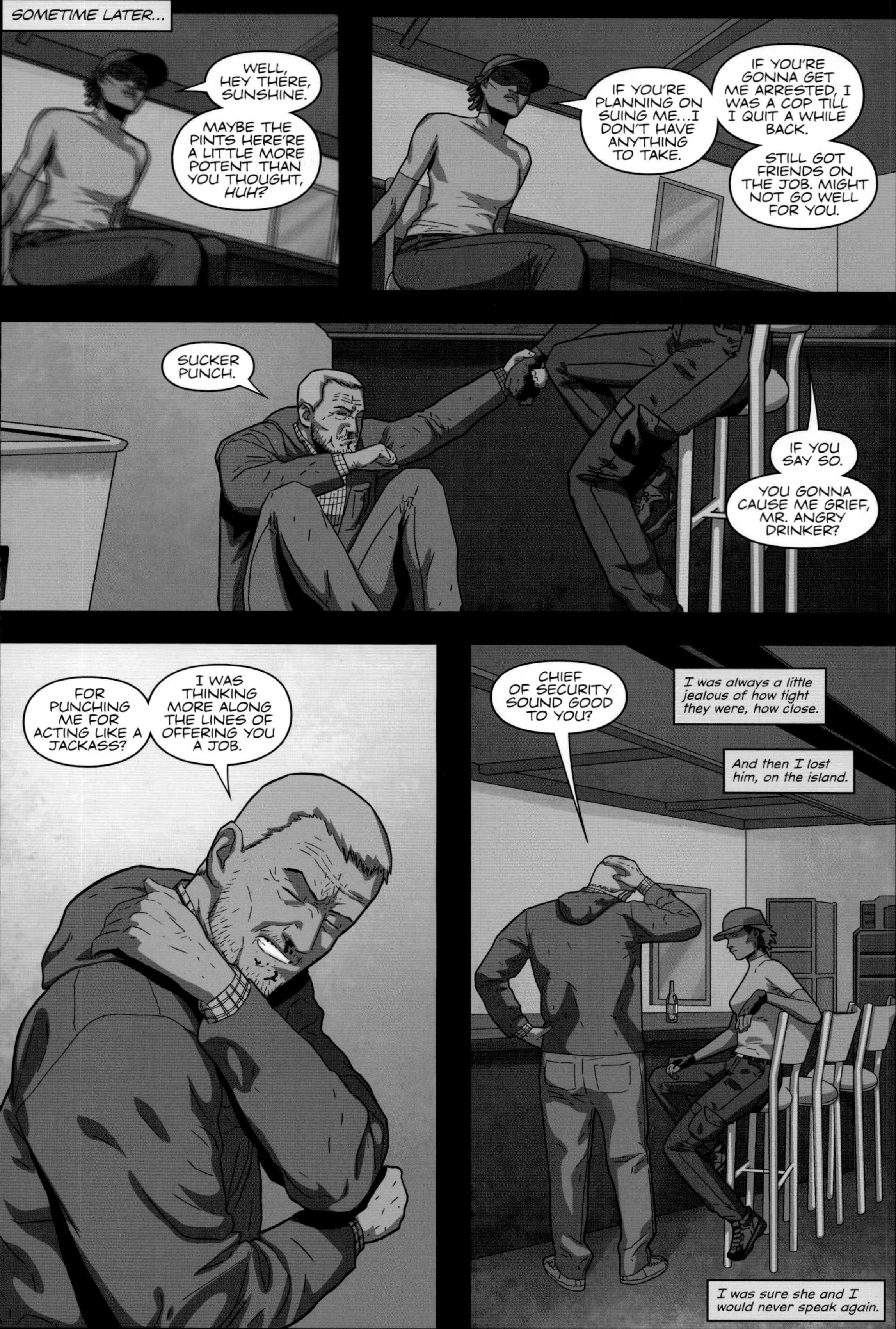
SOMETIME LATER...
WELL, HEY THERE, SUNSHINE.
MAYBE THE PINTS HERE'RE A LITTLE MORE POTENT THAN YOU THOUGHT, HUH?
IF YOU'RE PLANNING ON SUING ME...I DON'T HAVE ANYTHING TO TAKE.
IF YOU'RE GONNA GET ME ARRESTED, I WAS A COP TILL I QUIT A WHILE BACK.
STILL GOT FRIENDS ON THE JOB. MIGHT NOT GO WELL FOR YOU.
SUCKER PUNCH.
IF YOU SAY SO.
YOU GONNA CAUSE ME GRIEF, MR. ANGRY DRINKER?
FOR PUNCHING ME FOR ACTING LIKE A JACKASS?
I WAS THINKING MORE ALONG THE LINES OF OFFERING YOU A JOB.
CHIEF OF SECURITY SOUND GOOD TO YOU?
I was always a little jealous of how tight they were, how close.
And then I lost him, on the island.
I was sure she and I would never speak again.

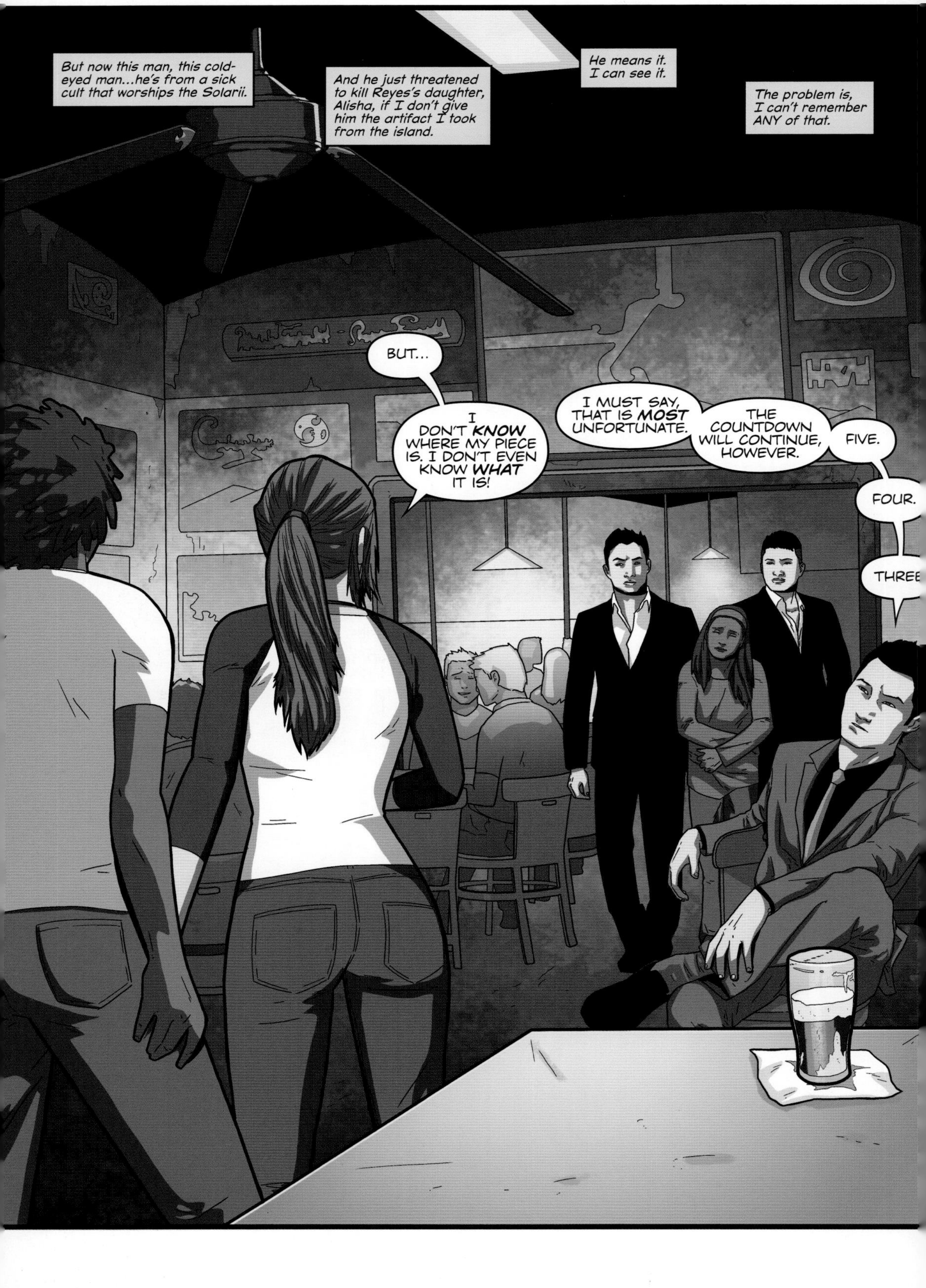

But now this man, this cold-eyed man...he's from a sick cult that worships the Solarii.
And he just threatened to kill Reyes's daughter, Alisha, if I don't give him the artifact I took from the island.
He means it. I can see it.
The problem is, I can't remember ANY of that.
BUT...
I DON'T **KNOW** WHERE MY PIECE IS. I DON'T EVEN KNOW **WHAT** IT IS!
I MUST SAY, THAT IS **MOST** UNFORTUNATE.
THE COUNTDOWN WILL CONTINUE, HOWEVER.
FIVE.
FOUR.
THREE

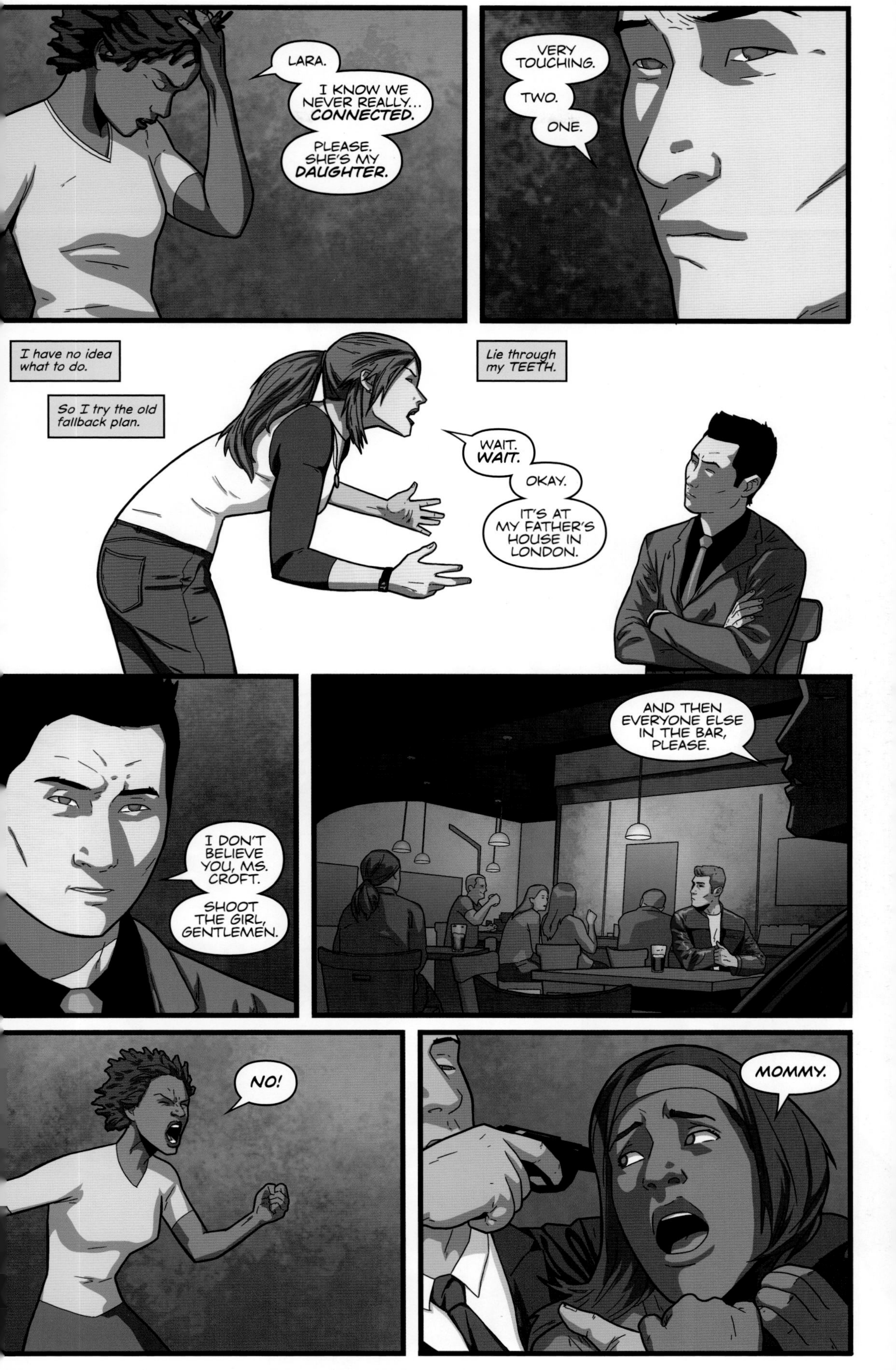
LARA.
I KNOW WE NEVER REALLY... CONNECTED.
PLEASE. SHE'S MY DAUGHTER.
VERY TOUCHING.
TWO.
ONE.
I have no idea what to do.
So I try the old fallback plan.
Lie through my TEETH.
WAIT. WAIT.
OKAY.
IT'S AT MY FATHER'S HOUSE IN LONDON.
I DON'T BELIEVE YOU, MS. CROFT.
SHOOT THE GIRL, GENTLEMEN.
AND THEN EVERYONE ELSE IN THE BAR, PLEASE.
NO!
MOMMY.

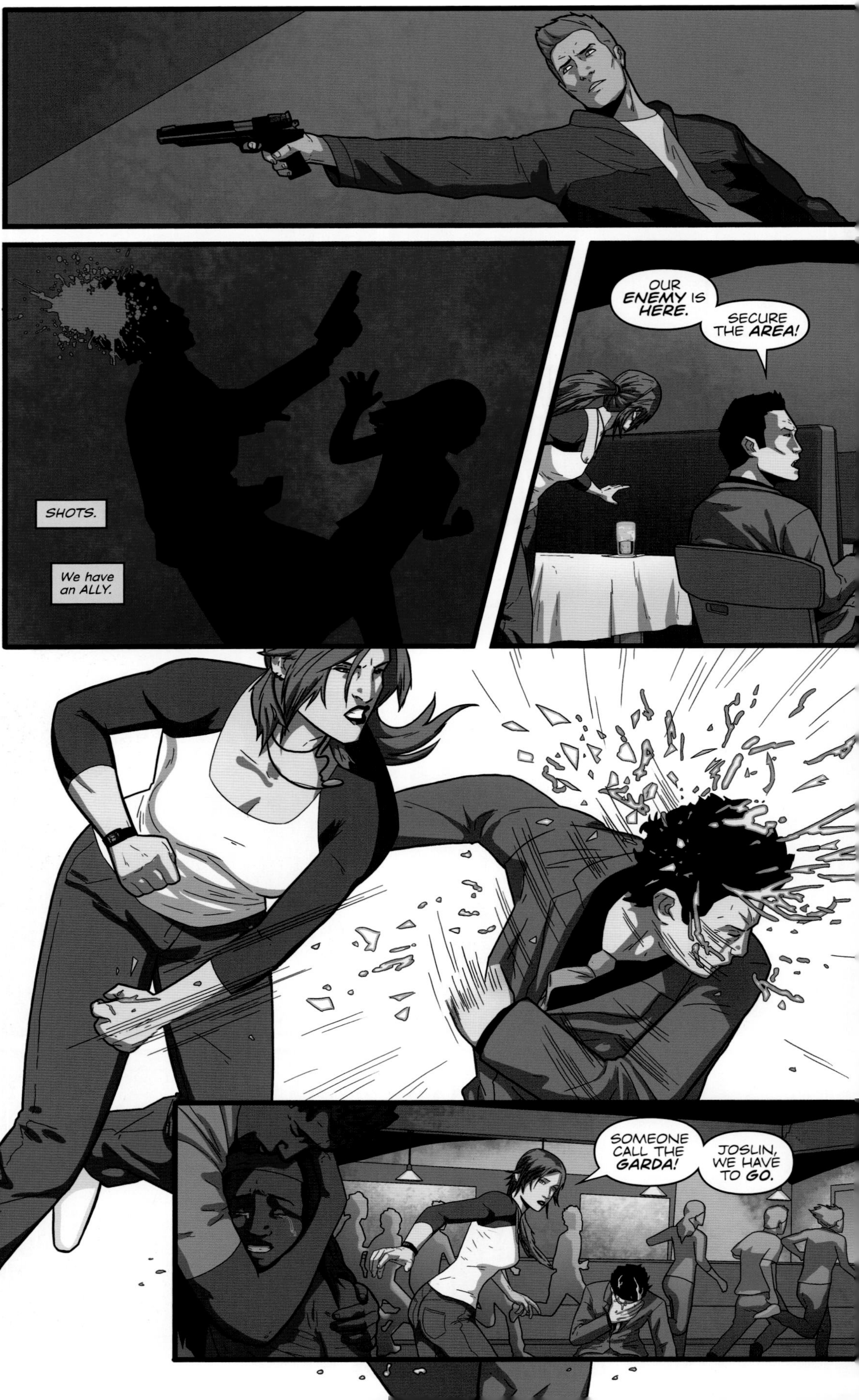
SHOTS.
We have an ALLY.
OUR ENEMY IS HERE.
SECURE THE AREA!
SOMEONE CALL THE GARDA!
JOSLIN, WE HAVE TO GO.

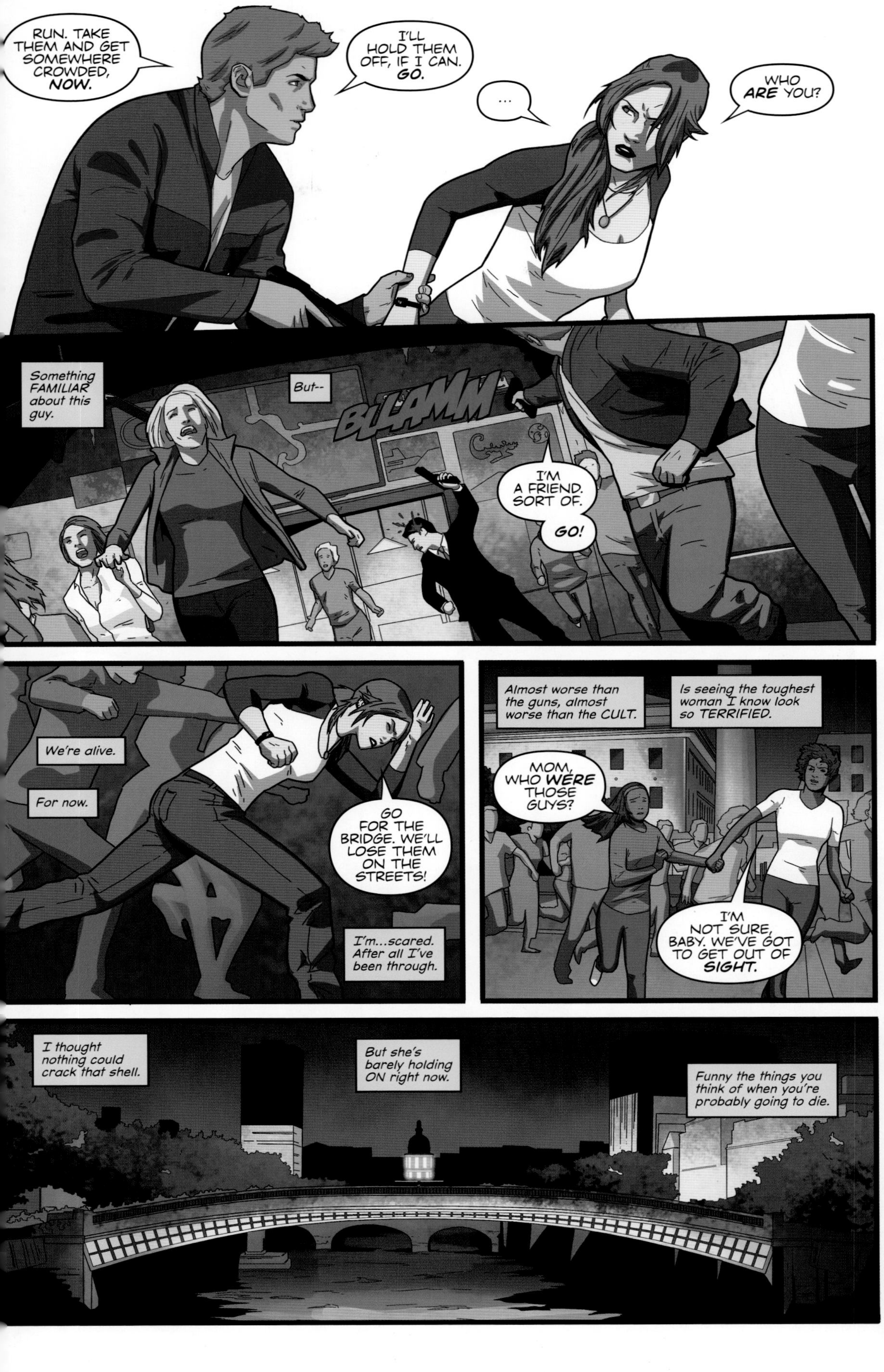
RUN. TAKE THEM AND GET SOMEWHERE CROWDED, NOW.
I'LL HOLD THEM OFF, IF I CAN. GO.
...
WHO ARE YOU?
Something FAMILIAR about this guy.
But--
BLLAMM
I'M A FRIEND. SORT OF.
GO!
We're alive.
For now.
GO FOR THE BRIDGE. WE'LL LOSE THEM ON THE STREETS!
I'm...scared. After all I've been through.
Almost worse than the guns, almost worse than the CULT.
Is seeing the toughest woman I know look so TERRIFIED.
MOM, WHO WERE THOSE GUYS?
I'M NOT SURE, BABY. WE'VE GOT TO GET OUT OF SIGHT.
I thought nothing could crack that shell.
But she's barely holding ON right now.
Funny the things you think of when you're probably going to die.

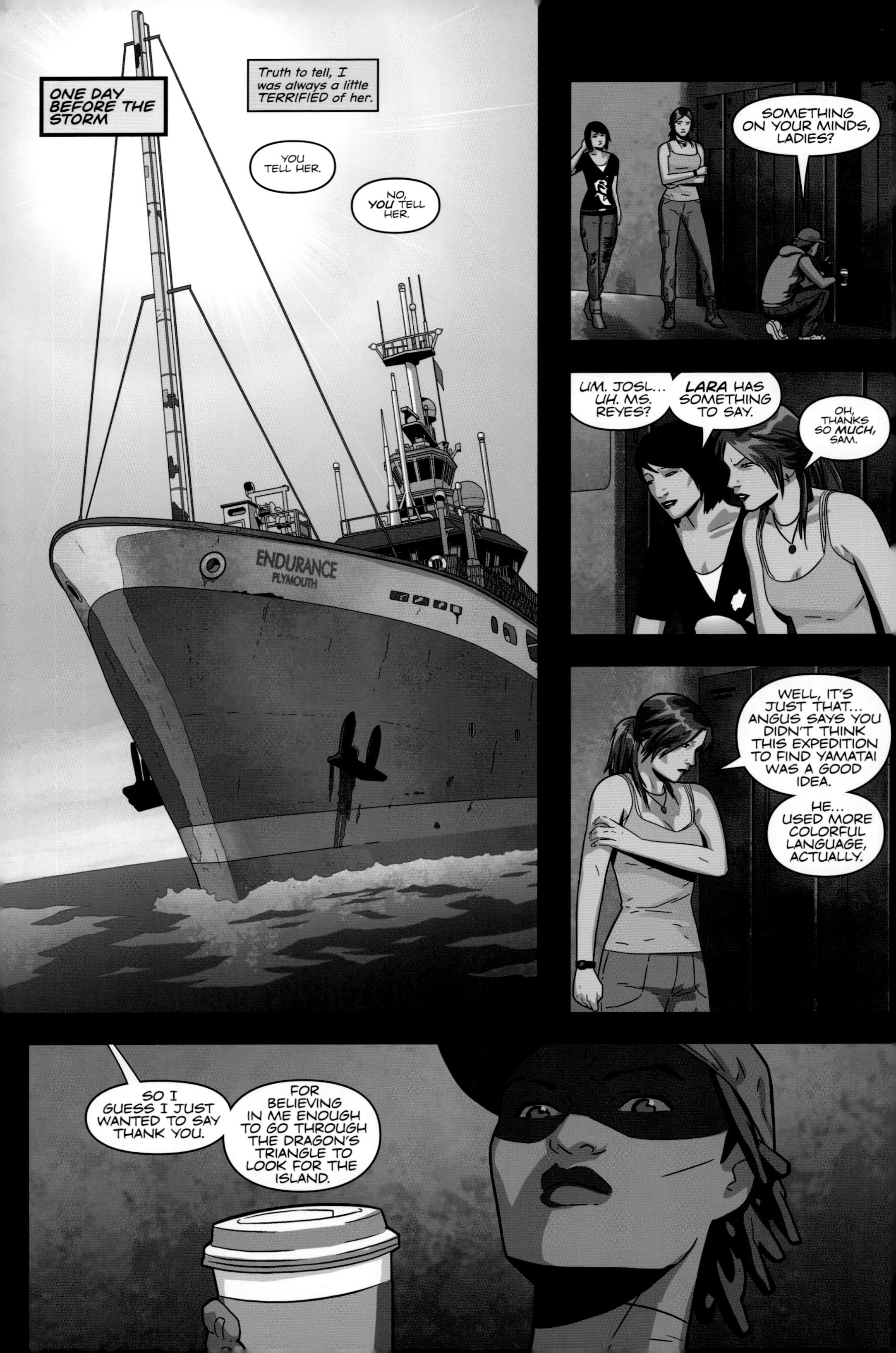
ONE DAY BEFORE THE STORM
Truth to tell, I was always a little TERRIFIED of her.
YOU TELL HER.
NO, YOU TELL HER.
ENDURANCE
PLYMOUTH
SOMETHING ON YOUR MINDS, LADIES?
UM. JOSL... UH. MS. REYES?
LARA HAS SOMETHING TO SAY.
OH, THANKS SO MUCH, SAM.
WELL, IT'S JUST THAT... ANGUS SAYS YOU DIDN'T THINK THIS EXPEDITION TO FIND YAMATAI WAS A GOOD IDEA.
HE... USED MORE COLORFUL LANGUAGE, ACTUALLY.
SO I GUESS I JUST WANTED TO SAY THANK YOU.
FOR BELIEVING IN ME ENOUGH TO GO THROUGH THE DRAGON'S TRIANGLE TO LOOK FOR THE ISLAND.

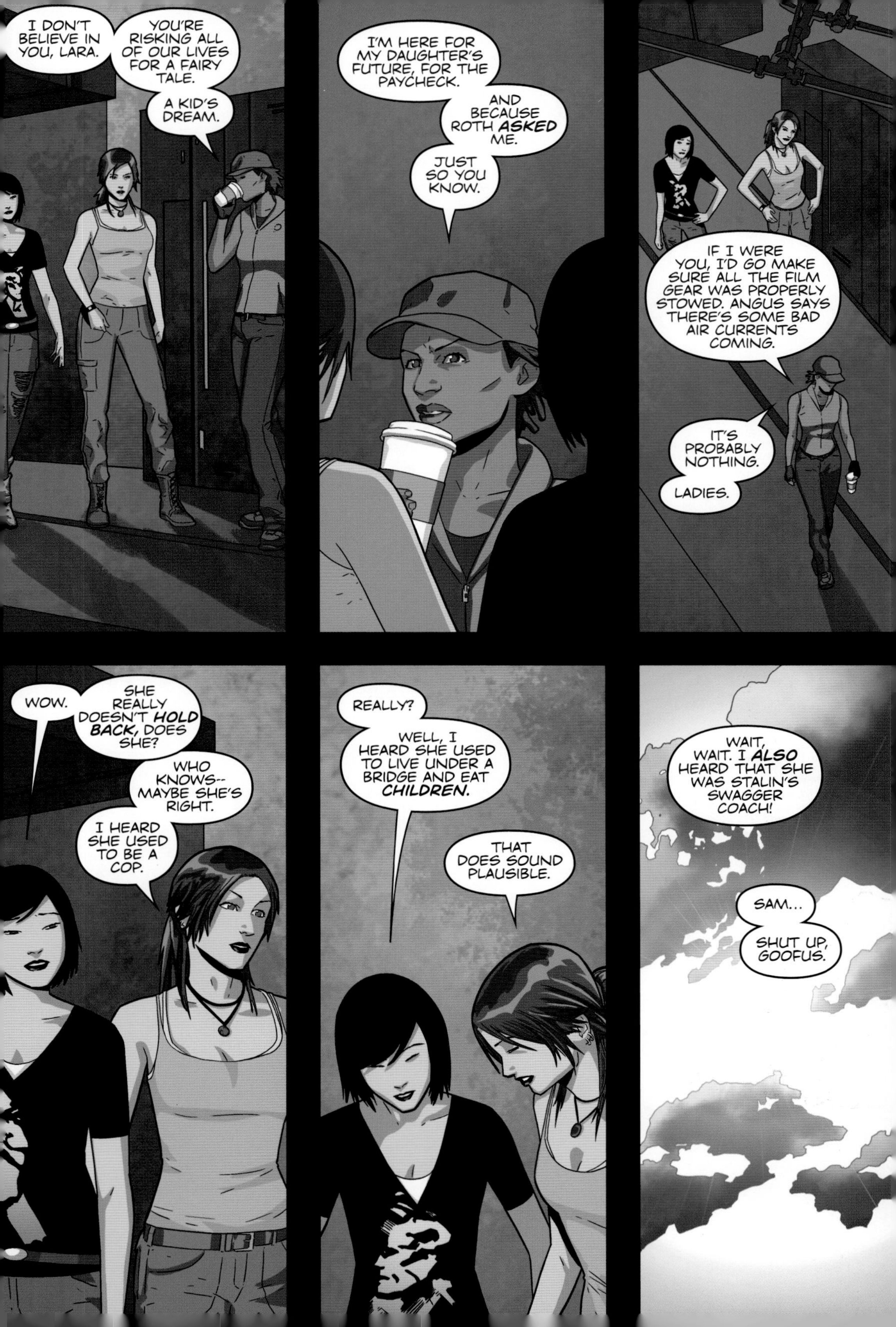

I DON'T BELIEVE IN YOU, LARA.
YOU'RE RISKING ALL OF OUR LIVES FOR A FAIRY TALE.
A KID'S DREAM.
I'M HERE FOR MY DAUGHTER'S FUTURE, FOR THE PAYCHECK.
AND BECAUSE ROTH **ASKED** ME.
JUST SO YOU KNOW.
IF I WERE YOU, I'D GO MAKE SURE ALL THE FILM GEAR WAS PROPERLY STOWED. ANGUS SAYS THERE'S SOME BAD AIR CURRENTS COMING.
IT'S PROBABLY NOTHING.
LADIES.
WOW.
SHE REALLY DOESN'T **HOLD BACK,** DOES SHE?
WHO KNOWS-- MAYBE SHE'S RIGHT.
I HEARD SHE USED TO BE A COP.
REALLY?
WELL, I HEARD SHE USED TO LIVE UNDER A BRIDGE AND EAT **CHILDREN.**
THAT DOES SOUND PLAUSIBLE.
WAIT, WAIT. I **ALSO** HEARD THAT SHE WAS STALIN'S SWAGGER COACH!
SAM...
SHUT UP, GOOFUS.

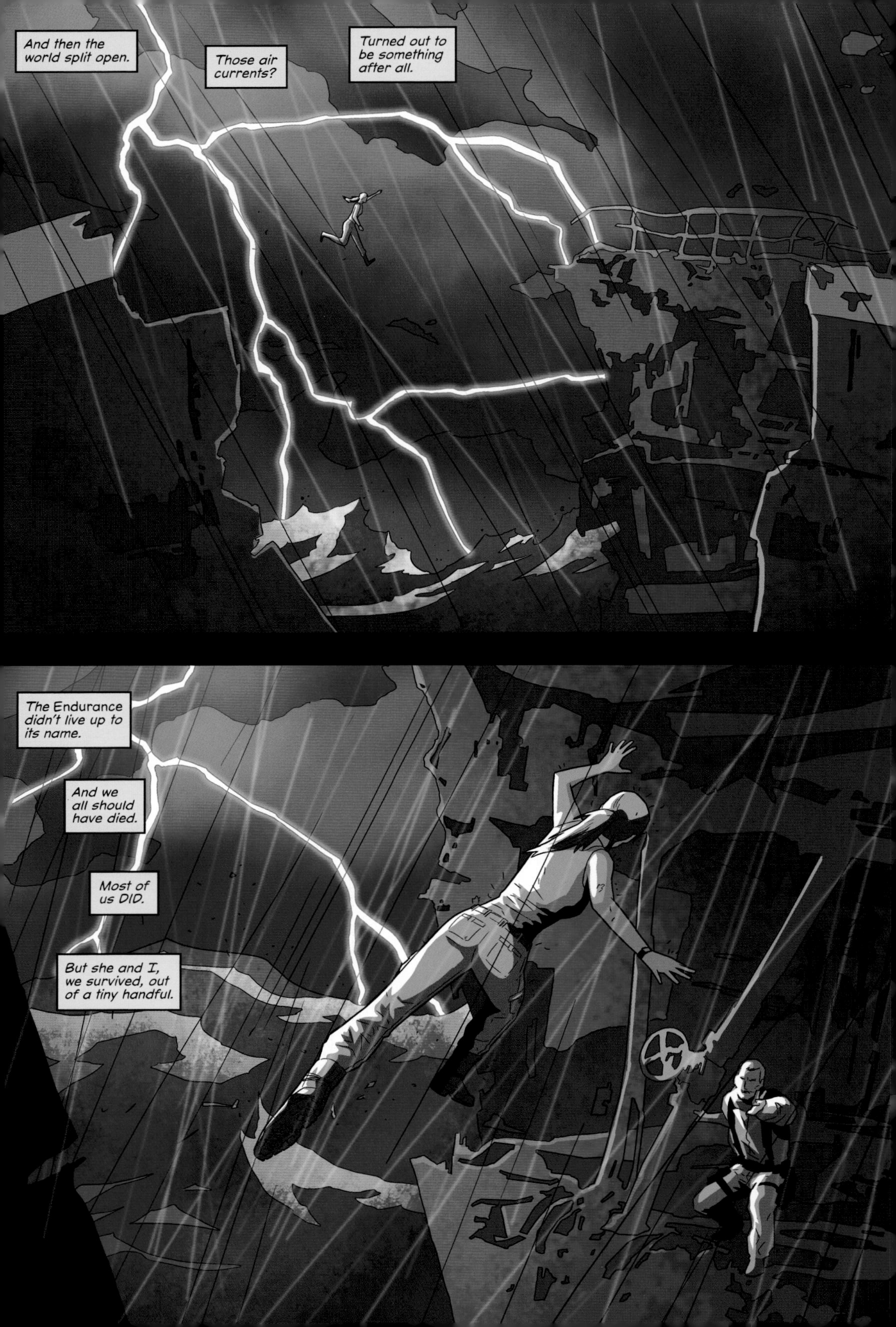
And then the world split open.
Those air currents?
Turned out to be something after all.
The Endurance didn't live up to its name.
And we all should have died.
Most of us DID.
But she and I, we survived, out of a tiny handful.

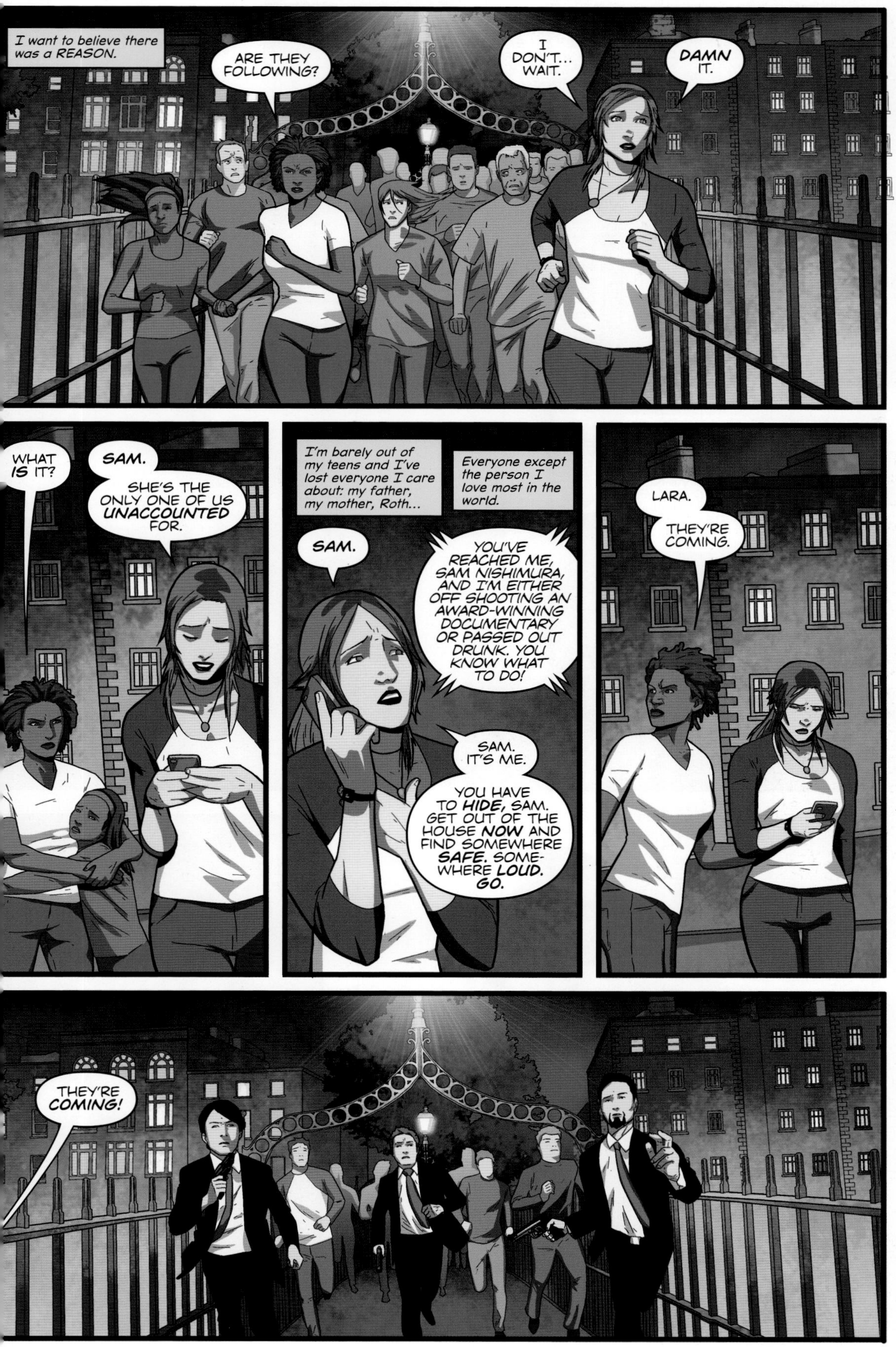
I want to believe there was a REASON.
ARE THEY FOLLOWING?
I DON'T... WAIT.
DAMN IT.
WHAT IS IT?
SAM.
SHE'S THE ONLY ONE OF US UNACCOUNTED FOR.
I'm barely out of my teens and I've lost everyone I care about: my father, my mother, Roth...
Everyone except the person I love most in the world.
SAM.
YOU'VE REACHED ME, SAM NISHIMURA, AND I'M EITHER OFF SHOOTING AN AWARD-WINNING DOCUMENTARY OR PASSED OUT DRUNK. YOU KNOW WHAT TO DO!
SAM. IT'S ME.
YOU HAVE TO HIDE, SAM. GET OUT OF THE HOUSE NOW AND FIND SOMEWHERE SAFE. SOMEWHERE LOUD. GO.
LARA.
THEY'RE COMING.
THEY'RE COMING!

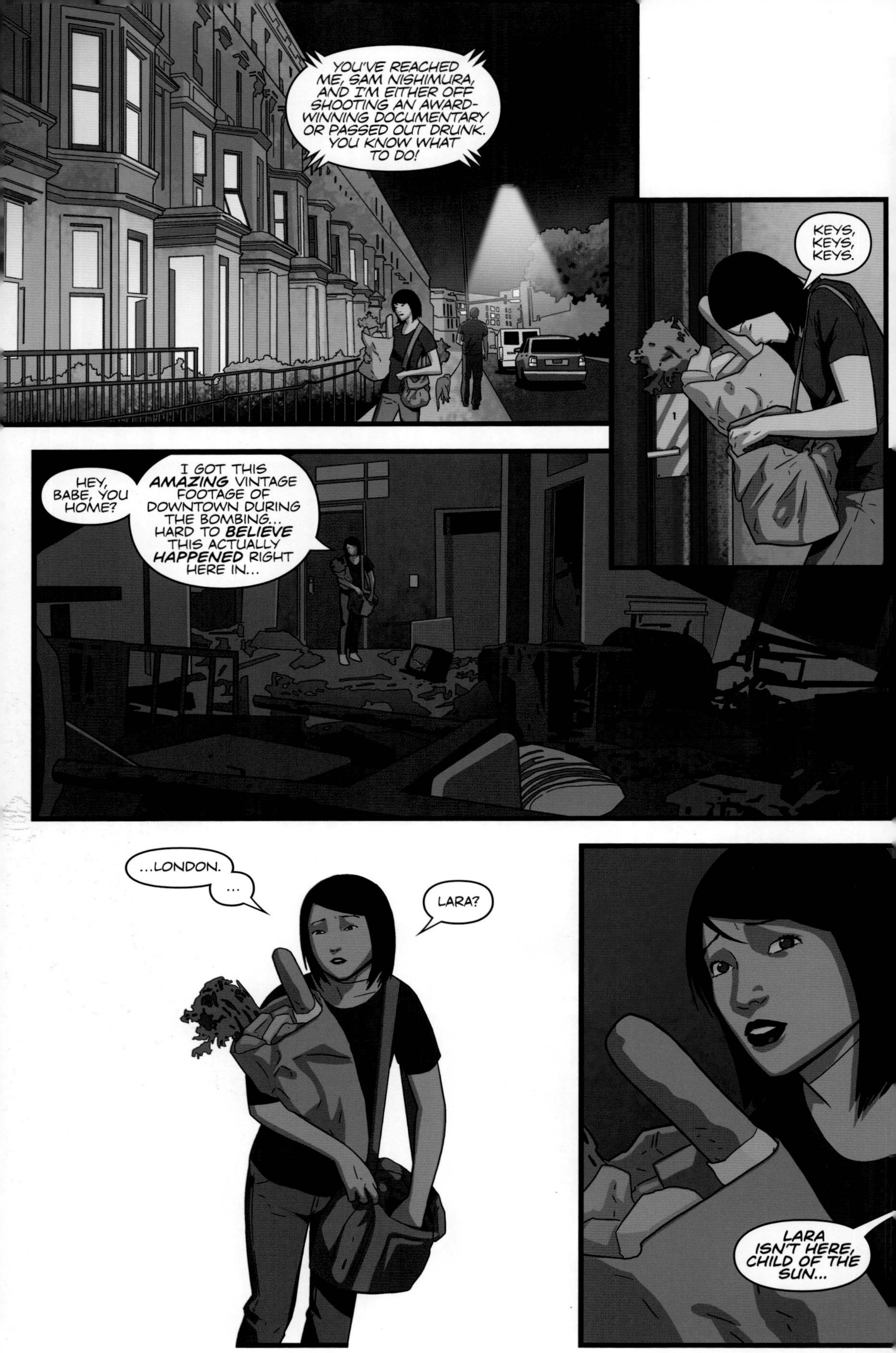
YOU'VE REACHED ME, SAM NISHIMURA, AND I'M EITHER OFF SHOOTING AN AWARD-WINNING DOCUMENTARY OR PASSED OUT DRUNK. YOU KNOW WHAT TO DO!
KEYS, KEYS, KEYS.
HEY, BABE, YOU HOME?
I GOT THIS AMAZING VINTAGE FOOTAGE OF DOWNTOWN DURING THE BOMBING... HARD TO BELIEVE THIS ACTUALLY HAPPENED RIGHT HERE IN...
...LONDON.
...
LARA?
LARA ISN'T HERE, CHILD OF THE SUN...

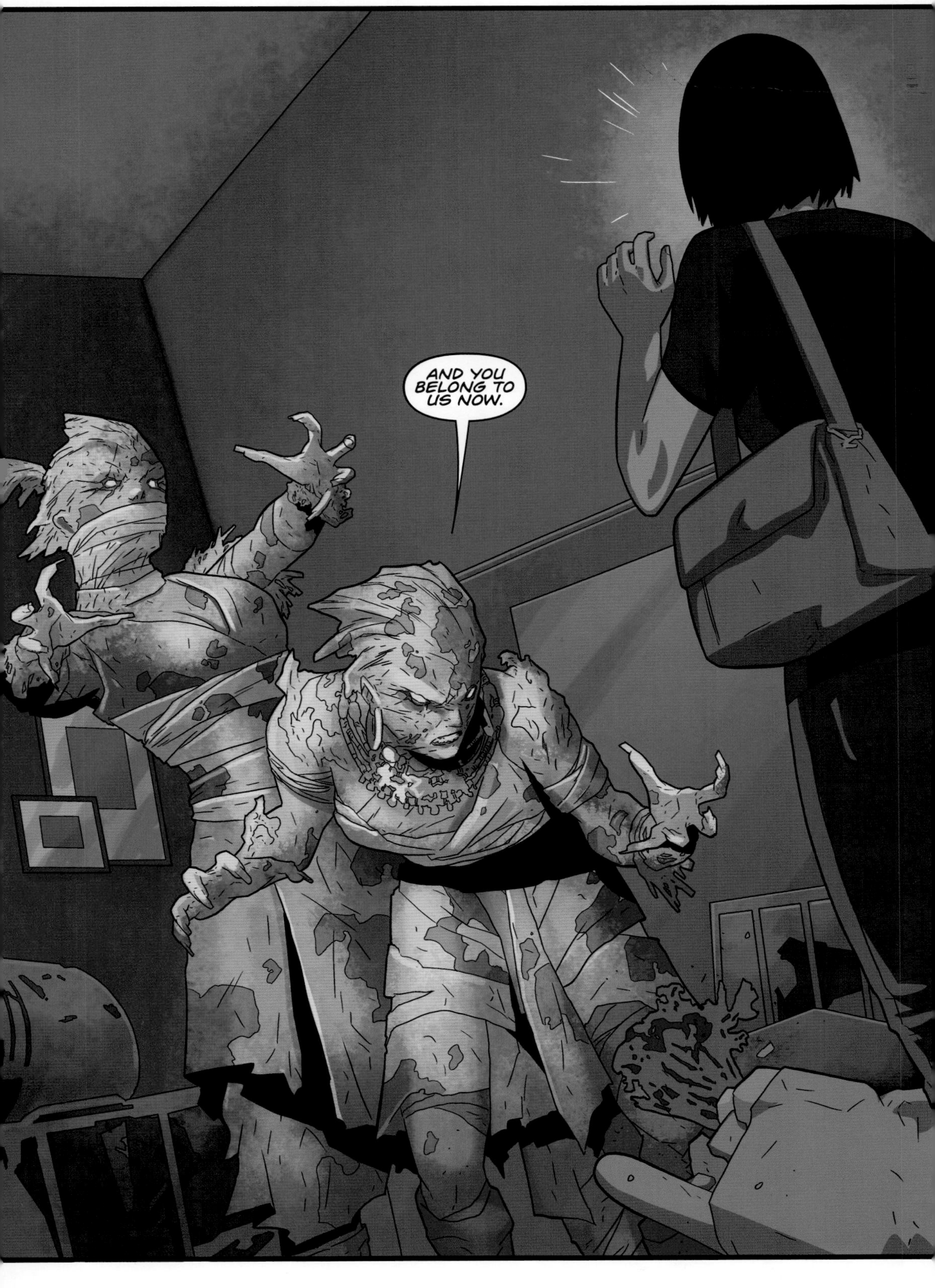
AND YOU BELONG TO US NOW.

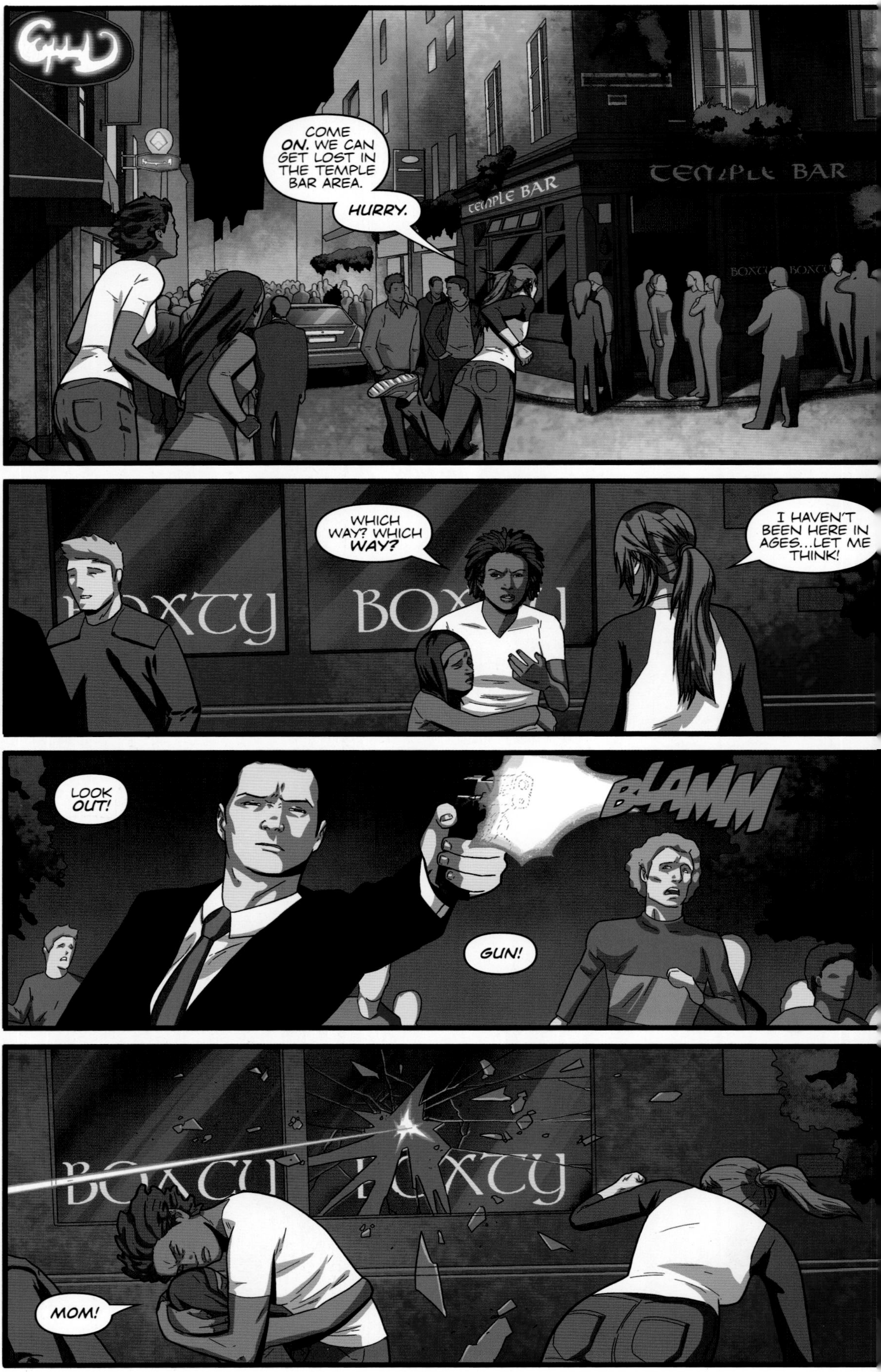
COME ON. WE CAN GET LOST IN THE TEMPLE BAR AREA.
HURRY.
TEMPLE BAR
TEMPLE BAR
WHICH WAY? WHICH WAY?
I HAVEN'T BEEN HERE IN AGES...LET ME THINK!
BOXTY
LOOK OUT!
BLAMM
GUN!
MOM!

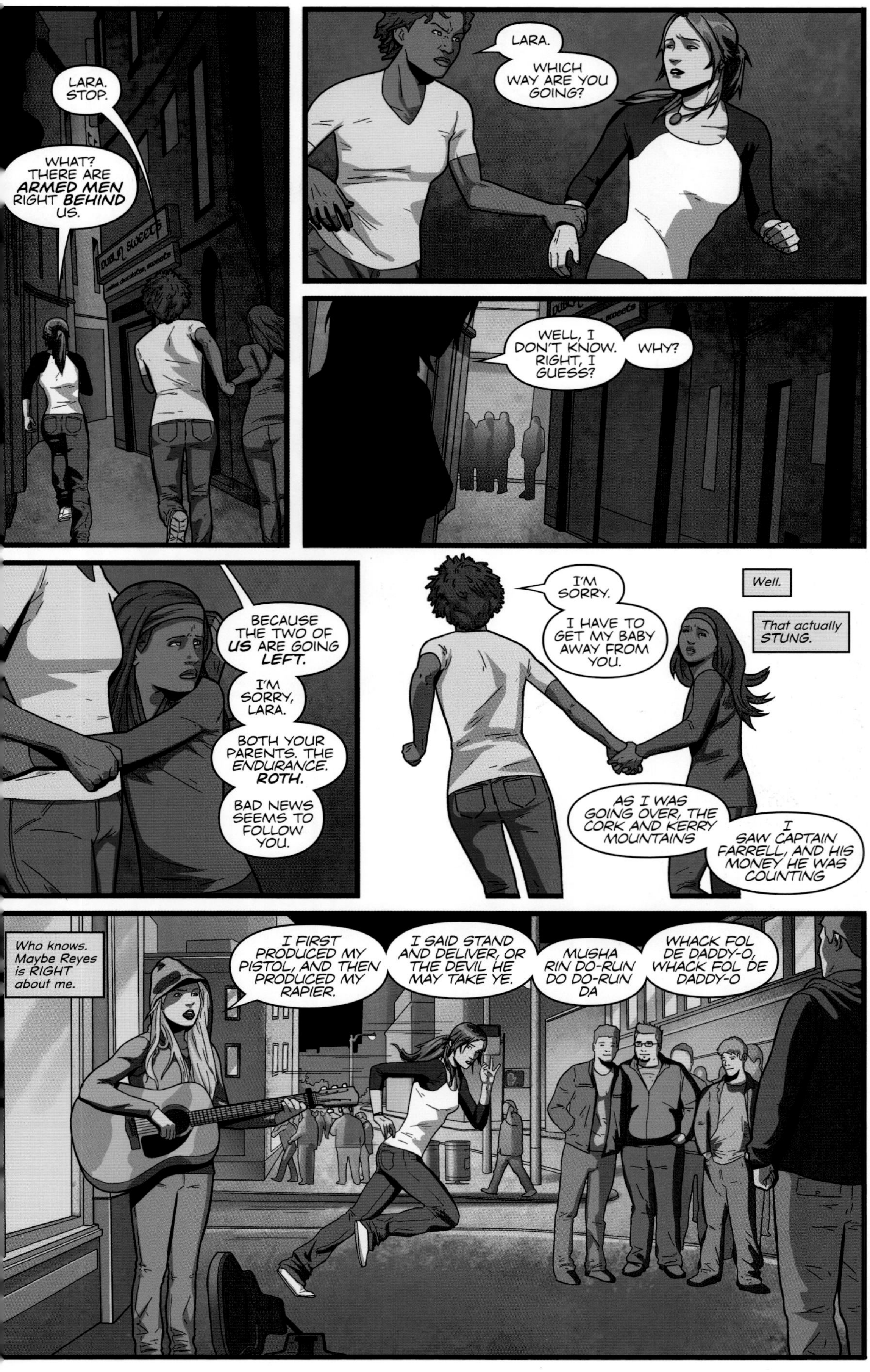
LARA. STOP.
WHAT? THERE ARE **ARMED MEN** RIGHT **BEHIND** US.
DUBLIN SWEETS
LARA.
WHICH WAY ARE YOU GOING?
WELL, I DON'T KNOW. RIGHT, I GUESS?
WHY?
BECAUSE THE TWO OF **US** ARE GOING **LEFT**.
I'M SORRY, LARA.
BOTH YOUR PARENTS. THE ENDURANCE. **ROTH**.
BAD NEWS SEEMS TO FOLLOW YOU.
I'M SORRY.
I HAVE TO GET MY BABY AWAY FROM YOU.
Well.
That actually STUNG.
AS I WAS GOING OVER, THE CORK AND KERRY MOUNTAINS
I SAW CAPTAIN FARRELL, AND HIS MONEY HE WAS COUNTING
Who knows. Maybe Reyes is RIGHT about me.
I FIRST PRODUCED MY PISTOL, AND THEN PRODUCED MY RAPIER.
I SAID STAND AND DELIVER, OR THE DEVIL HE MAY TAKE YE.
MUSHA RIN DO-RUN DO DO-RUN DA
WHACK FOL DE DADDY-O, WHACK FOL DE DADDY-O

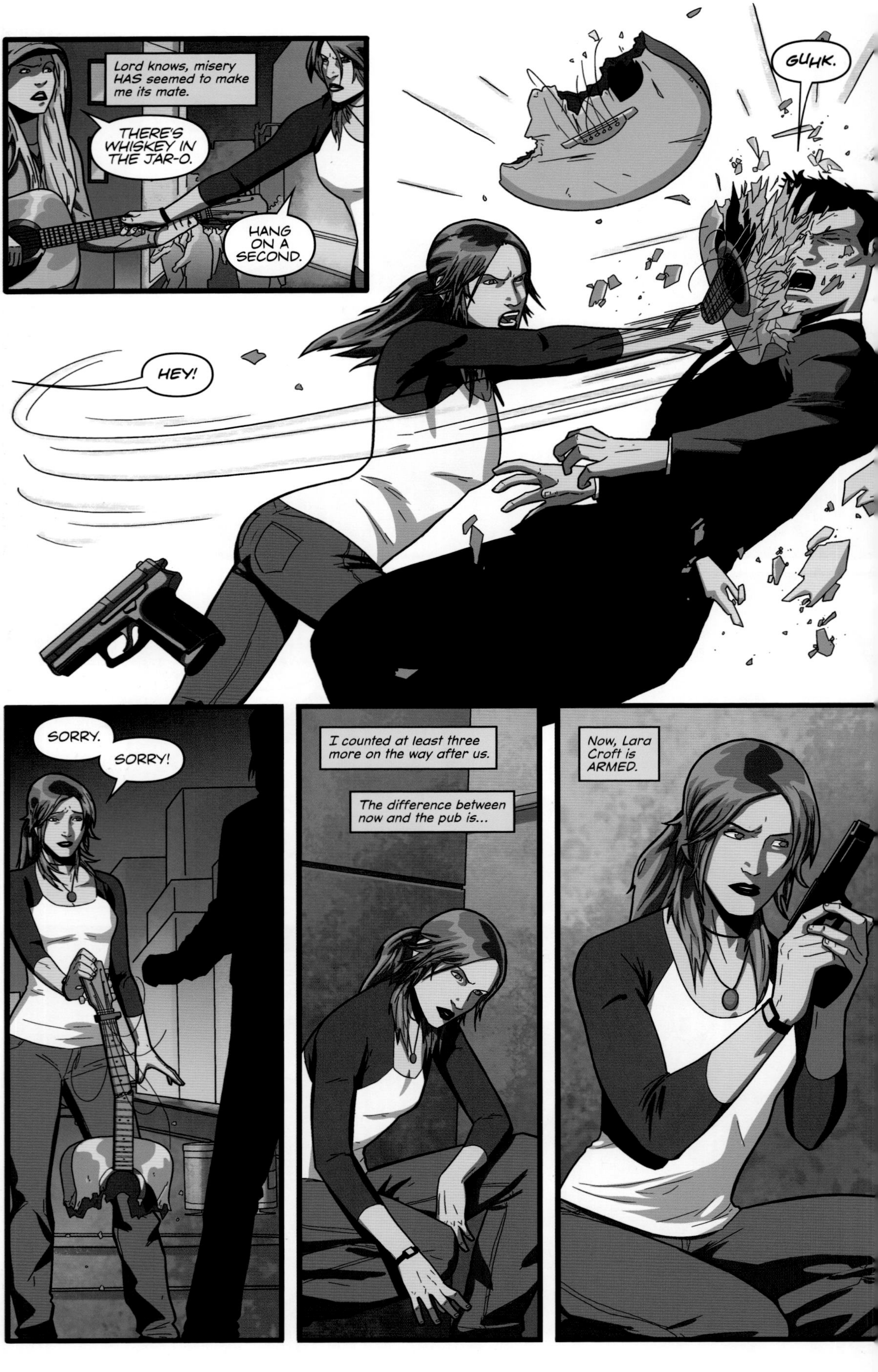
Lord knows, misery HAS seemed to make me its mate.
THERE'S WHISKEY IN THE JAR-O.
HANG ON A SECOND.
GUHK.
HEY!
SORRY.
SORRY!
I counted at least three more on the way after us.
The difference between now and the pub is...
Now, Lara Croft is ARMED.

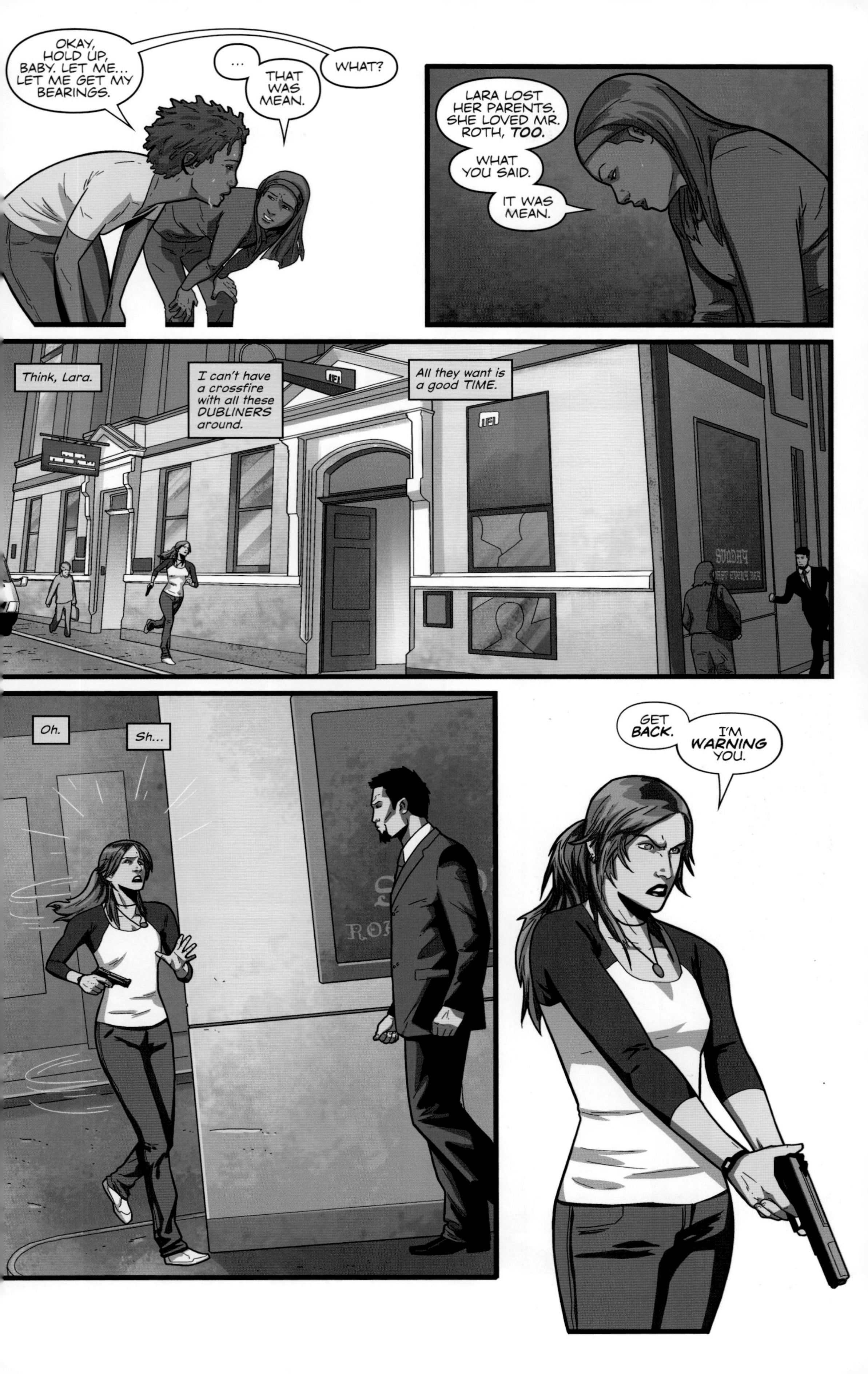
OKAY, HOLD UP, BABY. LET ME... LET ME GET MY BEARINGS.
...
THAT WAS MEAN.
WHAT?
LARA LOST HER PARENTS. SHE LOVED MR. ROTH, TOO.
WHAT YOU SAID.
IT WAS MEAN.
Think, Lara.
I can't have a crossfire with all these DUBLINERS around.
All they want is a good TIME.
Oh.
Sh...
GET BACK.
I'M WARNING YOU.

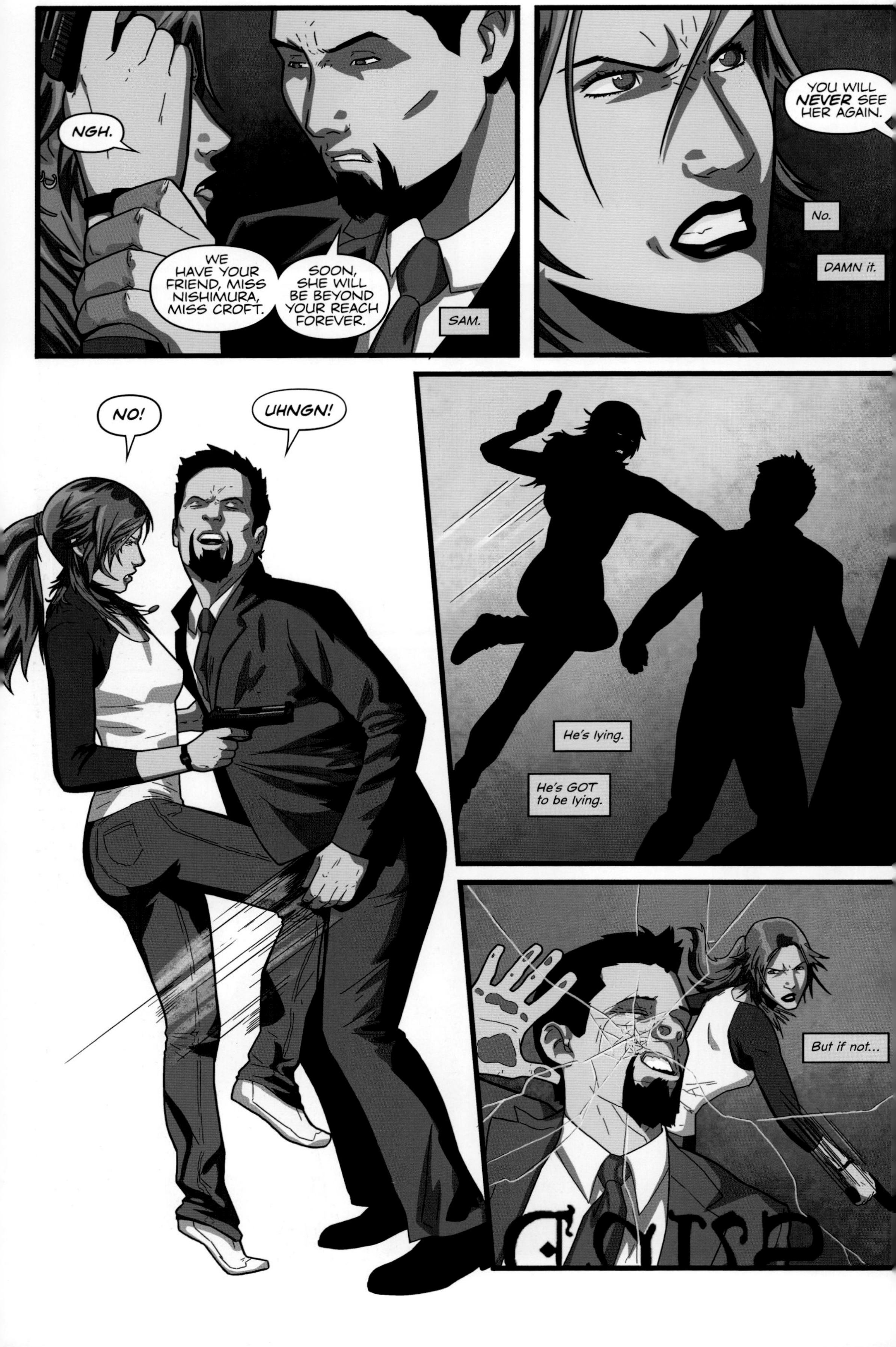
NGH.
WE HAVE YOUR FRIEND, MISS NISHIMURA, MISS CROFT.
SOON, SHE WILL BE BEYOND YOUR REACH FOREVER.
SAM.
YOU WILL **NEVER** SEE HER AGAIN.
No.
DAMN it.
NO!
UHNGN!
He's lying.
He's GOT to be lying.
But if not...

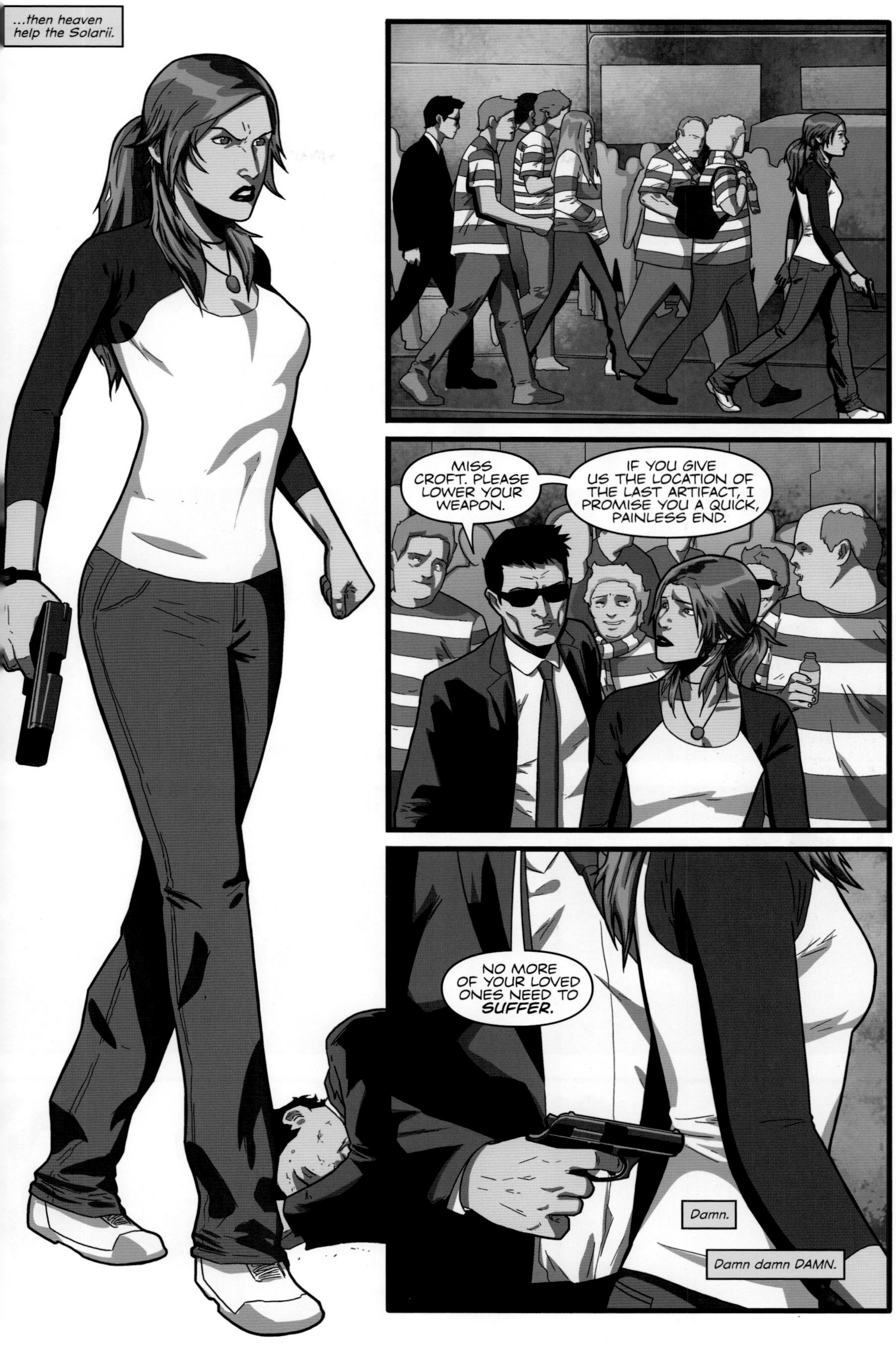
...then heaven help the Solarii.
MISS CROFT. PLEASE LOWER YOUR WEAPON.
IF YOU GIVE US THE LOCATION OF THE LAST ARTIFACT, I PROMISE YOU A QUICK, PAINLESS END.
NO MORE OF YOUR LOVED ONES NEED TO SUFFER.
Damn.
Damn damn DAMN.

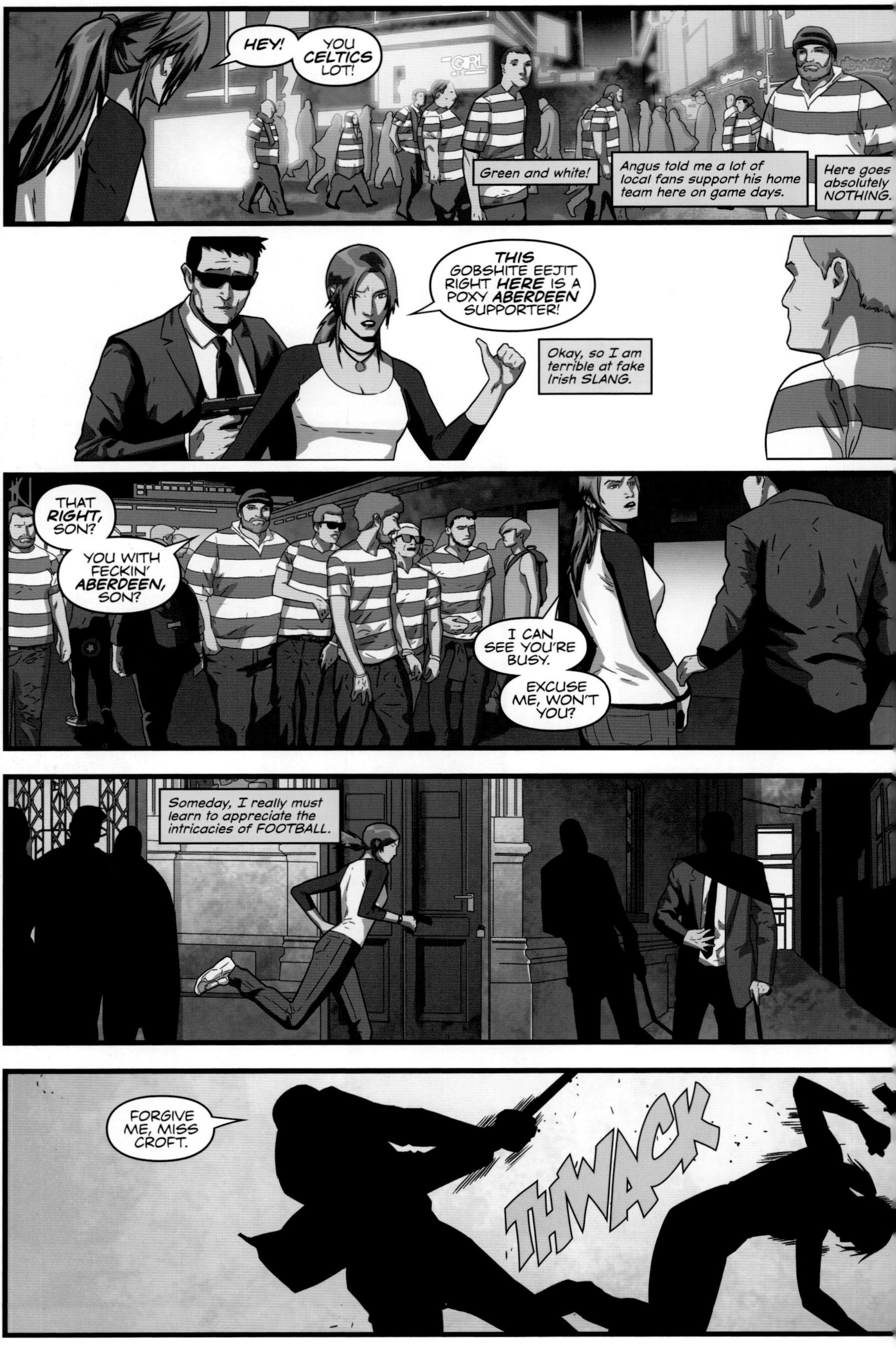
HEY!
YOU CELTICS LOT!
GIRL
Green and white!
Angus told me a lot of local fans support his home team here on game days.
Here goes absolutely NOTHING.
THIS GOBSHITE EEJIT RIGHT HERE IS A POXY ABERDEEN SUPPORTER!
Okay, so I am terrible at fake Irish SLANG.
THAT RIGHT, SON?
YOU WITH FECKIN' ABERDEEN, SON?
I CAN SEE YOU'RE BUSY.
EXCUSE ME, WON'T YOU?
Someday, I really must learn to appreciate the intricacies of FOOTBALL.
FORGIVE ME, MISS CROFT.
THWACK

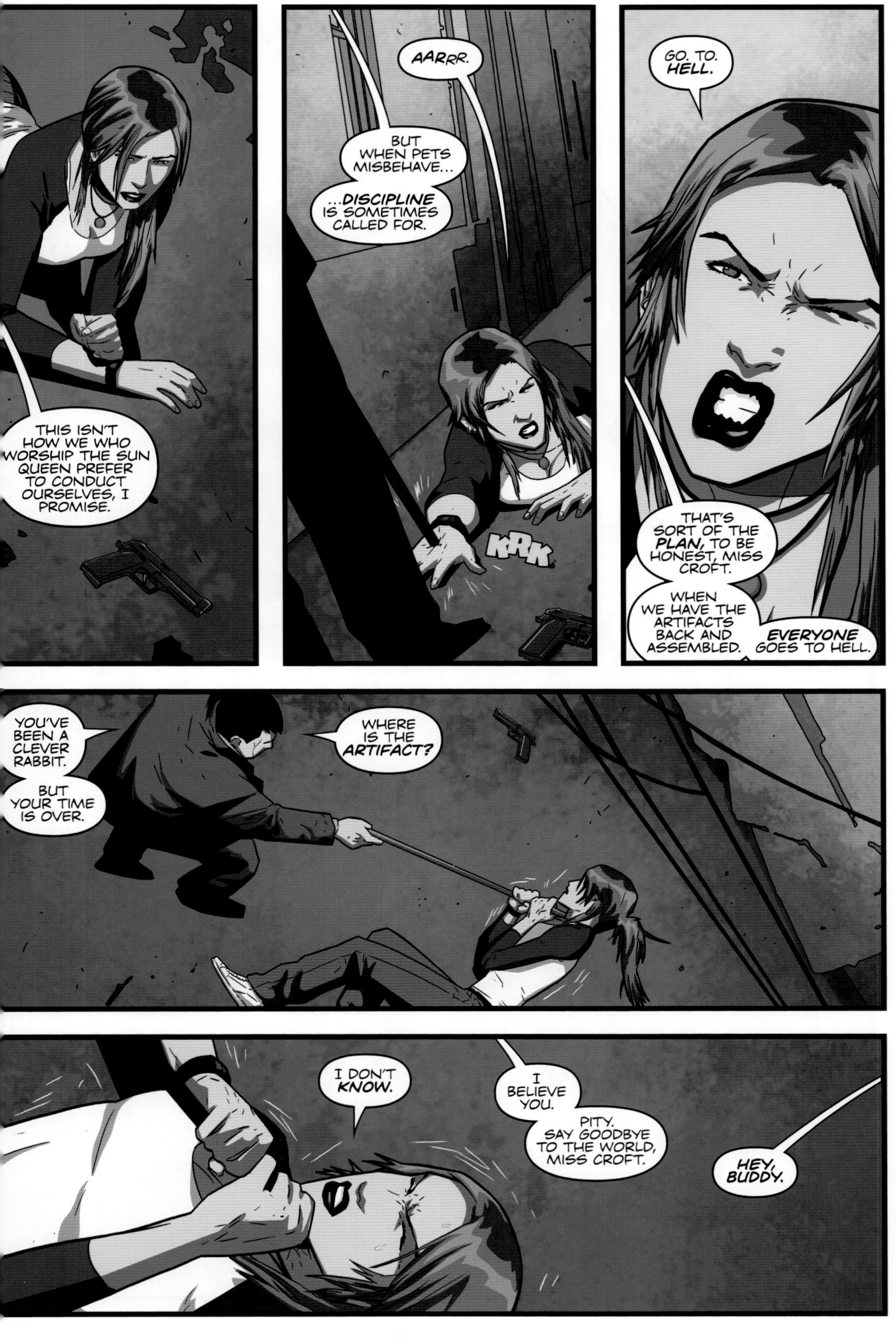
THIS ISN'T HOW WE WHO WORSHIP THE SUN QUEEN PREFER TO CONDUCT OURSELVES, I PROMISE.
AARRR.
BUT WHEN PETS MISBEHAVE...
...DISCIPLINE IS SOMETIMES CALLED FOR.
KRK
GO. TO. HELL.
THAT'S SORT OF THE PLAN, TO BE HONEST, MISS CROFT.
WHEN WE HAVE THE ARTIFACTS BACK AND ASSEMBLED.
EVERYONE GOES TO HELL.
YOU'VE BEEN A CLEVER RABBIT.
BUT YOUR TIME IS OVER.
WHERE IS THE ARTIFACT?
I DON'T KNOW.
I BELIEVE YOU.
PITY. SAY GOODBYE TO THE WORLD, MISS CROFT.
HEY, BUDDY.

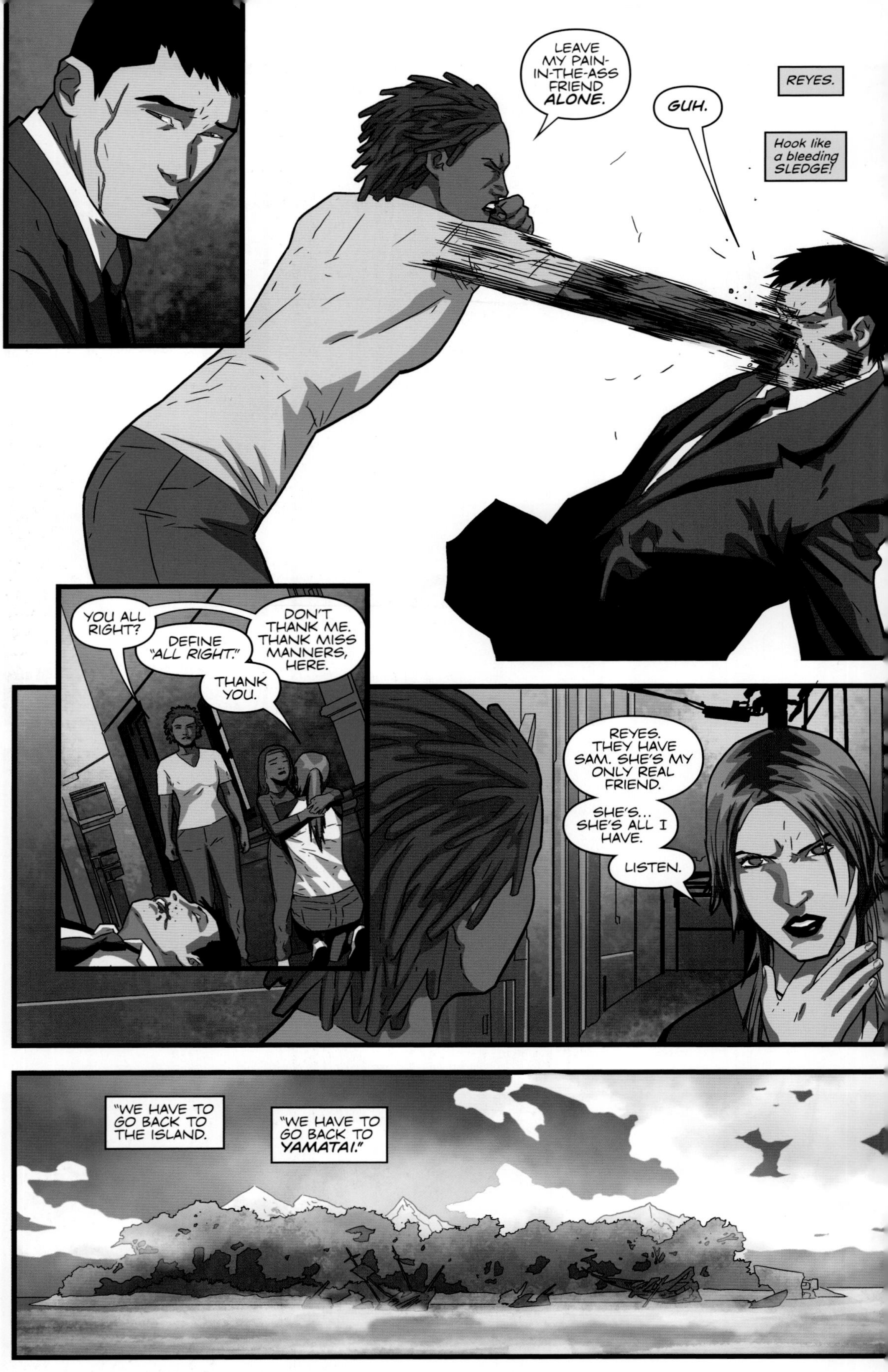
LEAVE MY PAIN-IN-THE-ASS FRIEND ALONE.
REYES.
GUH.
Hook like a bleeding SLEDGE!
YOU ALL RIGHT?
DEFINE "ALL RIGHT."
DON'T THANK ME. THANK MISS MANNERS, HERE.
THANK YOU.
REYES. THEY HAVE SAM. SHE'S MY ONLY REAL FRIEND.
SHE'S... SHE'S ALL I HAVE.
LISTEN.
"WE HAVE TO GO BACK TO THE ISLAND.
"WE HAVE TO GO BACK TO YAMATAI."

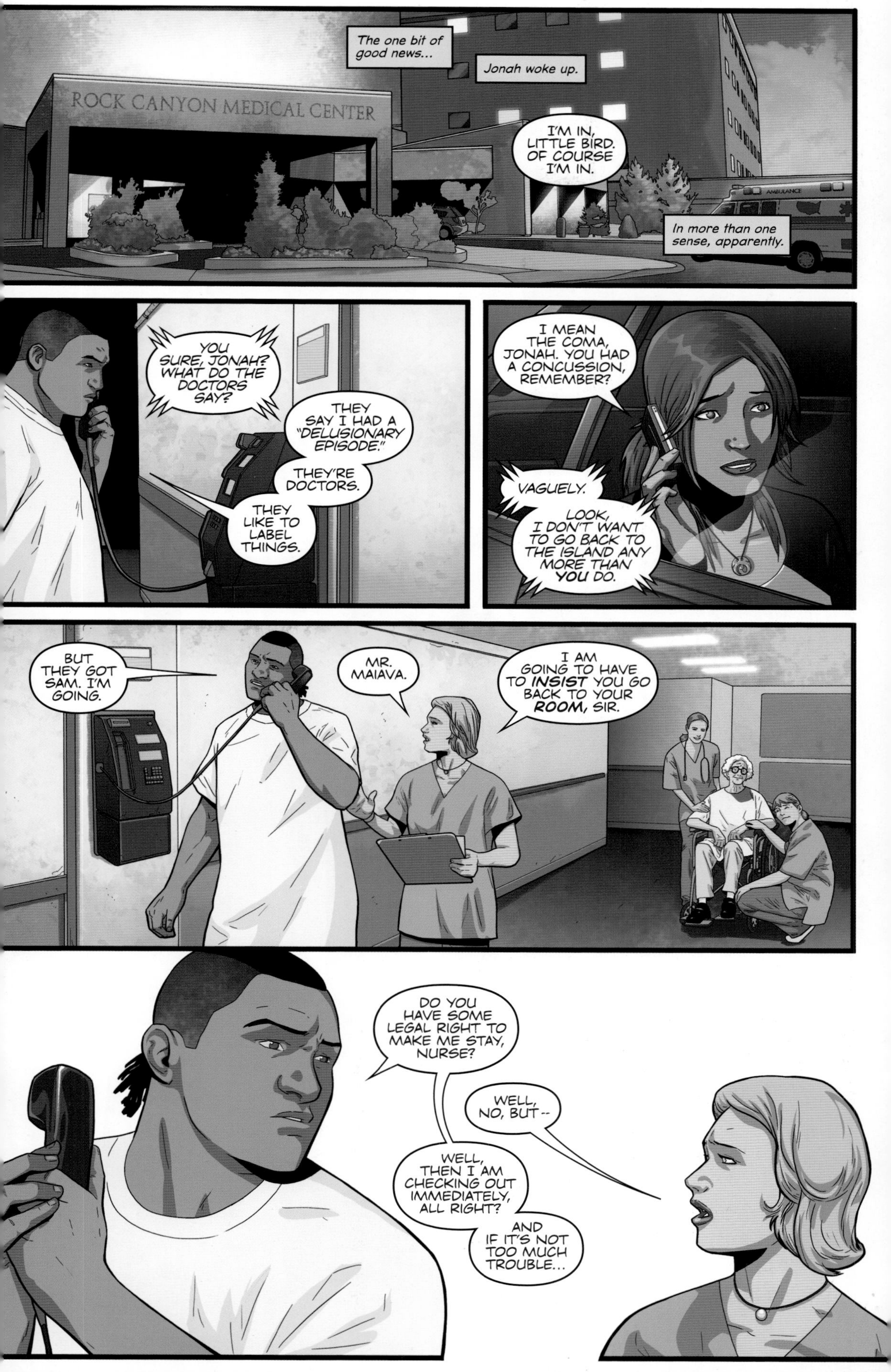
The one bit of good news...
Jonah woke up.
ROCK CANYON MEDICAL CENTER
I'M IN, LITTLE BIRD. OF COURSE I'M IN.
In more than one sense, apparently.
YOU SURE, JONAH? WHAT DO THE DOCTORS SAY?
THEY SAY I HAD A "DELUSIONARY EPISODE."
THEY'RE DOCTORS.
THEY LIKE TO LABEL THINGS.
I MEAN THE COMA, JONAH. YOU HAD A CONCUSSION, REMEMBER?
VAGUELY.
LOOK, I DON'T WANT TO GO BACK TO THE ISLAND ANY MORE THAN YOU DO.
BUT THEY GOT SAM. I'M GOING.
MR. MAIAVA.
I AM GOING TO HAVE TO INSIST YOU GO BACK TO YOUR ROOM, SIR.
DO YOU HAVE SOME LEGAL RIGHT TO MAKE ME STAY, NURSE?
WELL, NO, BUT --
WELL, THEN I AM CHECKING OUT IMMEDIATELY, ALL RIGHT?
AND IF IT'S NOT TOO MUCH TROUBLE...

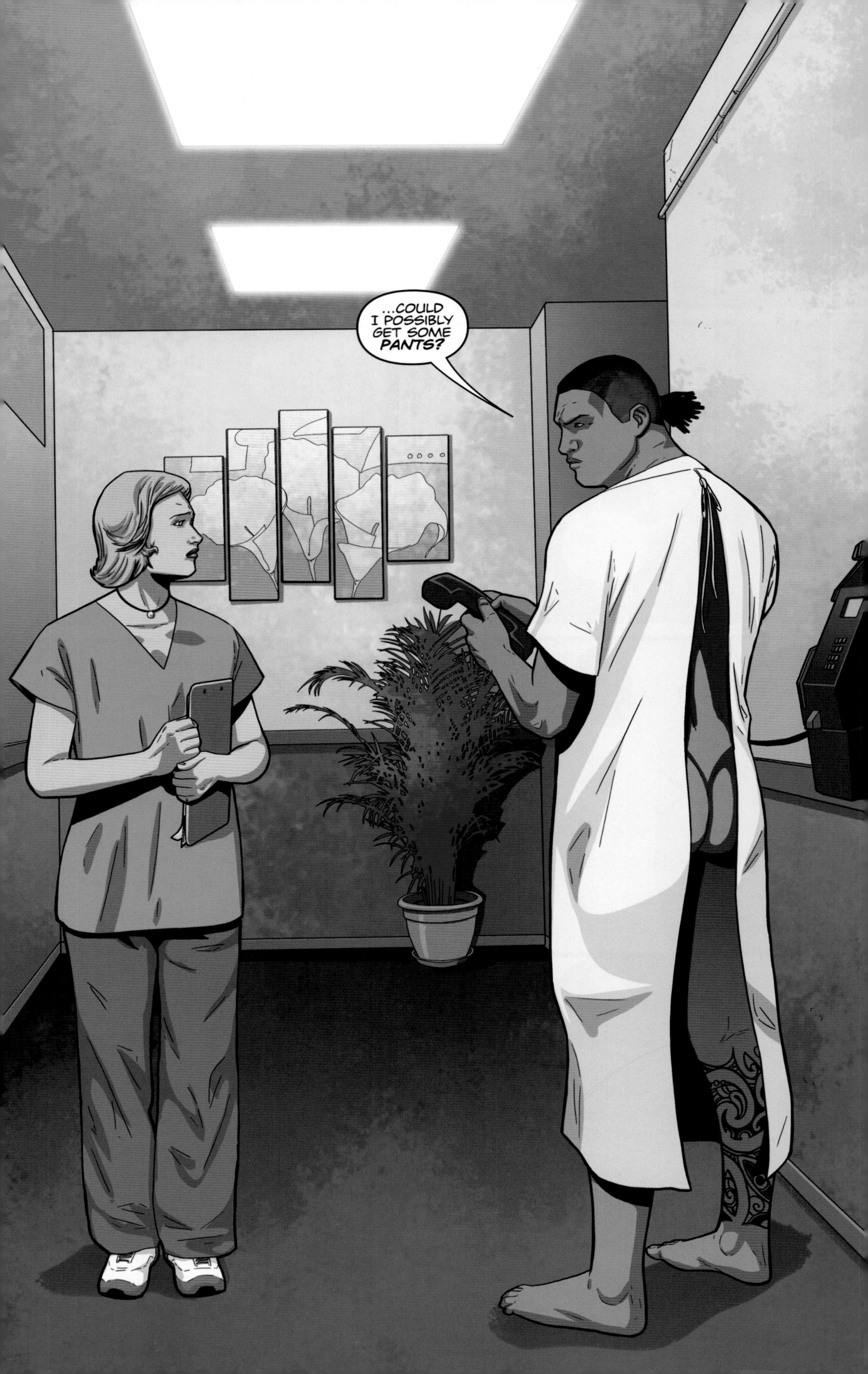
...COULD I POSSIBLY GET SOME PANTS?

I'M ON MY WAY TO SEE PROFESSOR CAHALANE, JONAH.

REYES GOT A BOAT, SAILING OUT OF INCHEON.

He doesn't remember the things he said, the premonitions.

Someone put them in his mind, somehow.

BE...BE CAREFUL, ALL RIGHT? THESE PEOPLE ARE STILL *OUT* THERE.

TRINITY COLLEGE, MISS.

The professor was a friend of my father's, and acts a bit like an overprotective uncle, sometimes.

I had him researching the little makara statue that Jonah found.

Hopefully, he'll have answers.

But no.

No answers this side of the afterlife.

The Solarii worshipers.

CRIME SCENE DO NOT CROSS   CRIME SCENE   CRIM

DO

CRIME SCENE DO NOT CROSS   CRIME SCENE

They GOT to him.

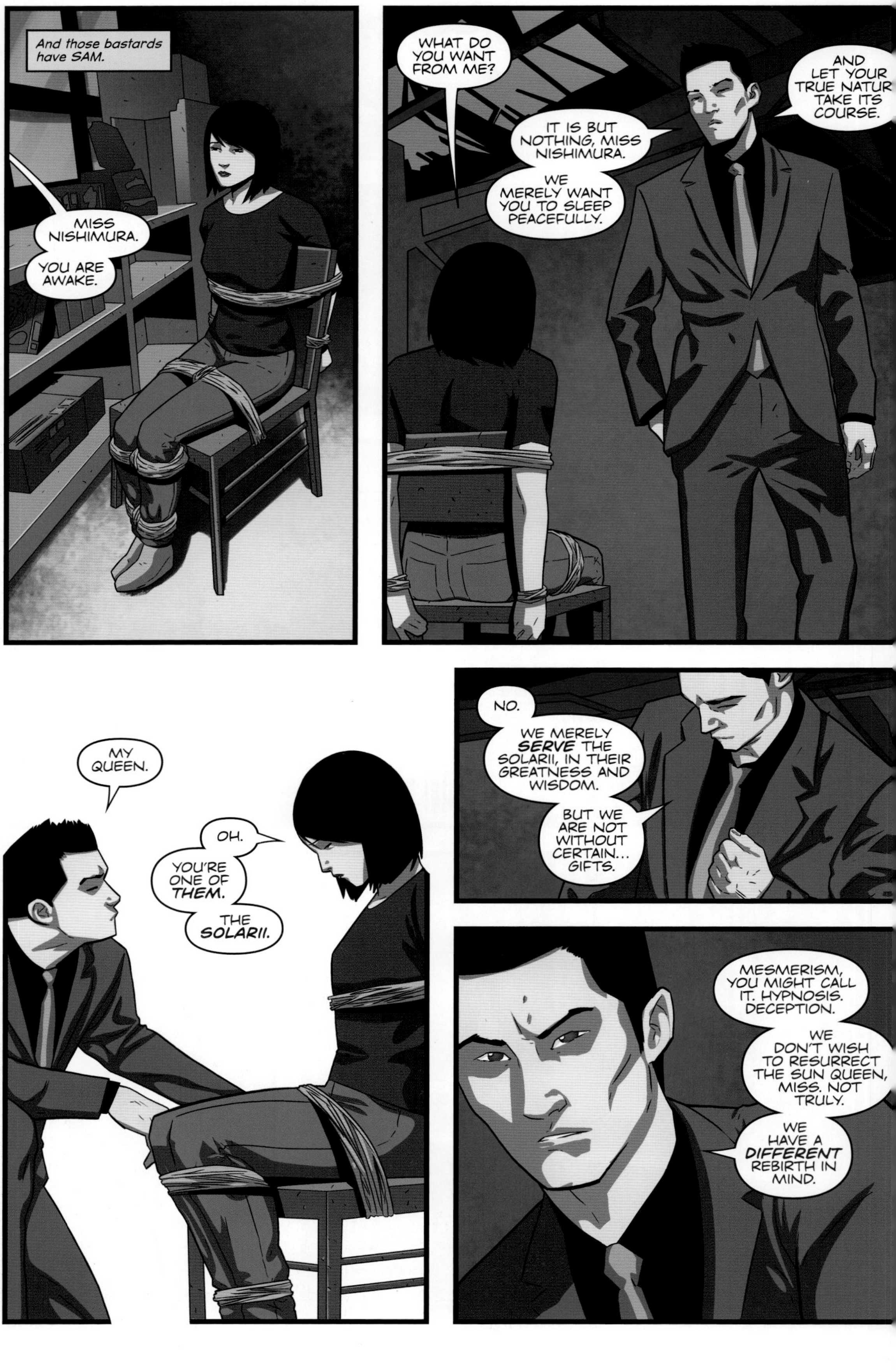
And those bastards have SAM.
MISS NISHIMURA.
YOU ARE AWAKE.
WHAT DO YOU WANT FROM ME?
IT IS BUT NOTHING, MISS NISHIMURA.
WE MERELY WANT YOU TO SLEEP PEACEFULLY.
AND LET YOUR TRUE NATUR
TAKE ITS COURSE.
MY QUEEN.
OH.
YOU'RE ONE OF THEM.
THE SOLARII.
NO.
WE MERELY SERVE THE SOLARII, IN THEIR GREATNESS AND WISDOM.
BUT WE ARE NOT WITHOUT CERTAIN... GIFTS.
MESMERISM, YOU MIGHT CALL IT. HYPNOSIS. DECEPTION.
WE DON'T WISH TO RESURRECT THE SUN QUEEN, MISS. NOT TRULY.
WE HAVE A DIFFERENT REBIRTH IN MIND.

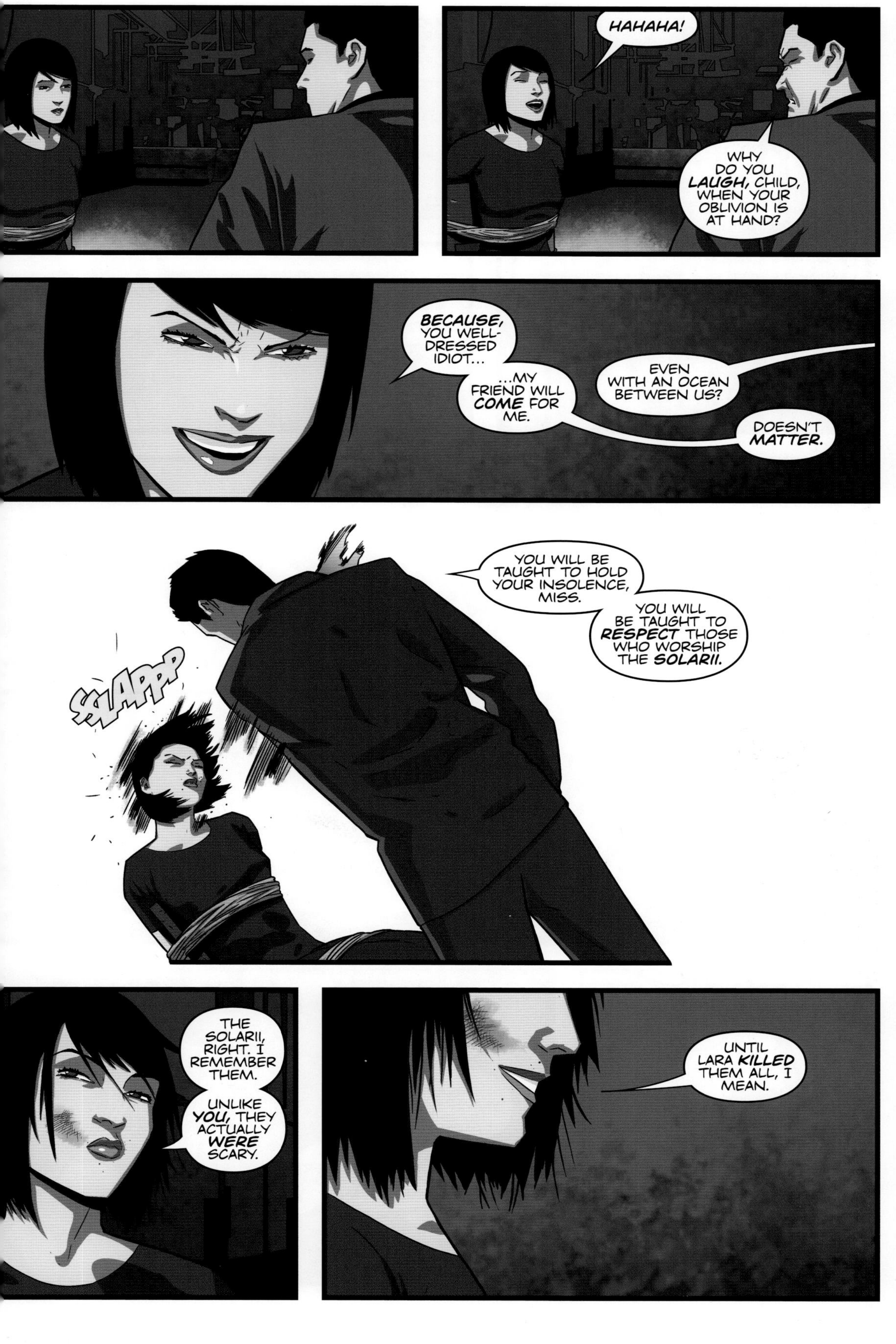
HAHAHA!
WHY DO YOU **LAUGH,** CHILD, WHEN YOUR OBLIVION IS AT HAND?
BECAUSE, YOU WELL-DRESSED IDIOT...
...MY FRIEND WILL **COME** FOR ME.
EVEN WITH AN OCEAN BETWEEN US?
DOESN'T **MATTER.**
YOU WILL BE TAUGHT TO HOLD YOUR INSOLENCE, MISS.
YOU WILL BE TAUGHT TO ***RESPECT*** THOSE WHO WORSHIP THE ***SOLARII.***
SLAPPP
THE SOLARII, RIGHT. I REMEMBER THEM.
UNLIKE ***YOU,*** THEY ACTUALLY ***WERE*** SCARY.
UNTIL LARA **KILLED** THEM ALL, I MEAN.

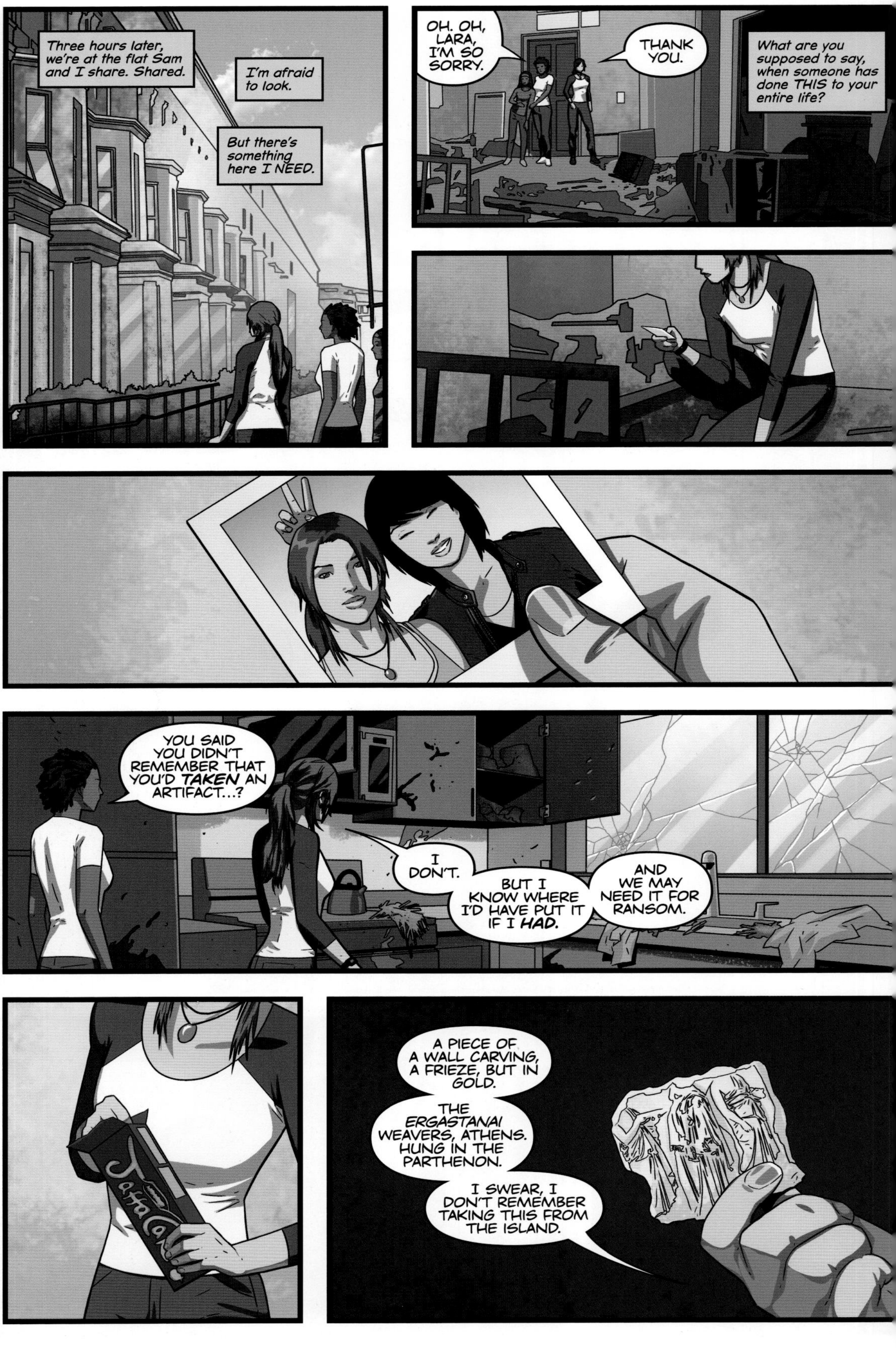
Three hours later, we're at the flat Sam and I share. Shared.
I'm afraid to look.
But there's something here I NEED.
OH. OH, LARA, I'M SO SORRY.
THANK YOU.
What are you supposed to say, when someone has done THIS to your entire life?
YOU SAID YOU DIDN'T REMEMBER THAT YOU'D TAKEN AN ARTIFACT...?
I DON'T.
BUT I KNOW WHERE I'D HAVE PUT IT IF I HAD.
AND WE MAY NEED IT FOR RANSOM.
A PIECE OF A WALL CARVING, A FRIEZE, BUT IN GOLD.
THE ERGASTANAI WEAVERS, ATHENS. HUNG IN THE PARTHENON.
I SWEAR, I DON'T REMEMBER TAKING THIS FROM THE ISLAND.

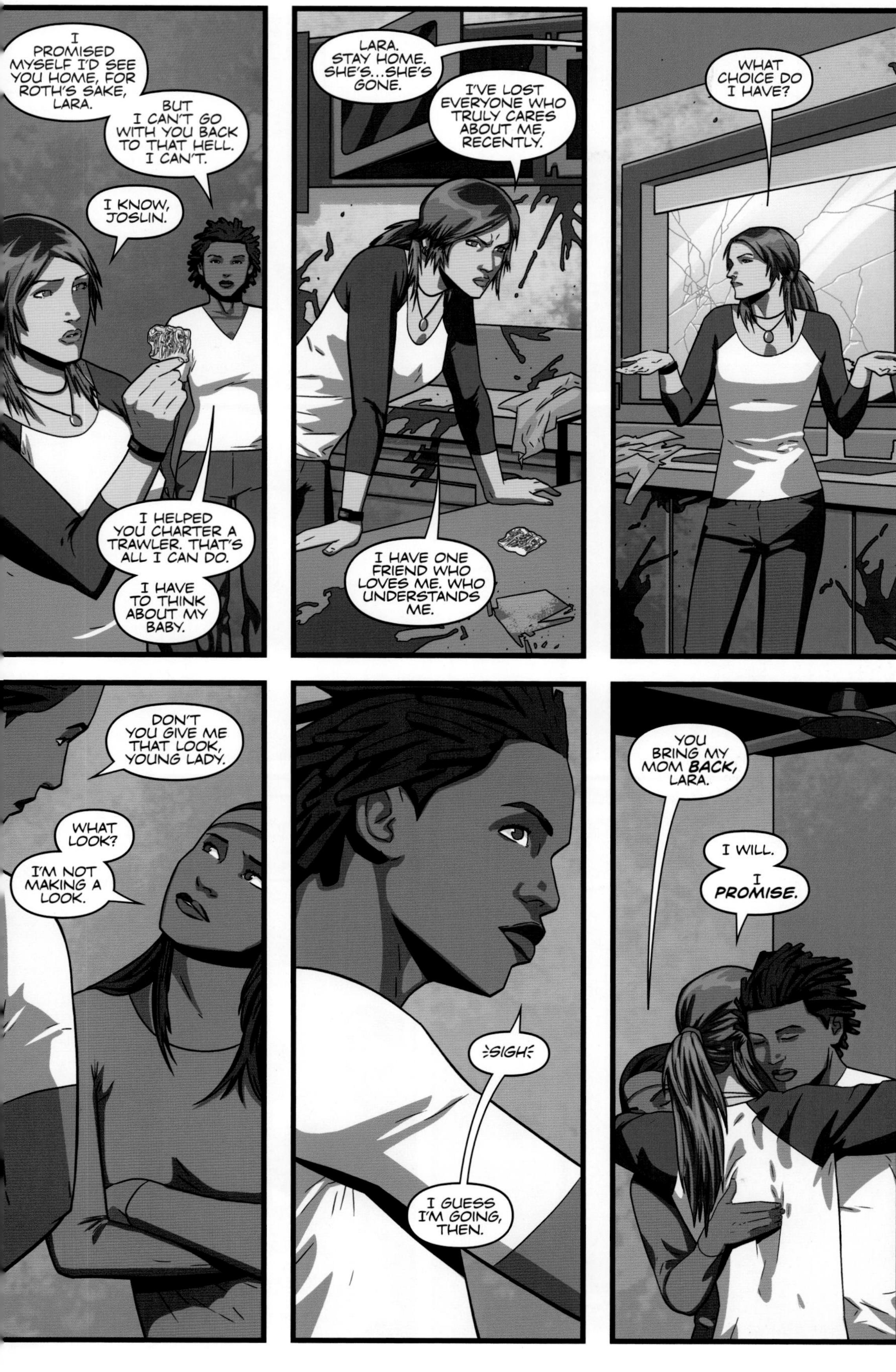
I PROMISED MYSELF I'D SEE YOU HOME, FOR ROTH'S SAKE, LARA.
BUT I CAN'T GO WITH YOU BACK TO THAT HELL. I CAN'T.
I KNOW, JOSLIN.
I HELPED YOU CHARTER A TRAWLER. THAT'S ALL I CAN DO.
I HAVE TO THINK ABOUT MY BABY.
LARA. STAY HOME. SHE'S...SHE'S GONE.
I'VE LOST EVERYONE WHO TRULY CARES ABOUT ME, RECENTLY.
I HAVE ONE FRIEND WHO LOVES ME. WHO UNDERSTANDS ME.
WHAT CHOICE DO I HAVE?
DON'T YOU GIVE ME THAT LOOK, YOUNG LADY.
WHAT LOOK?
I'M NOT MAKING A LOOK.
SIGH
I GUESS I'M GOING, THEN.
YOU BRING MY MOM BACK, LARA.
I WILL.
I PROMISE.

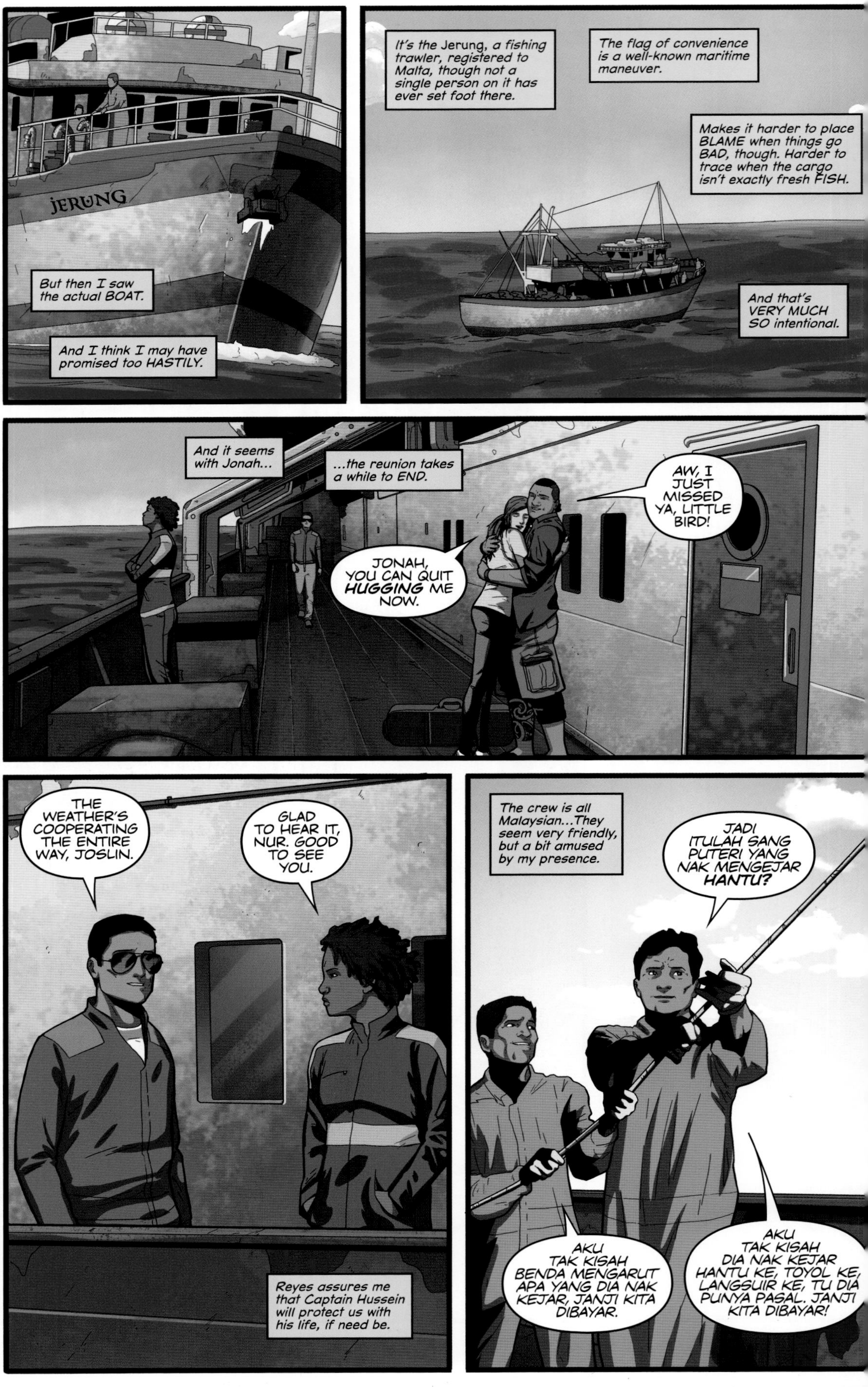

But then I saw the actual BOAT.
And I think I may have promised too HASTILY.
JERUNG
It's the Jerung, a fishing trawler, registered to Malta, though not a single person on it has ever set foot there.
The flag of convenience is a well-known maritime maneuver.
Makes it harder to place BLAME when things go BAD, though. Harder to trace when the cargo isn't exactly fresh FISH.
And that's VERY MUCH SO intentional.
And it seems with Jonah...
...the reunion takes a while to END.
AW, I JUST MISSED YA, LITTLE BIRD!
JONAH, YOU CAN QUIT HUGGING ME NOW.
THE WEATHER'S COOPERATING THE ENTIRE WAY, JOSLIN.
GLAD TO HEAR IT, NUR. GOOD TO SEE YOU.
Reyes assures me that Captain Hussein will protect us with his life, if need be.
The crew is all Malaysian...They seem very friendly, but a bit amused by my presence.
JADI ITULAH SANG PUTERI YANG NAK MENGEJAR HANTU?
AKU TAK KISAH BENDA MENGARUT APA YANG DIA NAK KEJAR, JANJI KITA DIBAYAR.
AKU TAK KISAH DIA NAK KEJAR HANTU KE, TOYOL KE, LANGSUIR KE, TU DIA PUNYA PASAL. JANJI KITA DIBAYAR!

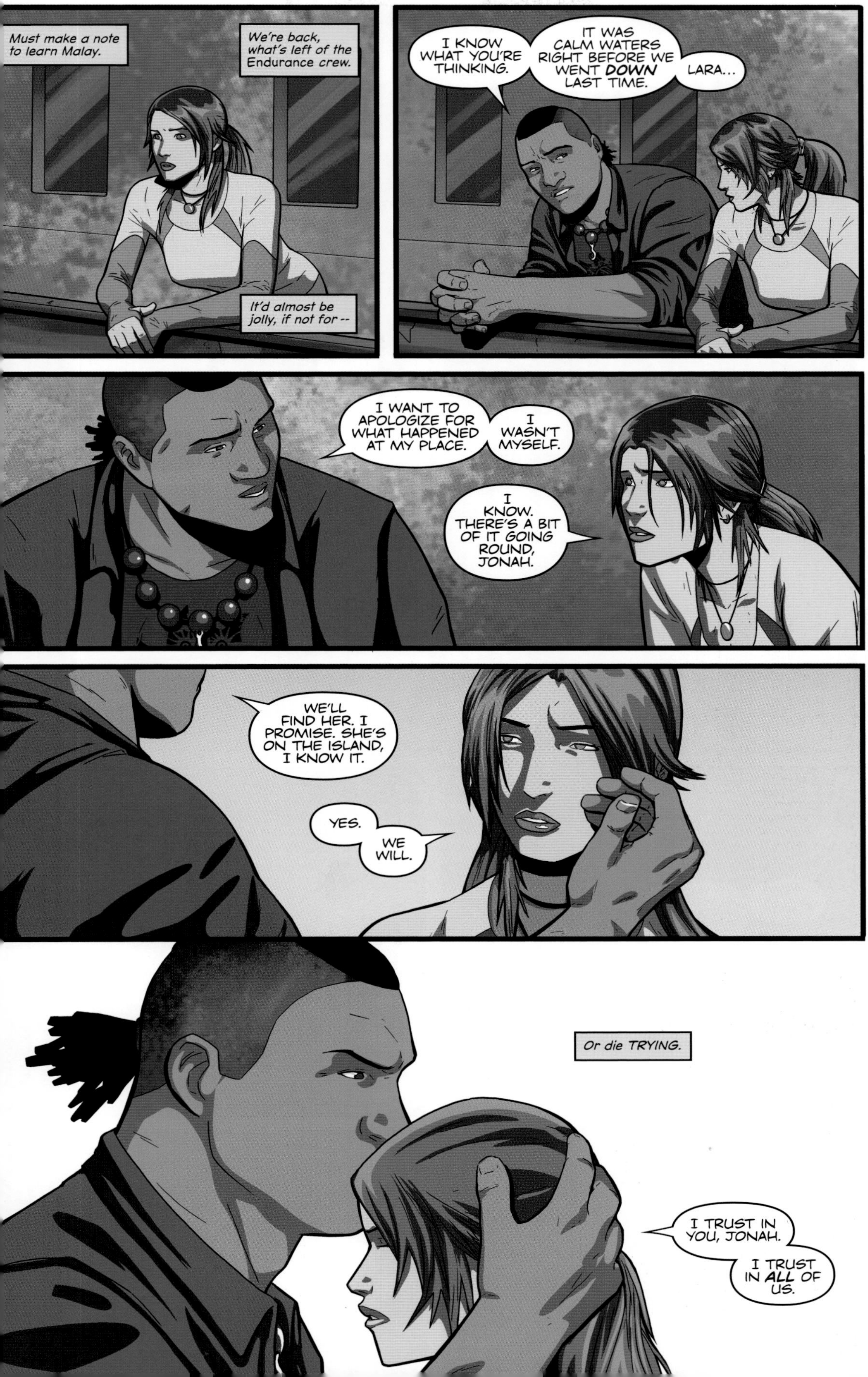
Must make a note to learn Malay.
We're back, what's left of the Endurance crew.
It'd almost be jolly, if not for --
I KNOW WHAT YOU'RE THINKING.
IT WAS CALM WATERS RIGHT BEFORE WE WENT DOWN LAST TIME.
LARA...
I WANT TO APOLOGIZE FOR WHAT HAPPENED AT MY PLACE.
I WASN'T MYSELF.
I KNOW. THERE'S A BIT OF IT GOING ROUND, JONAH.
WE'LL FIND HER. I PROMISE. SHE'S ON THE ISLAND, I KNOW IT.
YES.
WE WILL.
Or die TRYING.
I TRUST IN YOU, JONAH.
I TRUST IN ALL OF US.

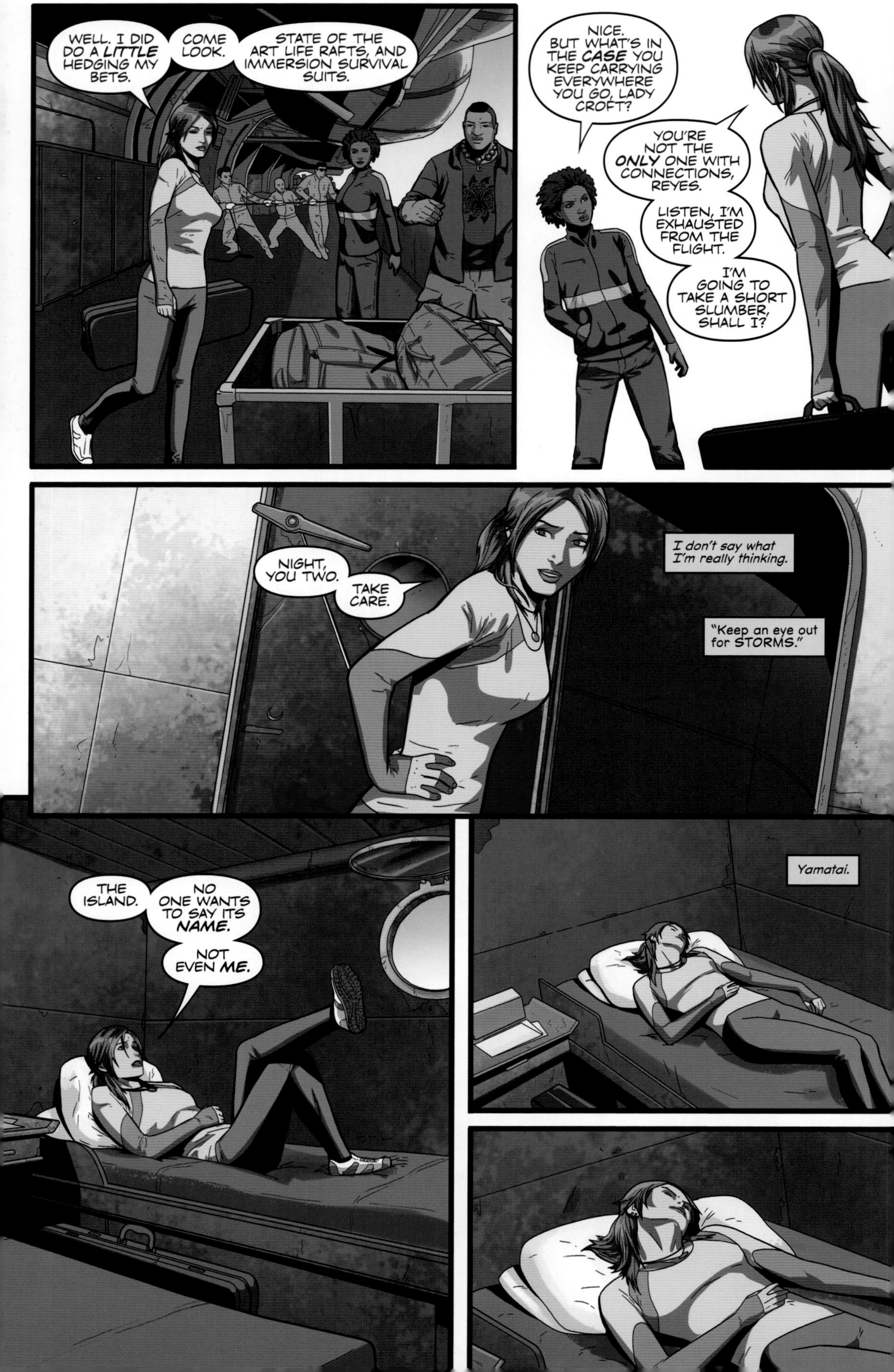
WELL. I DID DO A LITTLE HEDGING MY BETS.
COME LOOK.
STATE OF THE ART LIFE RAFTS, AND IMMERSION SURVIVAL SUITS.
NICE. BUT WHAT'S IN THE CASE YOU KEEP CARRYING EVERYWHERE YOU GO, LADY CROFT?
YOU'RE NOT THE ONLY ONE WITH CONNECTIONS, REYES.
LISTEN, I'M EXHAUSTED FROM THE FLIGHT.
I'M GOING TO TAKE A SHORT SLUMBER, SHALL I?
NIGHT, YOU TWO.
TAKE CARE.
I don't say what I'm really thinking.
"Keep an eye out for STORMS."
THE ISLAND.
NO ONE WANTS TO SAY ITS NAME.
NOT EVEN ME.
Yamatai.

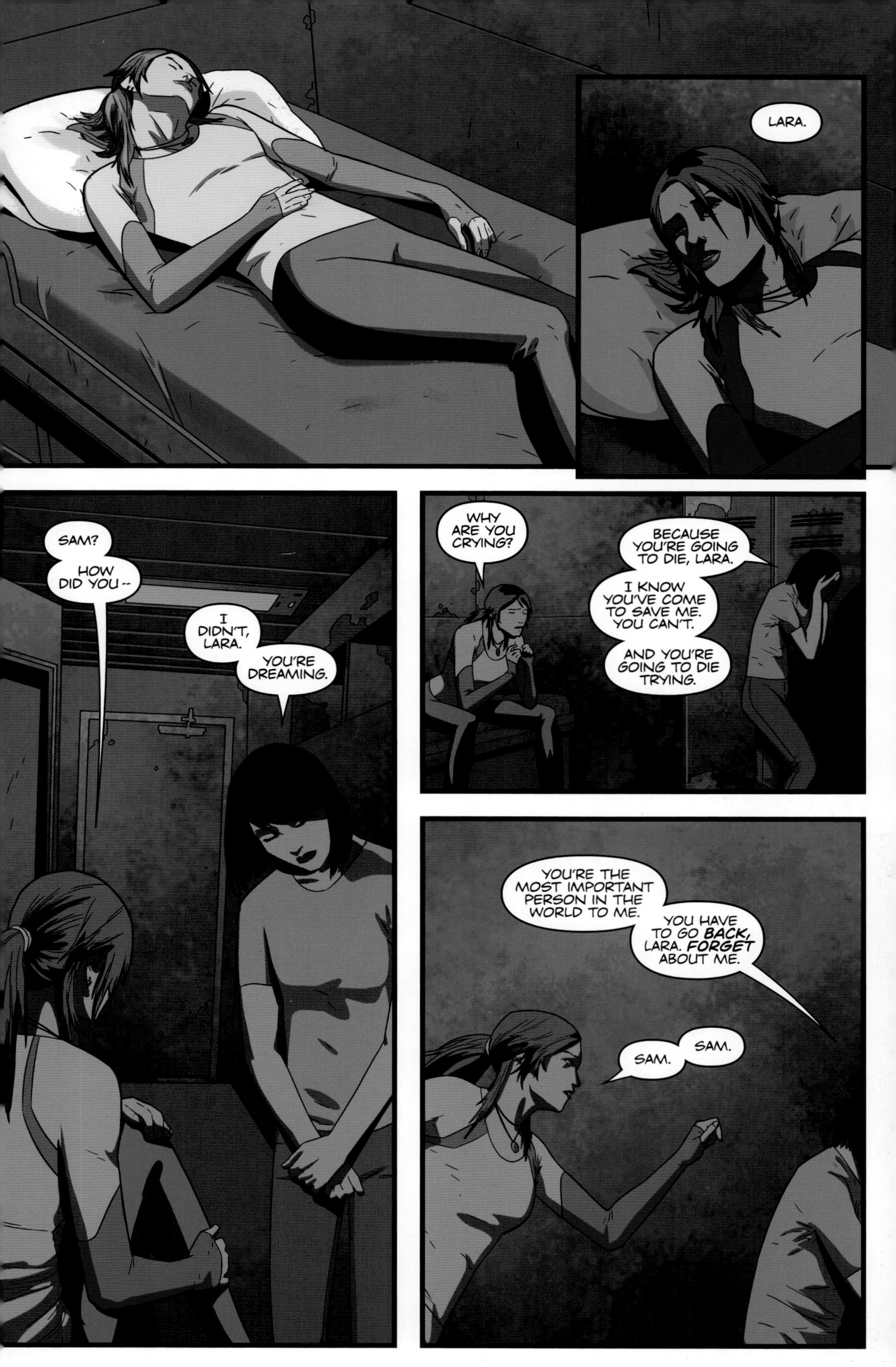
LARA.
SAM?
HOW DID YOU --
I DIDN'T, LARA.
YOU'RE DREAMING.
WHY ARE YOU CRYING?
BECAUSE YOU'RE GOING TO DIE, LARA.
I KNOW YOU'VE COME TO SAVE ME. YOU CAN'T.
AND YOU'RE GOING TO DIE TRYING.
YOU'RE THE MOST IMPORTANT PERSON IN THE WORLD TO ME.
YOU HAVE TO GO BACK, LARA. FORGET ABOUT ME.
SAM.
SAM.

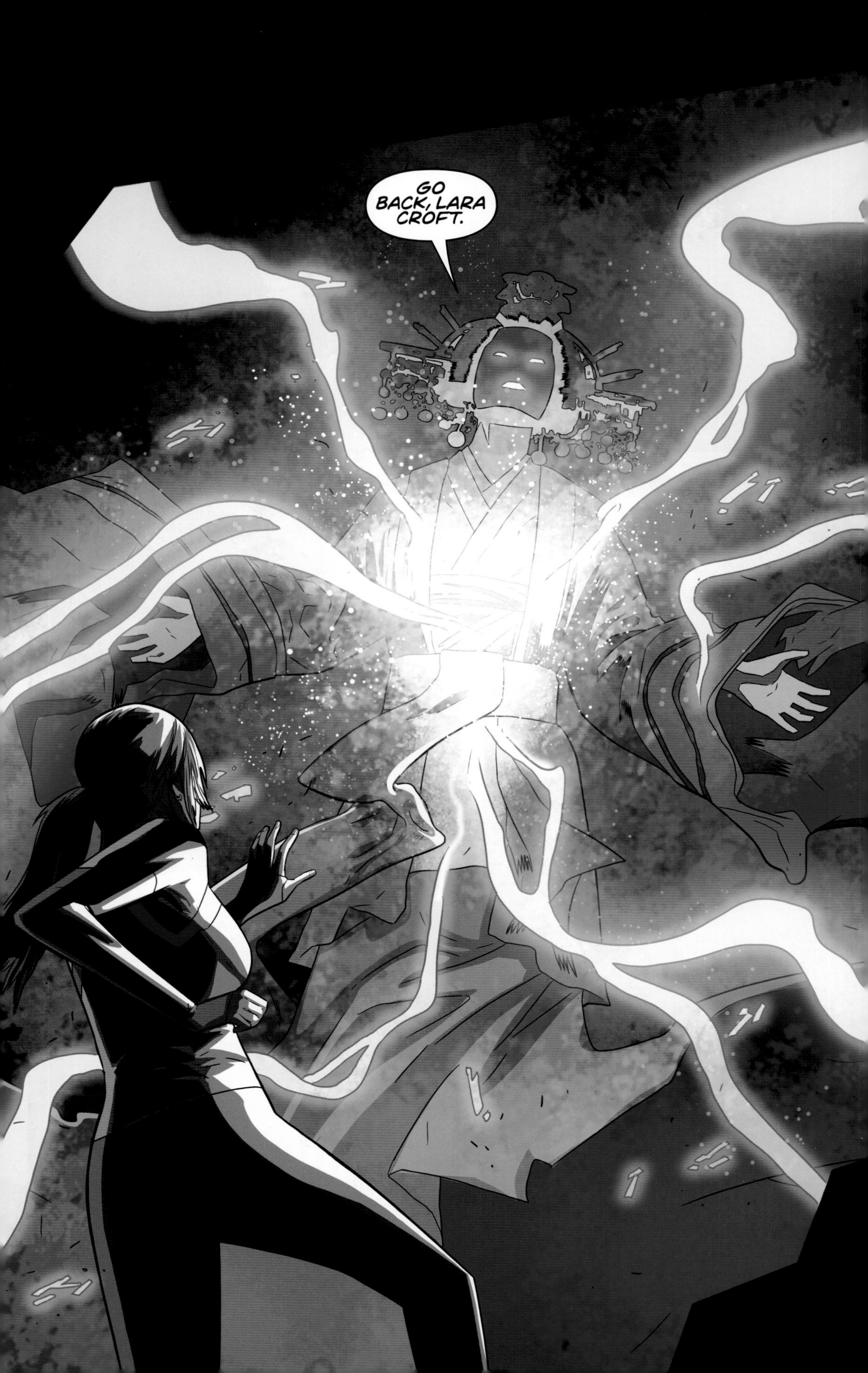
GO BACK, LARA CROFT.

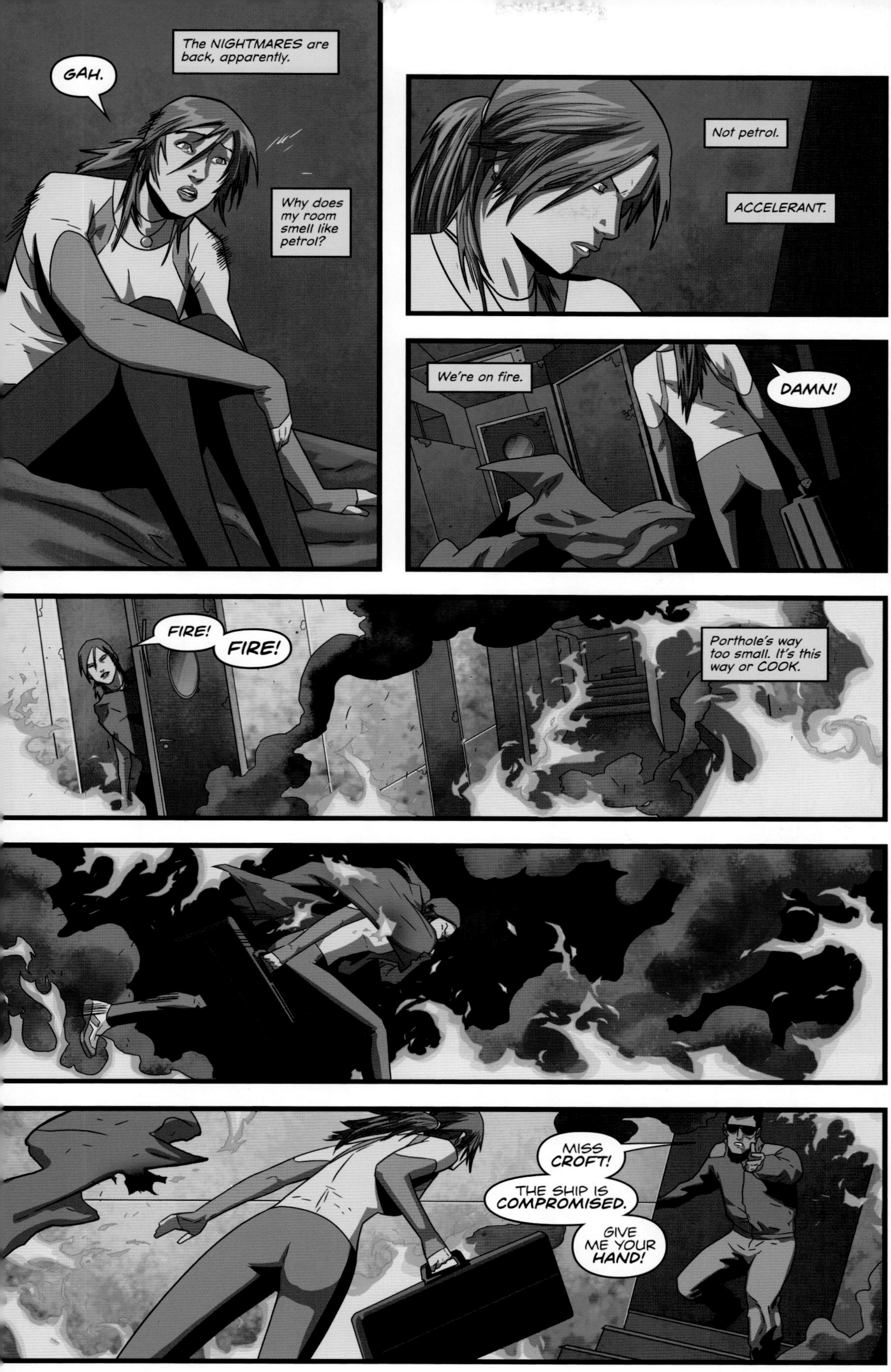
The NIGHTMARES are back, apparently.
GAH.
Why does my room smell like petrol?
Not petrol.
ACCELERANT.
We're on fire.
DAMN!
FIRE!
FIRE!
Porthole's way too small. It's this way or COOK.
MISS CROFT!
THE SHIP IS COMPROMISED.
GIVE ME YOUR HAND!

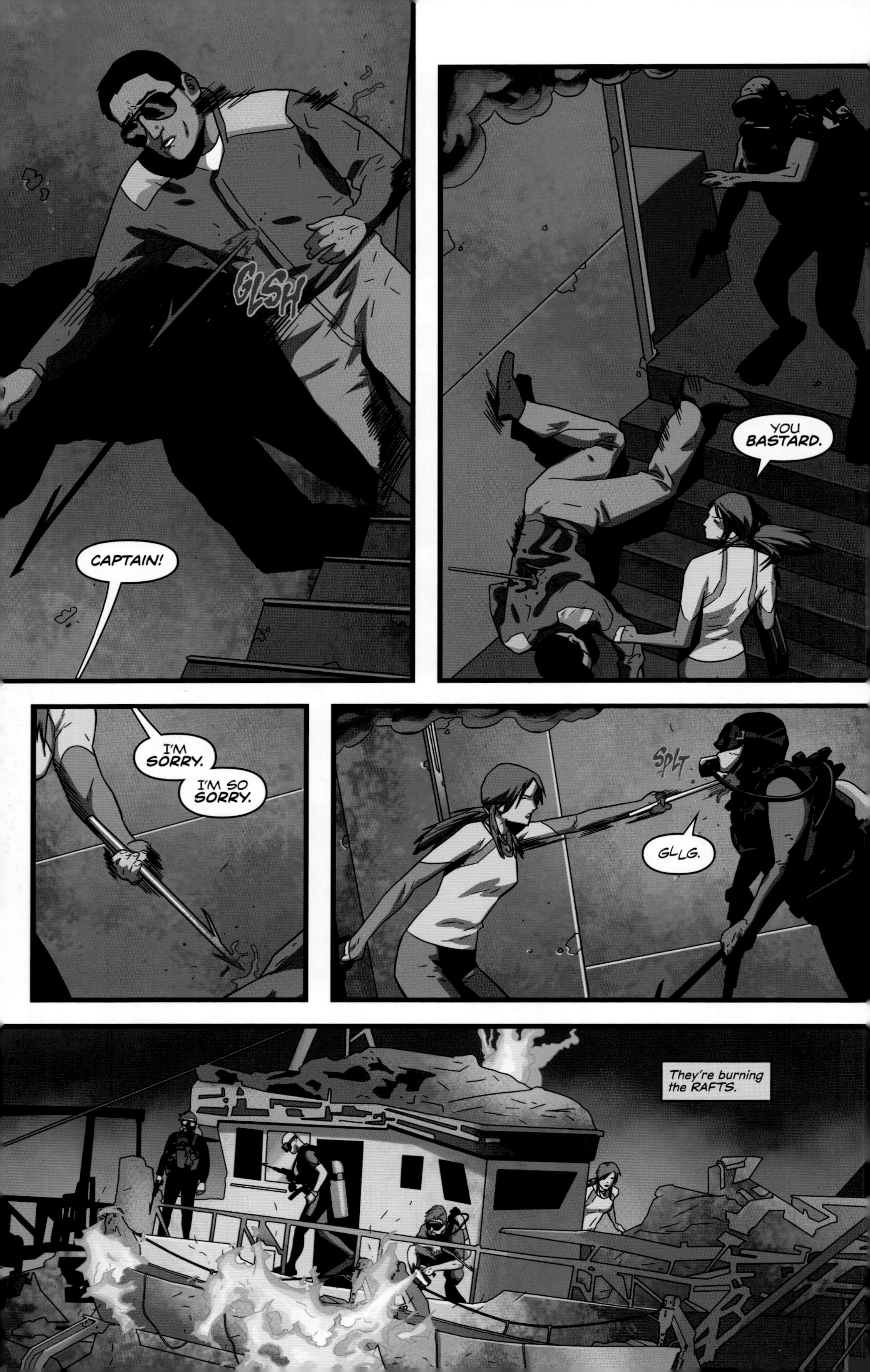
GLSH
CAPTAIN!
YOU BASTARD.
I'M SORRY.
I'M SO SORRY.
SPLT
GLLG.
They're burning the RAFTS.

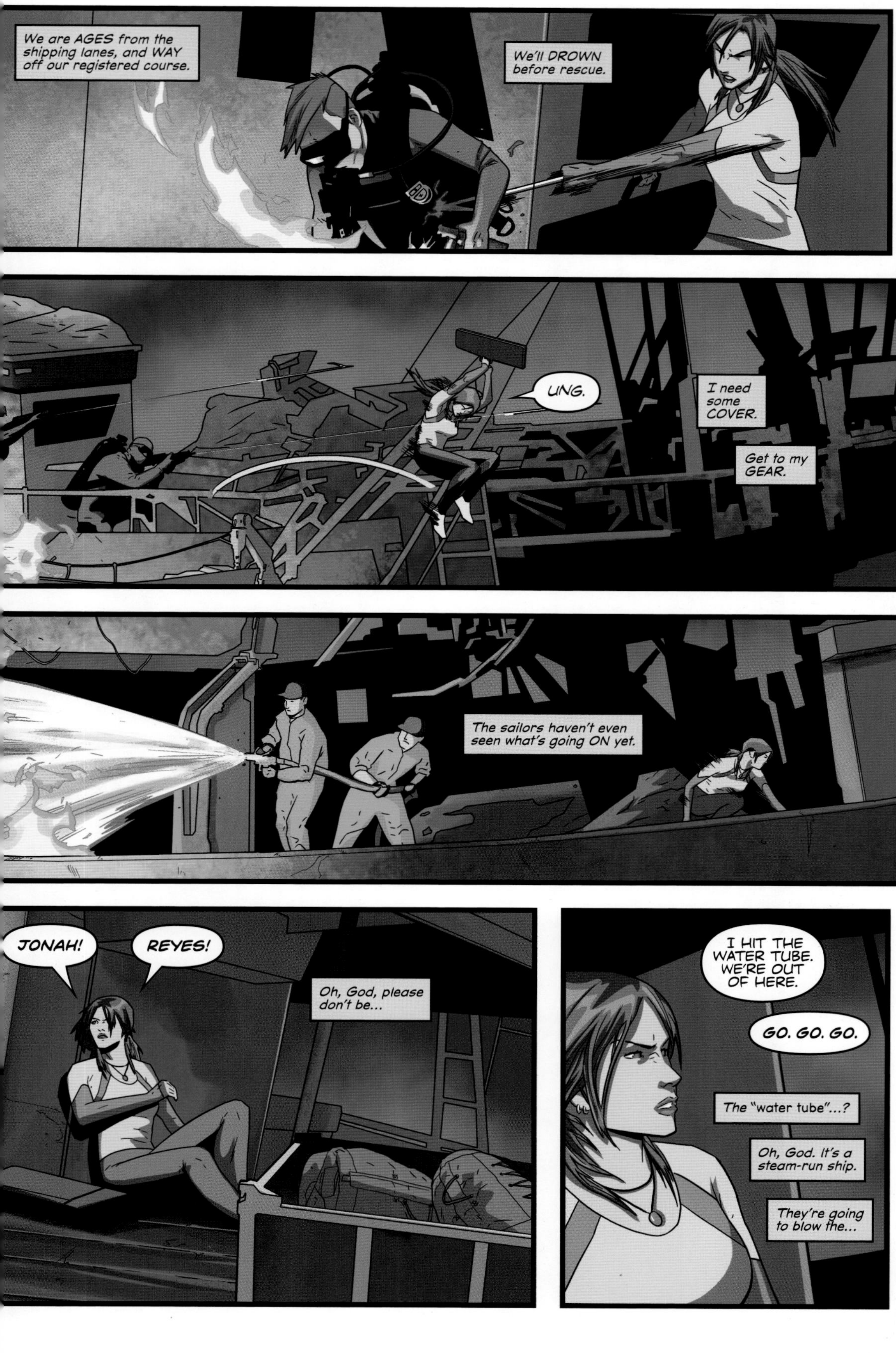

We are AGES from the shipping lanes, and WAY off our registered course.
We'll DROWN before rescue.
UNG.
I need some COVER.
Get to my GEAR.
The sailors haven't even seen what's going ON yet.
JONAH!
REYES!
Oh, God, please don't be...
I HIT THE WATER TUBE. WE'RE OUT OF HERE.
GO. GO. GO.
The "water tube"...?
Oh, God. It's a steam-run ship.
They're going to blow the...

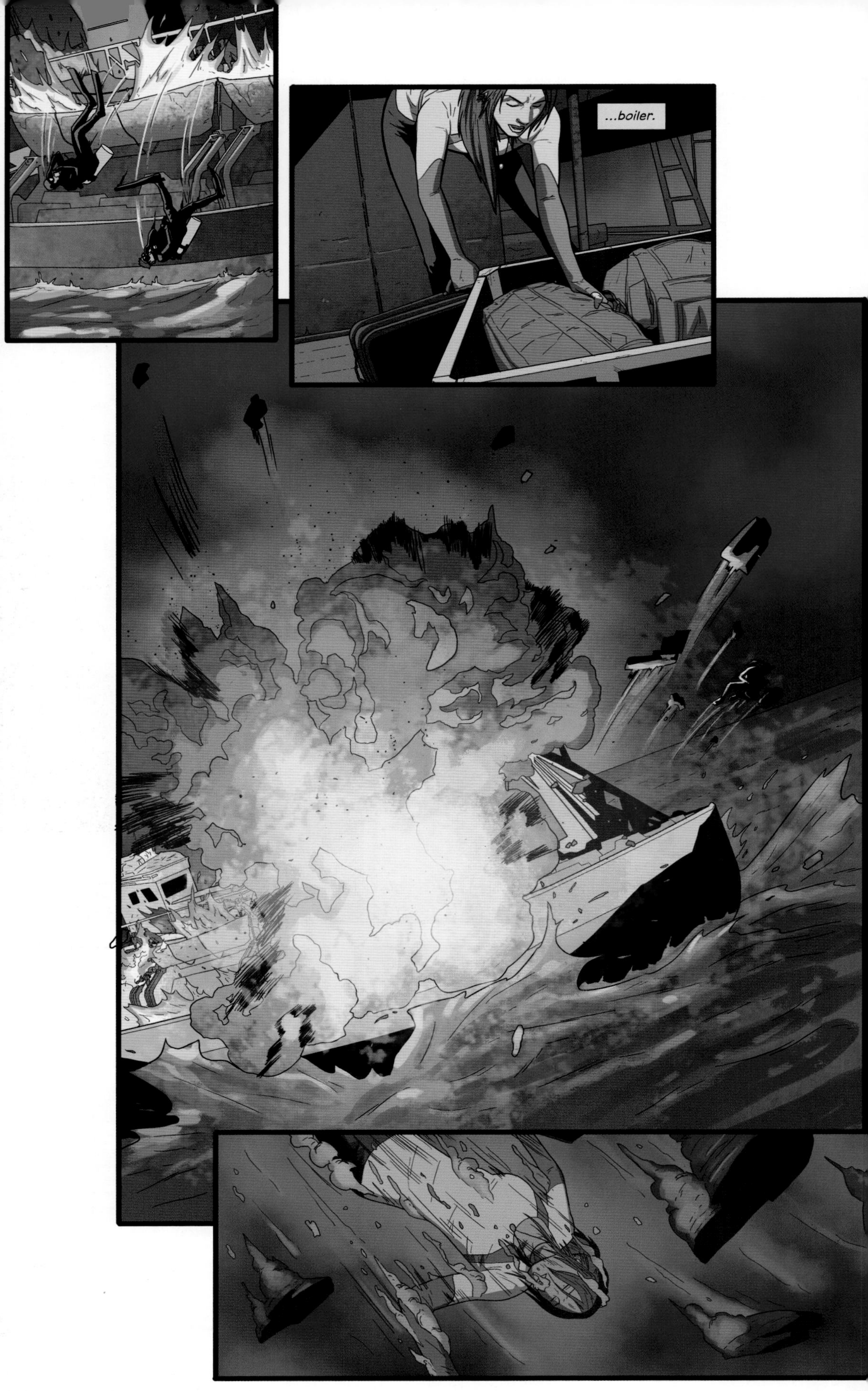
...boiler.

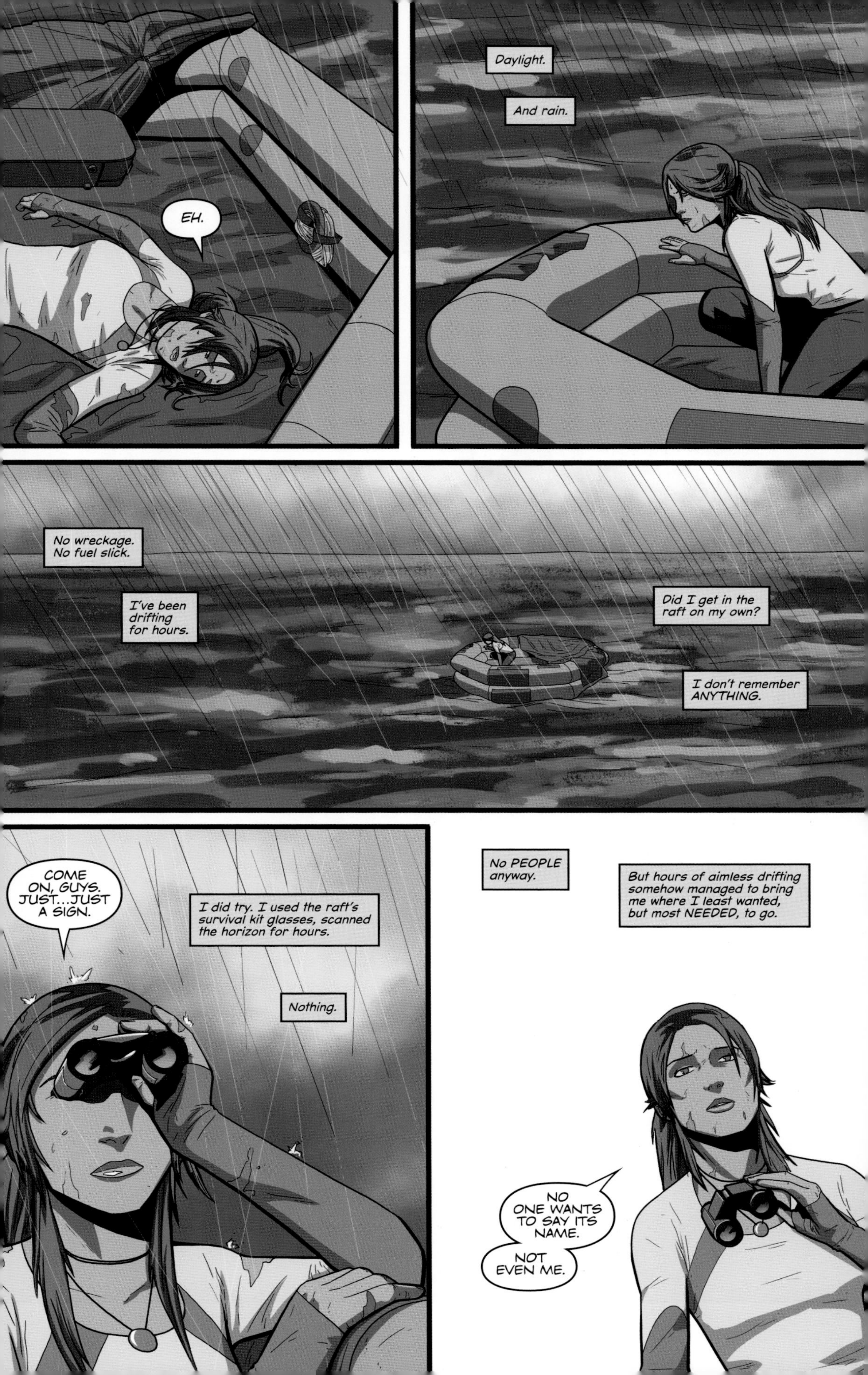
EH.
Daylight.
And rain.
No wreckage.
No fuel slick.
I've been drifting for hours.
Did I get in the raft on my own?
I don't remember ANYTHING.
COME ON, GUYS. JUST...JUST A SIGN.
I did try. I used the raft's survival kit glasses, scanned the horizon for hours.
Nothing.
No PEOPLE anyway.
But hours of aimless drifting somehow managed to bring me where I least wanted, but most NEEDED, to go.
NO ONE WANTS TO SAY ITS NAME.
NOT EVEN ME.

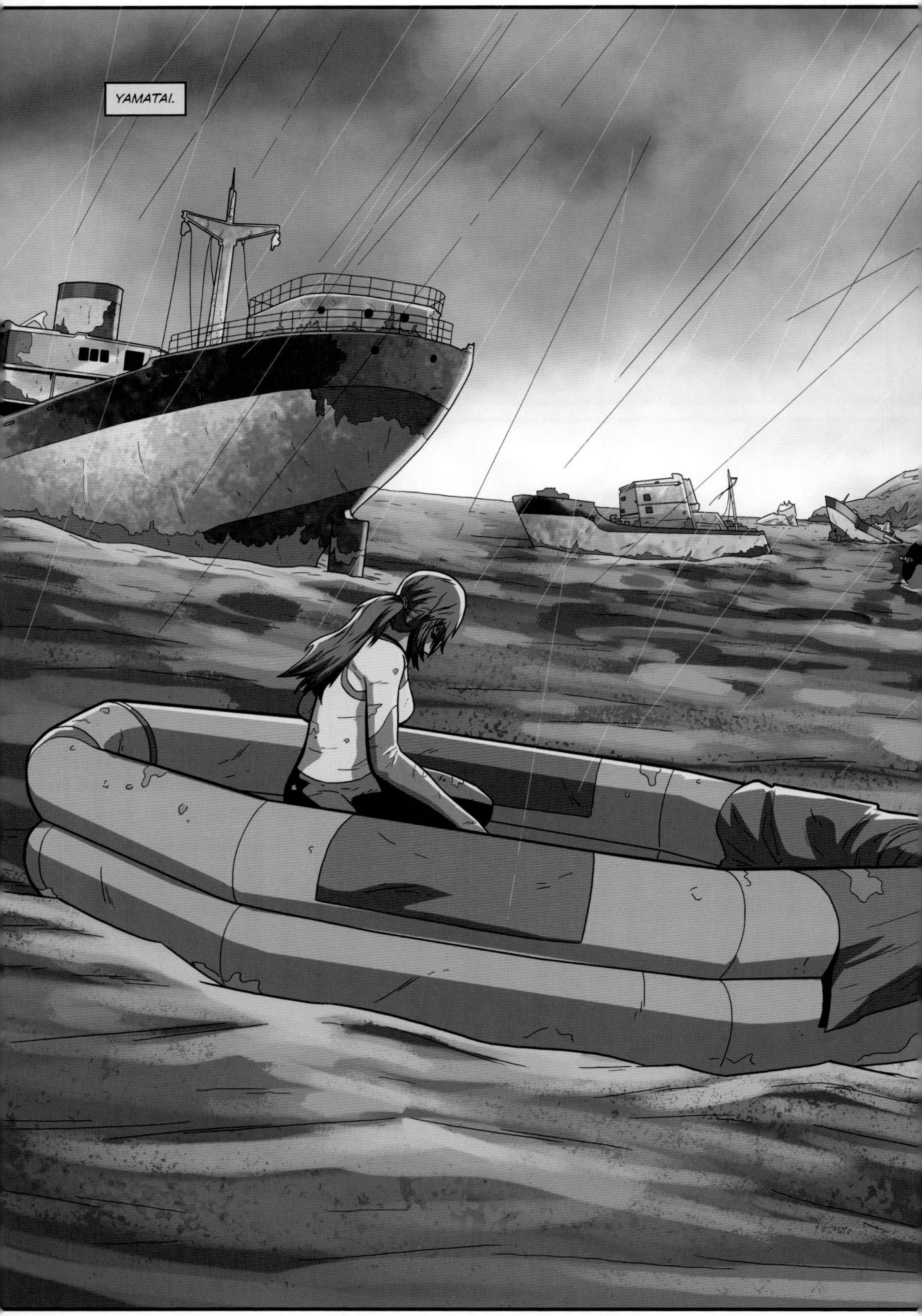
YAMATAI.

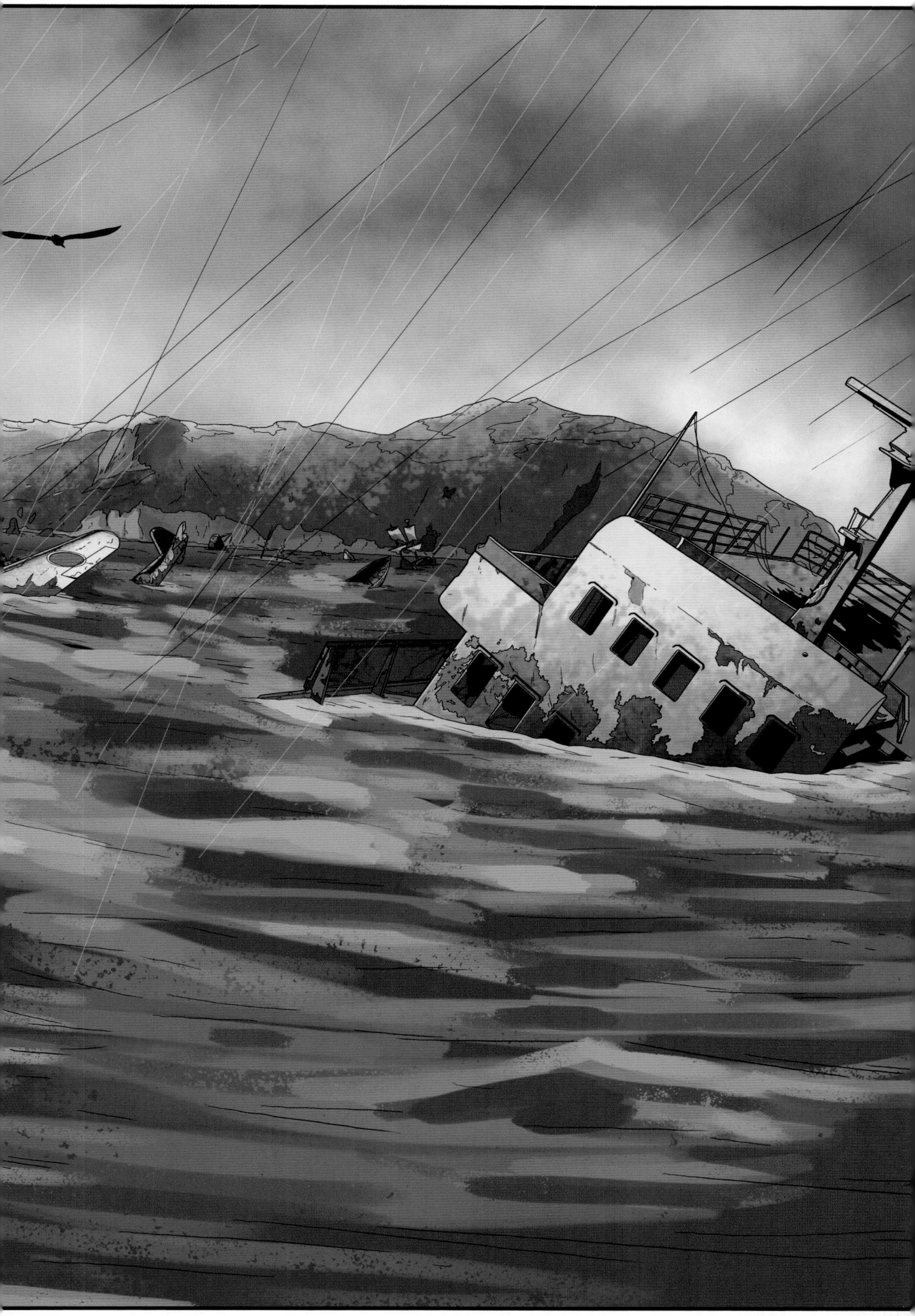

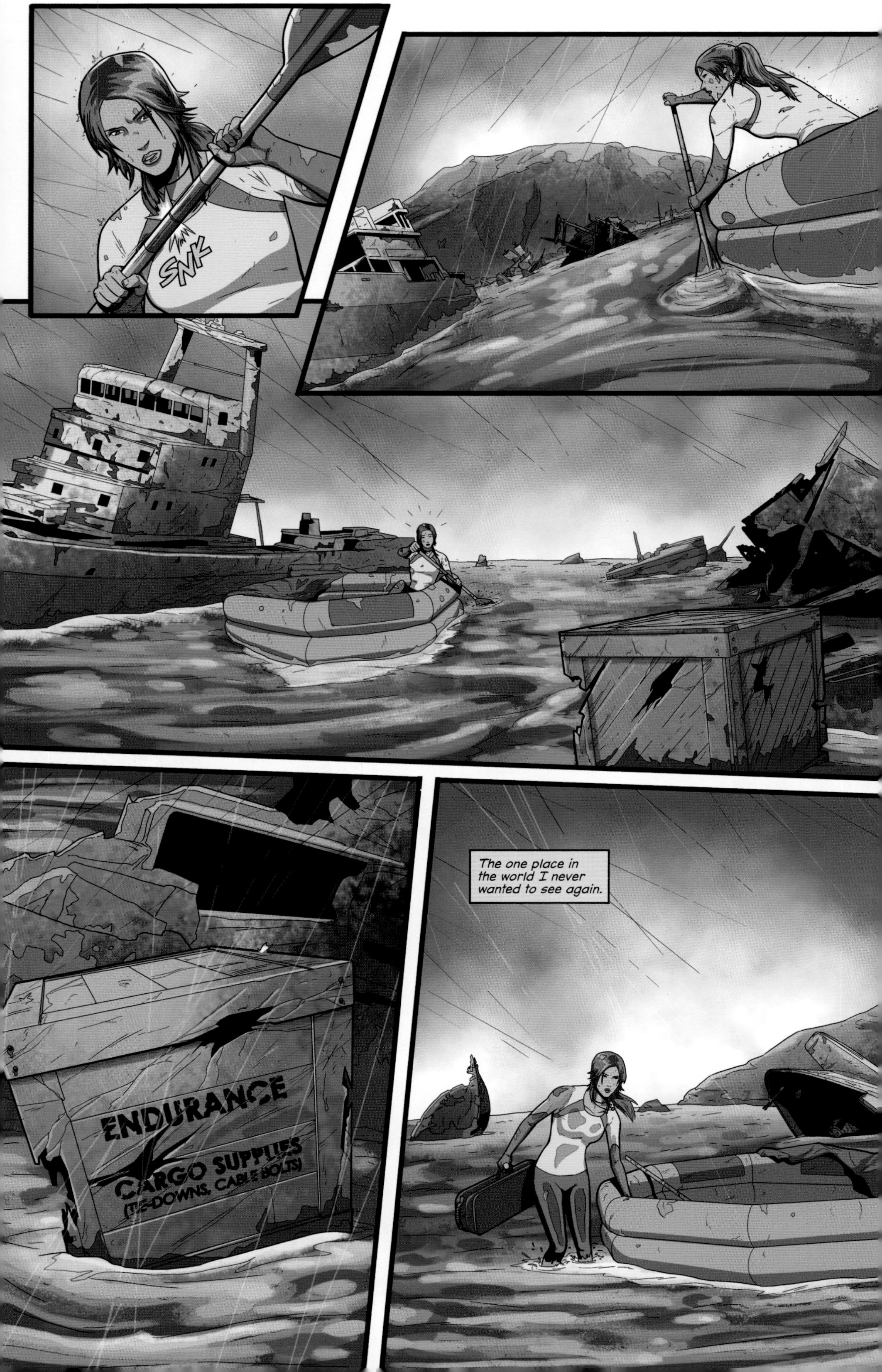
SNK
ENDURANCE
CARGO SUPPLIES
(TIE-DOWNS, CABLE BOLTS)
The one place in the world I never wanted to see again.

Where I lost my friends.

Alex. Grim. Roth.

Where I lost my INNOCENCE.

But there's a difference this time.

KLKK

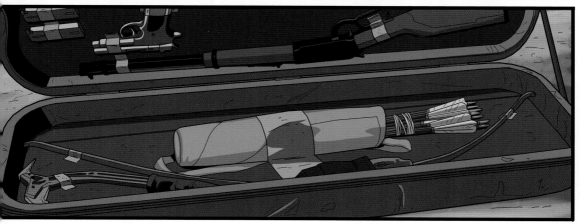

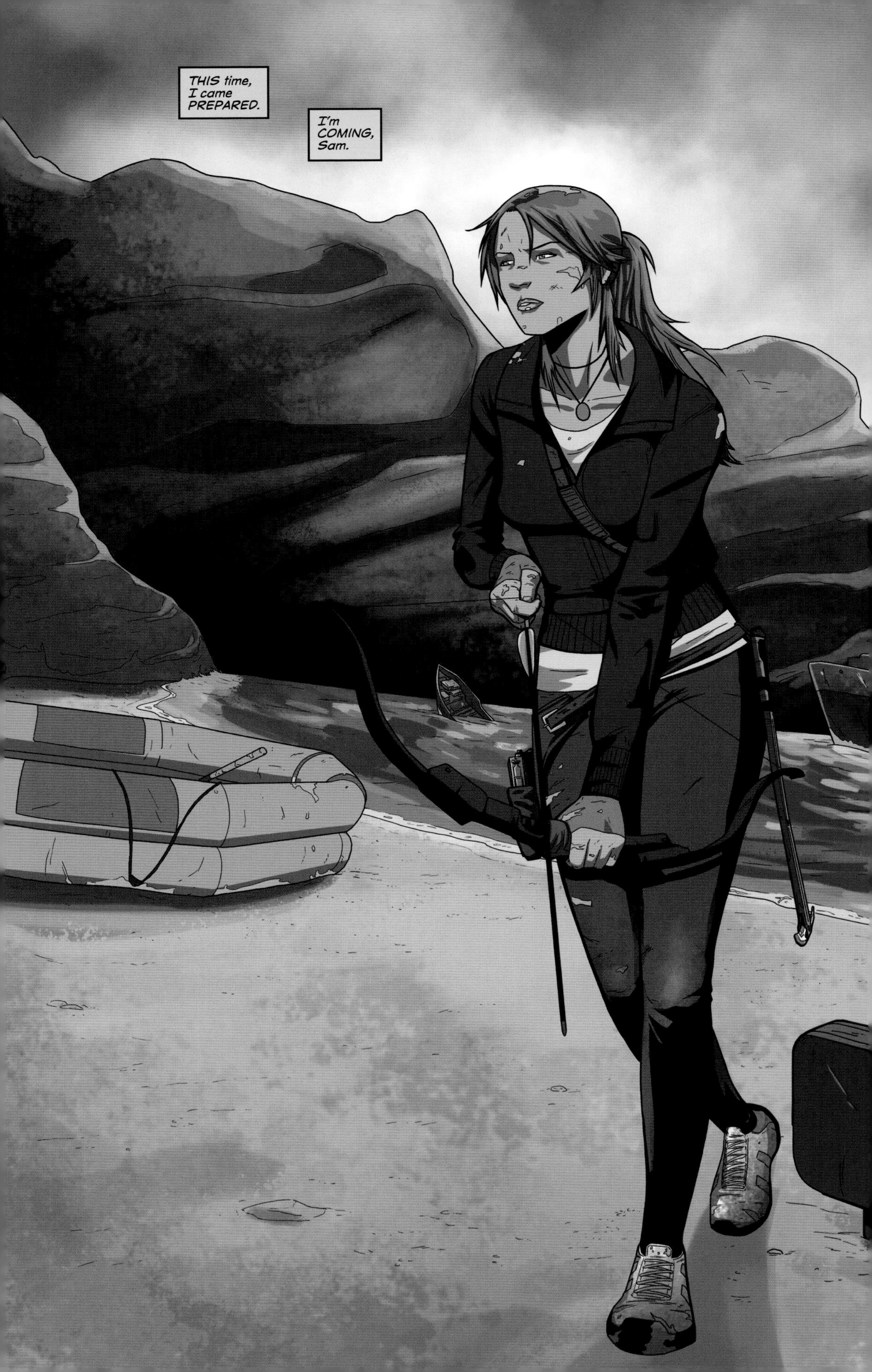
THIS time, I came PREPARED.
I'm COMING, Sam.

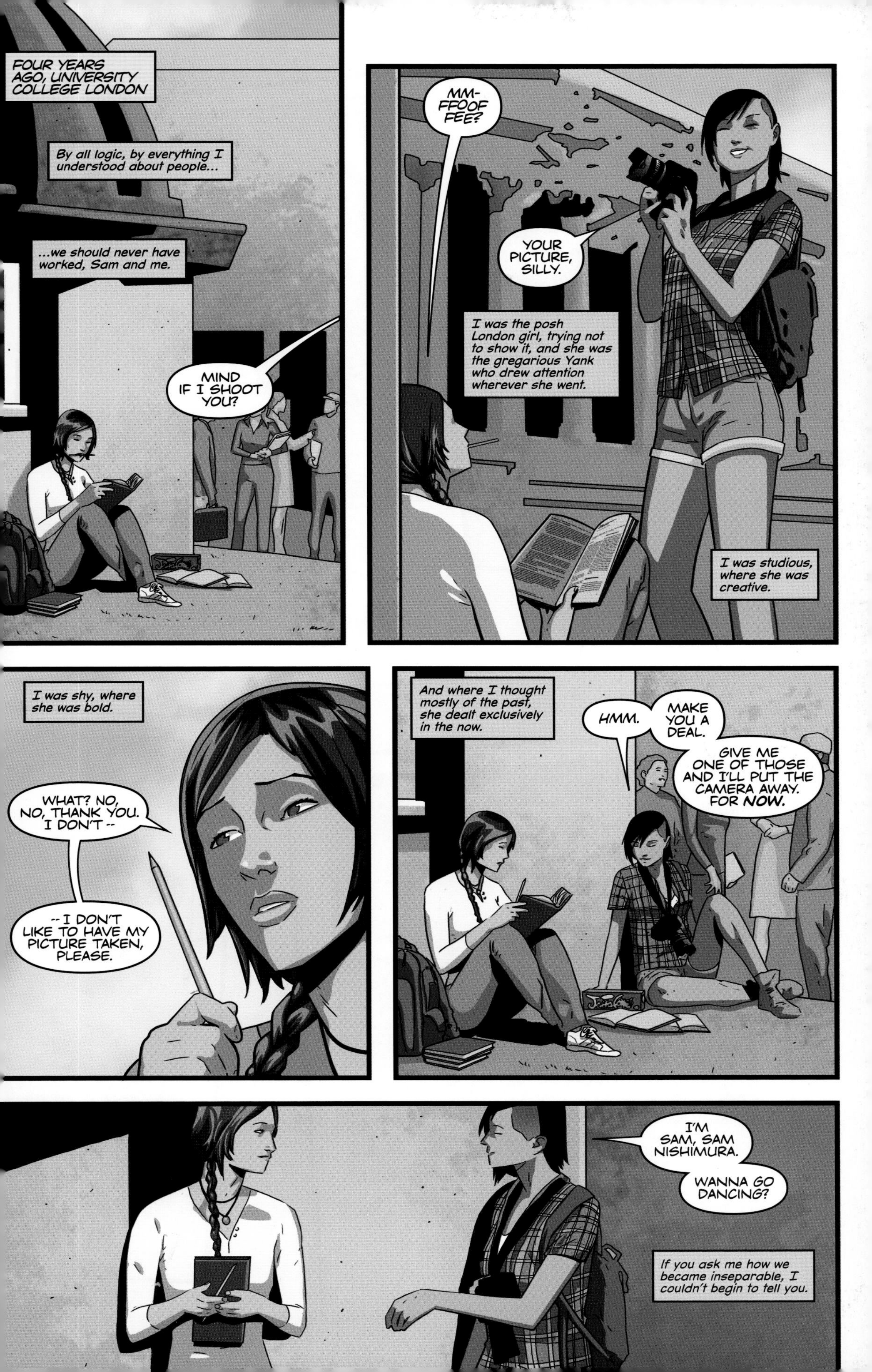
FOUR YEARS AGO, UNIVERSITY COLLEGE LONDON
By all logic, by everything I understood about people...
...we should never have worked, Sam and me.
MIND IF I SHOOT YOU?
MM-FFOOF FEE?
YOUR PICTURE, SILLY.
I was the posh London girl, trying not to show it, and she was the gregarious Yank who drew attention wherever she went.
I was studious, where she was creative.
I was shy, where she was bold.
WHAT? NO, NO, THANK YOU. I DON'T --
-- I DON'T LIKE TO HAVE MY PICTURE TAKEN, PLEASE.
And where I thought mostly of the past, she dealt exclusively in the now.
HMM.
MAKE YOU A DEAL.
GIVE ME ONE OF THOSE AND I'LL PUT THE CAMERA AWAY. FOR NOW.
I'M SAM, SAM NISHIMURA.
WANNA GO DANCING?
If you ask me how we became inseparable, I couldn't begin to tell you.

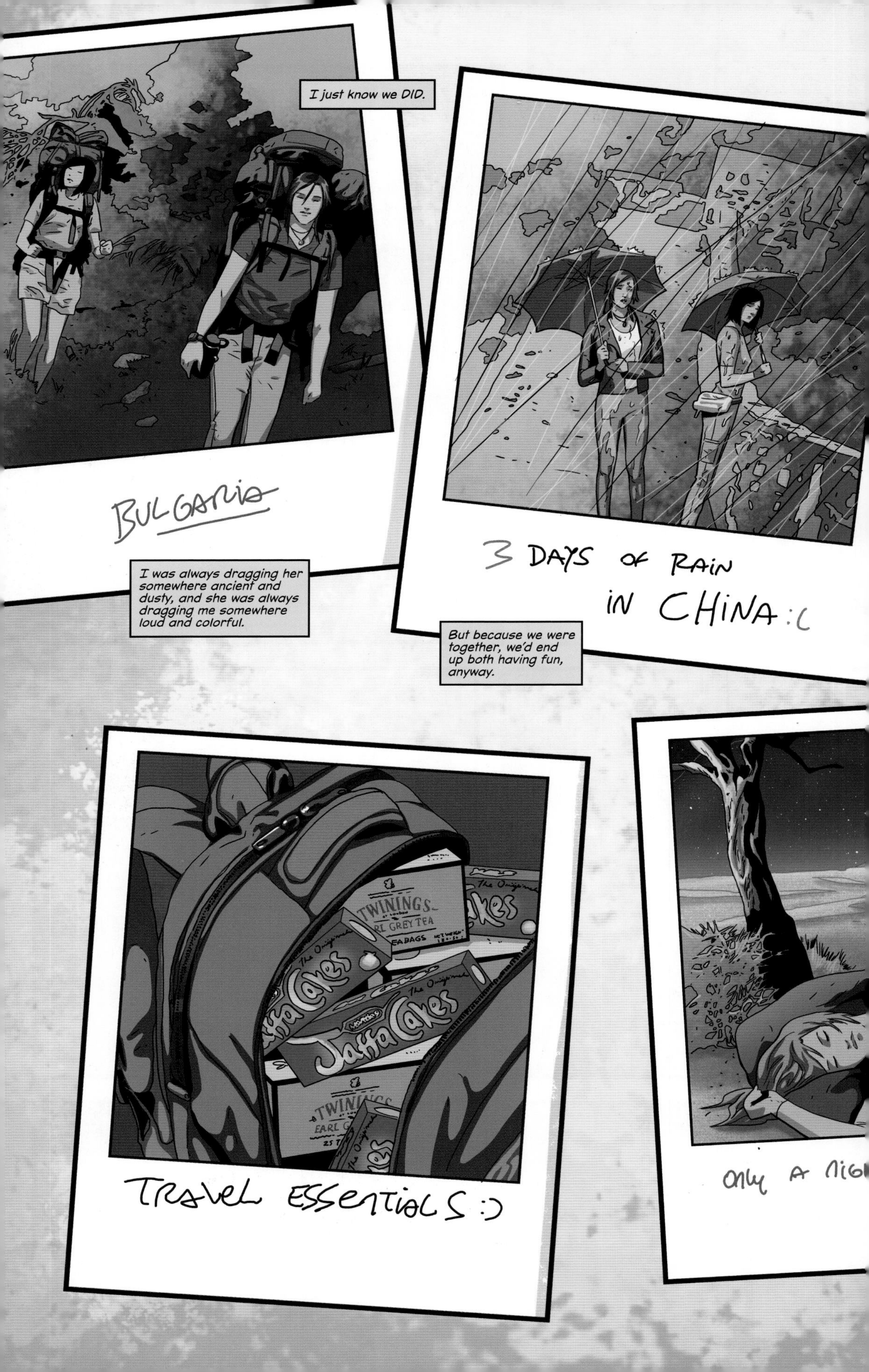

I just know we DID.
BULGARIA
I was always dragging her somewhere ancient and dusty, and she was always dragging me somewhere loud and colorful.
3 DAYS OF RAIN IN CHINA :(
But because we were together, we'd end up both having fun, anyway.
TWININGS EARL GREY TEA
Jaffa Cakes
TRAVEL ESSENTIALS :)
ONLY A NIG

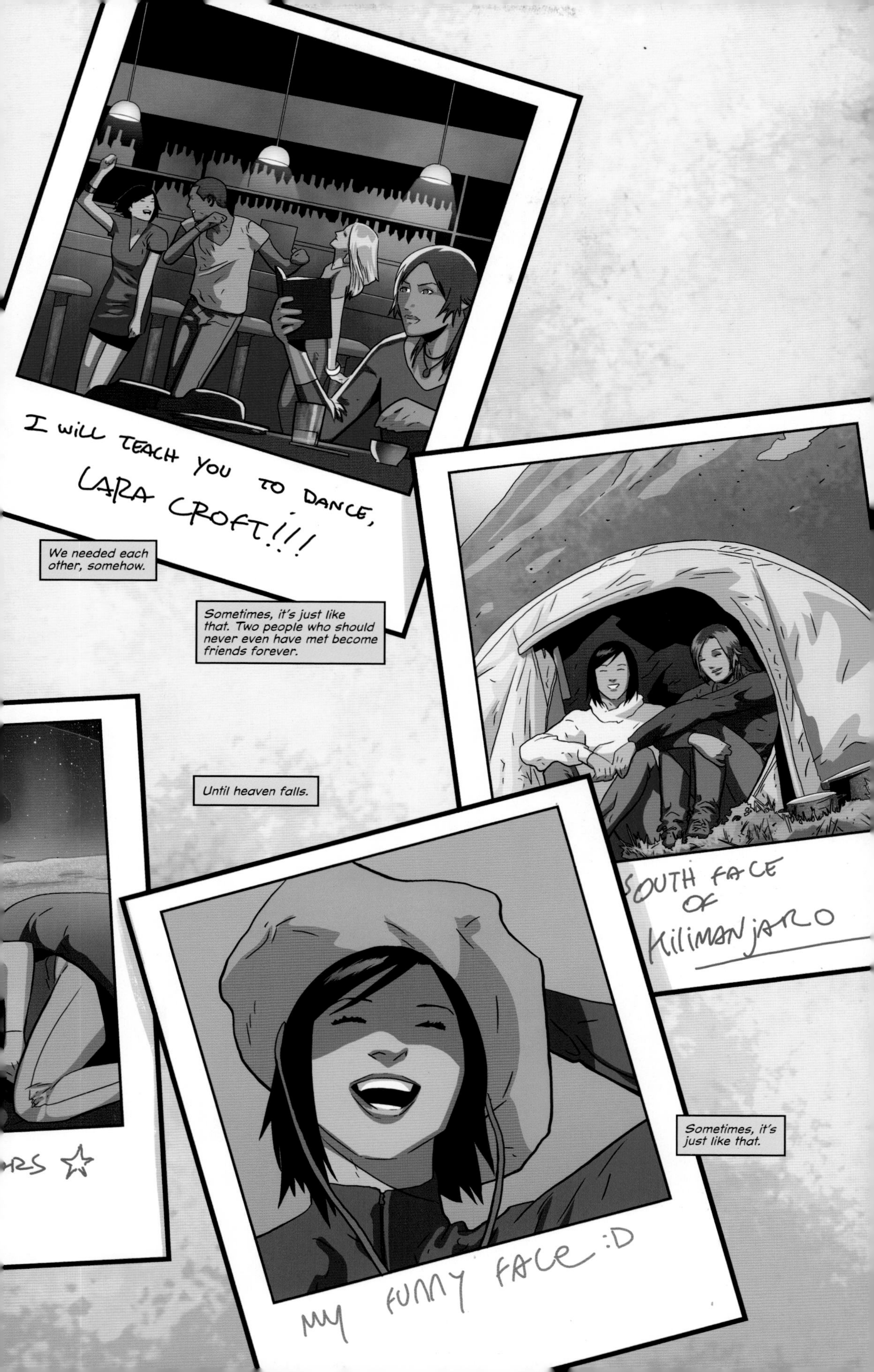
I WILL TEACH YOU TO DANCE, LARA CROFT!!!
We needed each other, somehow.
Sometimes, it's just like that. Two people who should never even have met become friends forever.
SOUTH FACE OF KILIMANJARO
Until heaven falls.
Sometimes, it's just like that.
MY FUNNY FACE :D

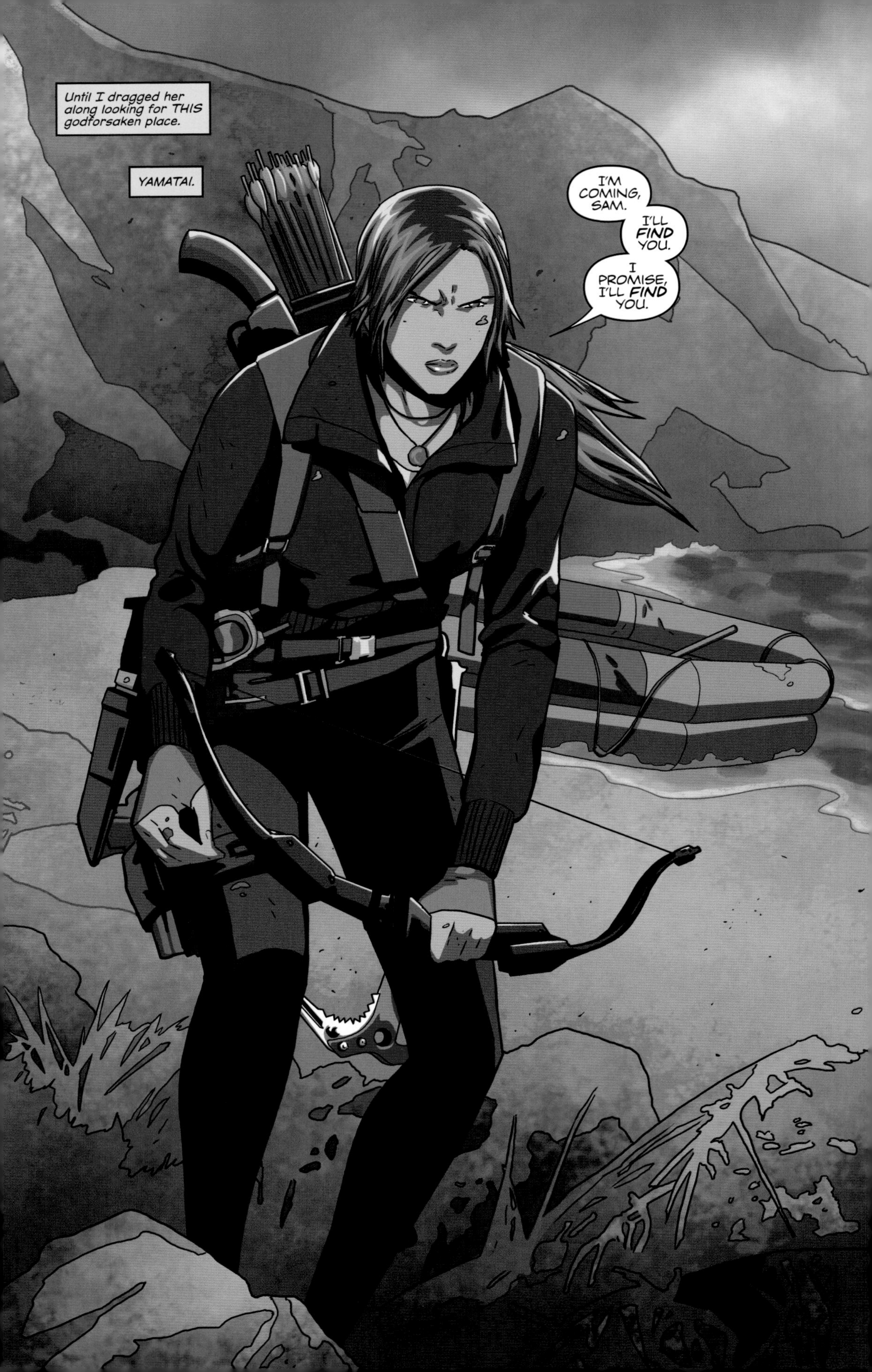
Until I dragged her along looking for THIS godforsaken place.
YAMATAI.
I'M COMING, SAM.
I'LL FIND YOU.
I PROMISE, I'LL FIND YOU.

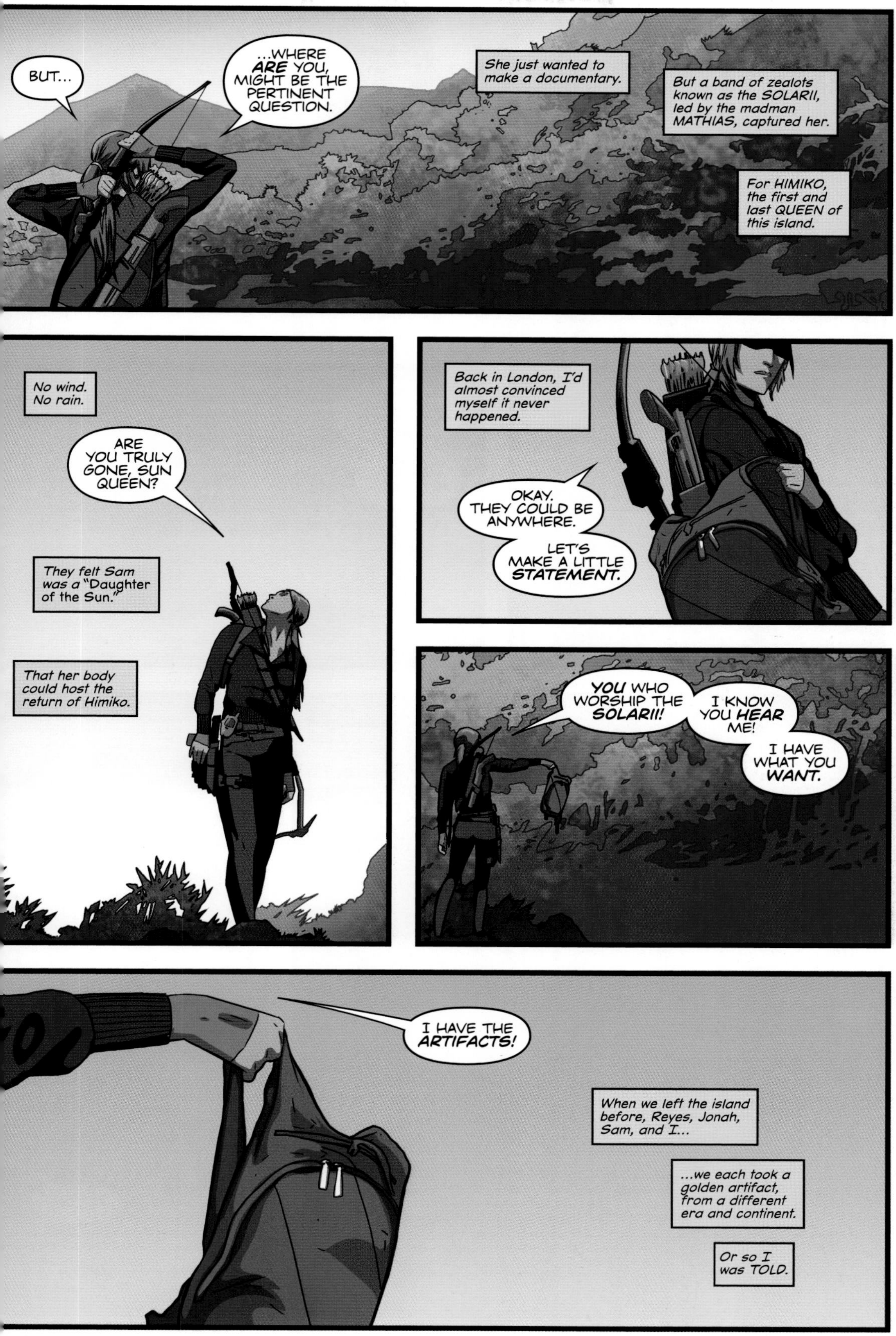
BUT...
...WHERE ARE YOU, MIGHT BE THE PERTINENT QUESTION.
She just wanted to make a documentary.
But a band of zealots known as the SOLARII, led by the madman MATHIAS, captured her.
For HIMIKO, the first and last QUEEN of this island.
No wind. No rain.
ARE YOU TRULY GONE, SUN QUEEN?
They felt Sam was a "Daughter of the Sun."
That her body could host the return of Himiko.
Back in London, I'd almost convinced myself it never happened.
OKAY. THEY COULD BE ANYWHERE.
LET'S MAKE A LITTLE STATEMENT.
YOU WHO WORSHIP THE SOLARII!
I KNOW YOU HEAR ME!
I HAVE WHAT YOU WANT.
I HAVE THE ARTIFACTS!
When we left the island before, Reyes, Jonah, Sam, and I...
...we each took a golden artifact, from a different era and continent.
Or so I was TOLD.

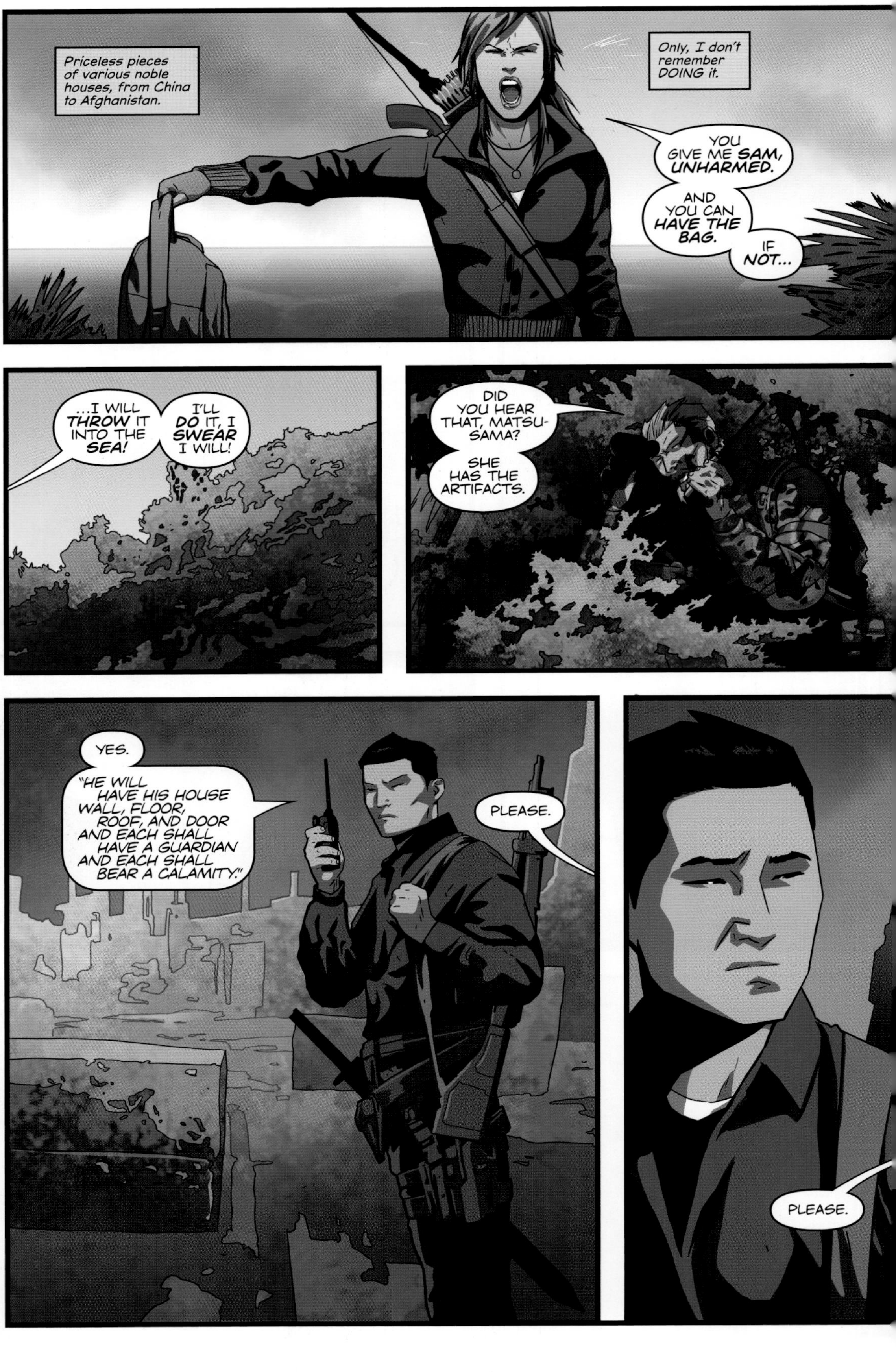
Priceless pieces of various noble houses, from China to Afghanistan.
Only, I don't remember DOING it.
YOU GIVE ME SAM, UNHARMED.
AND YOU CAN HAVE THE BAG.
IF NOT...
...I WILL THROW IT INTO THE SEA!
I'LL DO IT, I SWEAR I WILL!
DID YOU HEAR THAT, MATSU-SAMA?
SHE HAS THE ARTIFACTS.
YES.
"HE WILL HAVE HIS HOUSE WALL, FLOOR, ROOF, AND DOOR AND EACH SHALL HAVE A GUARDIAN AND EACH SHALL BEAR A CALAMITY."
PLEASE.
PLEASE.

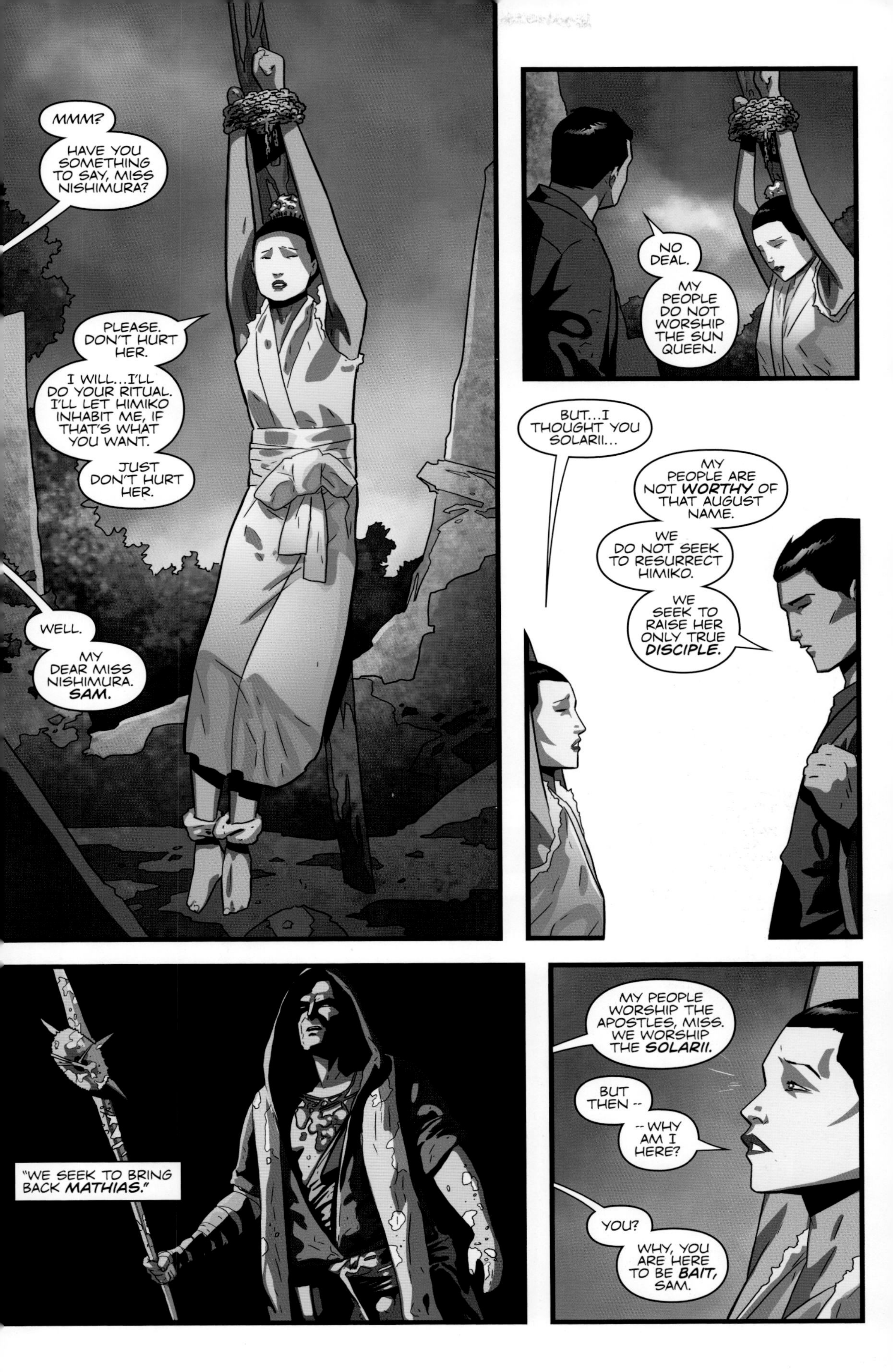
MMM?
HAVE YOU SOMETHING TO SAY, MISS NISHIMURA?
PLEASE. DON'T HURT HER.
I WILL...I'LL DO YOUR RITUAL. I'LL LET HIMIKO INHABIT ME, IF THAT'S WHAT YOU WANT.
JUST DON'T HURT HER.
WELL.
MY DEAR MISS NISHIMURA. **SAM.**
NO DEAL.
MY PEOPLE DO NOT WORSHIP THE SUN QUEEN.
BUT...I THOUGHT YOU SOLARII...
MY PEOPLE ARE NOT ***WORTHY*** OF THAT AUGUST NAME.
WE DO NOT SEEK TO RESURRECT HIMIKO.
WE SEEK TO RAISE HER ONLY TRUE ***DISCIPLE.***
"WE SEEK TO BRING BACK ***MATHIAS.***"
MY PEOPLE WORSHIP THE APOSTLES, MISS. WE WORSHIP THE ***SOLARII.***
BUT THEN --
-- WHY AM I HERE?
YOU?
WHY, YOU ARE HERE TO BE ***BAIT,*** SAM.

YOUR FRIEND, MISS.

LARA CROFT.

SHE'LL COME RIGHT TO THE *KILLING FLOOR* FOR YOU, DON'T YOU SEE THAT?

NO. *NO.*

"OH, YES. WE STILL NEED BLOOD FOR OUR SACRIFICE.

"BUT IT HAS TO BE *HER* BLOOD, IN THE TEMPLE WHERE SHE *MURDERED* OUR SAVIOR.

"WE DON'T EVEN HAVE TO BRING HER HERE.

"SHE'LL COME IN AND BEG TO GIVE HERSELF UP TO US.

"FOR *YOU*, MISS NISHIMURA."

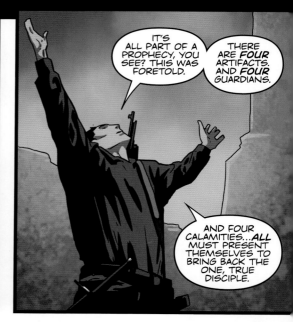

IT'S ALL PART OF A PROPHECY, YOU SEE? THIS WAS FORETOLD.

THERE ARE *FOUR* ARTIFACTS. AND *FOUR* GUARDIANS.

AND FOUR CALAMITIES...*ALL* MUST PRESENT THEMSELVES TO BRING BACK THE ONE, TRUE DISCIPLE.

"THE FOUR ARTIFACTS YOU KNOW.

"I AM THE FIRST OF THE GUARDIANS."

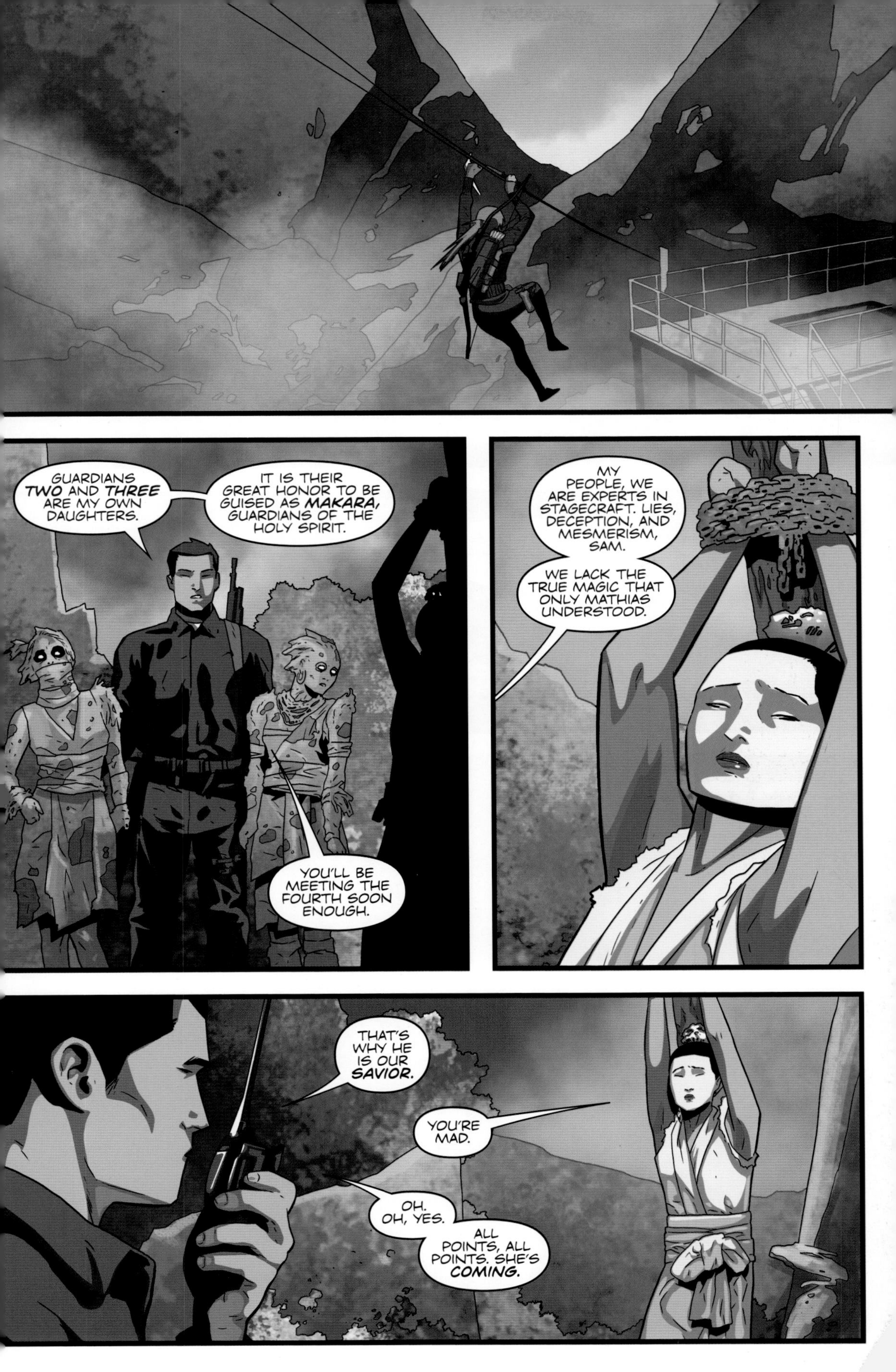
GUARDIANS TWO AND THREE ARE MY OWN DAUGHTERS.
IT IS THEIR GREAT HONOR TO BE GUISED AS MAKARA, GUARDIANS OF THE HOLY SPIRIT.
YOU'LL BE MEETING THE FOURTH SOON ENOUGH.
MY PEOPLE, WE ARE EXPERTS IN STAGECRAFT. LIES, DECEPTION, AND MESMERISM, SAM.
WE LACK THE TRUE MAGIC THAT ONLY MATHIAS UNDERSTOOD.
THAT'S WHY HE IS OUR SAVIOR.
YOU'RE MAD.
OH. OH, YES.
ALL POINTS, ALL POINTS. SHE'S COMING.

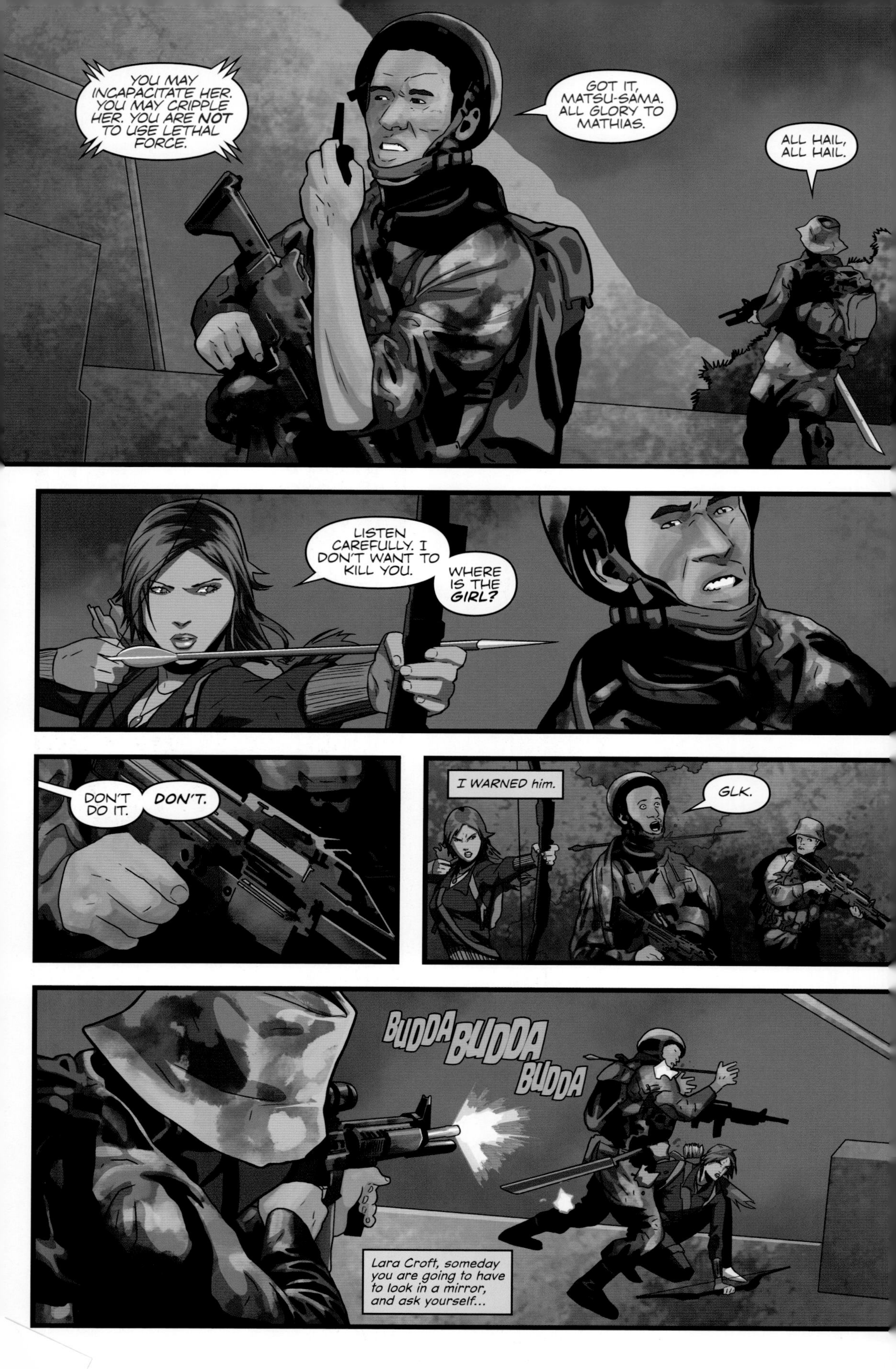

YOU MAY INCAPACITATE HER. YOU MAY CRIPPLE HER. YOU ARE **NOT** TO USE LETHAL FORCE.
GOT IT, MATSU-SAMA. ALL GLORY TO MATHIAS.
ALL HAIL, ALL HAIL.
LISTEN CAREFULLY. I DON'T WANT TO KILL YOU.
WHERE IS THE ***GIRL?***
DON'T DO IT.
DON'T.
I WARNED him.
GLK.
BUDDA BUDDA BUDDA
Lara Croft, someday you are going to have to look in a mirror, and ask yourself...

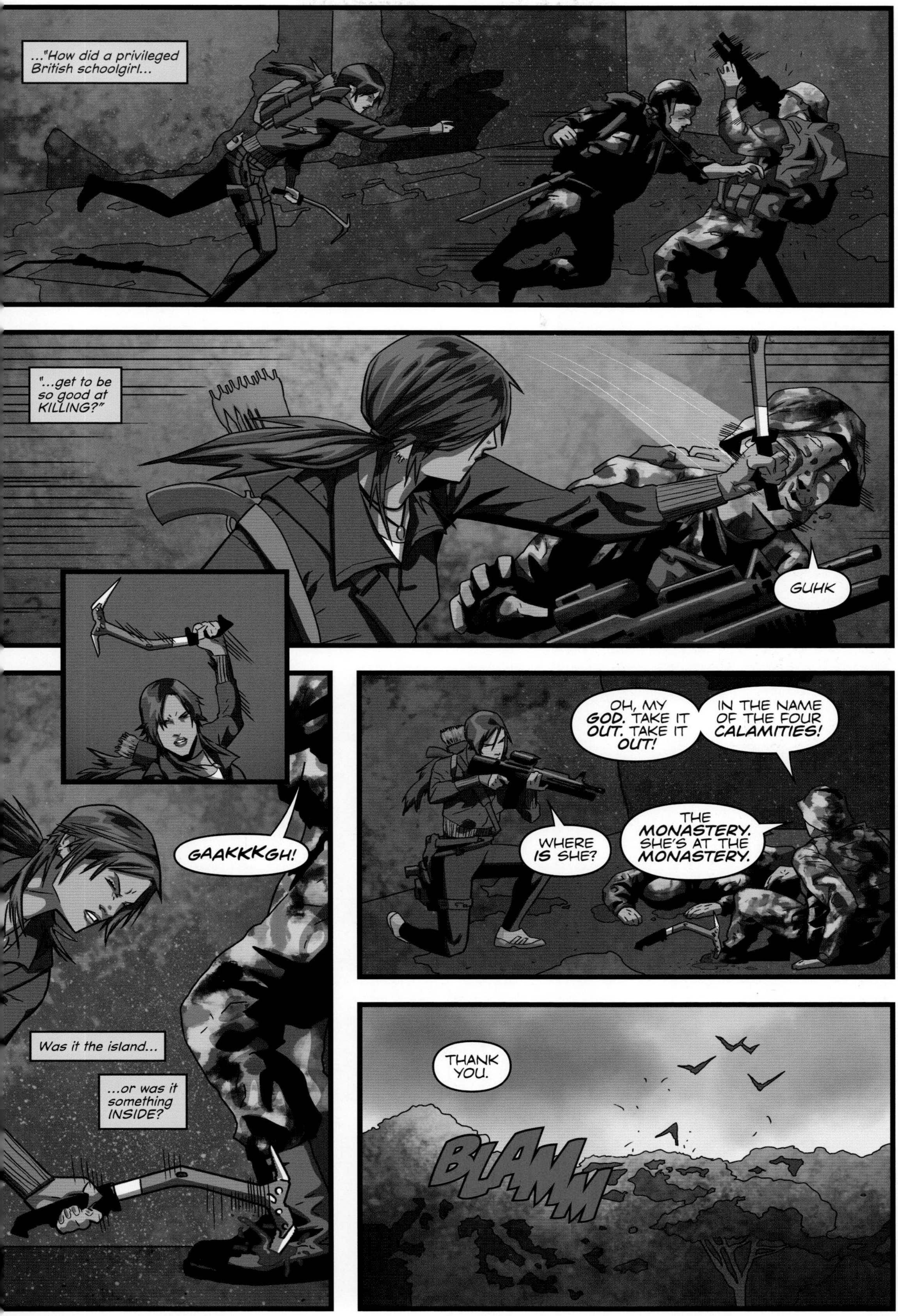
..."How did a privileged British schoolgirl...
"...get to be so good at KILLING?"
GUHK
GAAKKKGH!
Was it the island...
...or was it something INSIDE?
OH, MY GOD. TAKE IT OUT. TAKE IT OUT!
IN THE NAME OF THE FOUR CALAMITIES!
WHERE IS SHE?
THE MONASTERY. SHE'S AT THE MONASTERY.
THANK YOU.
BLAMM

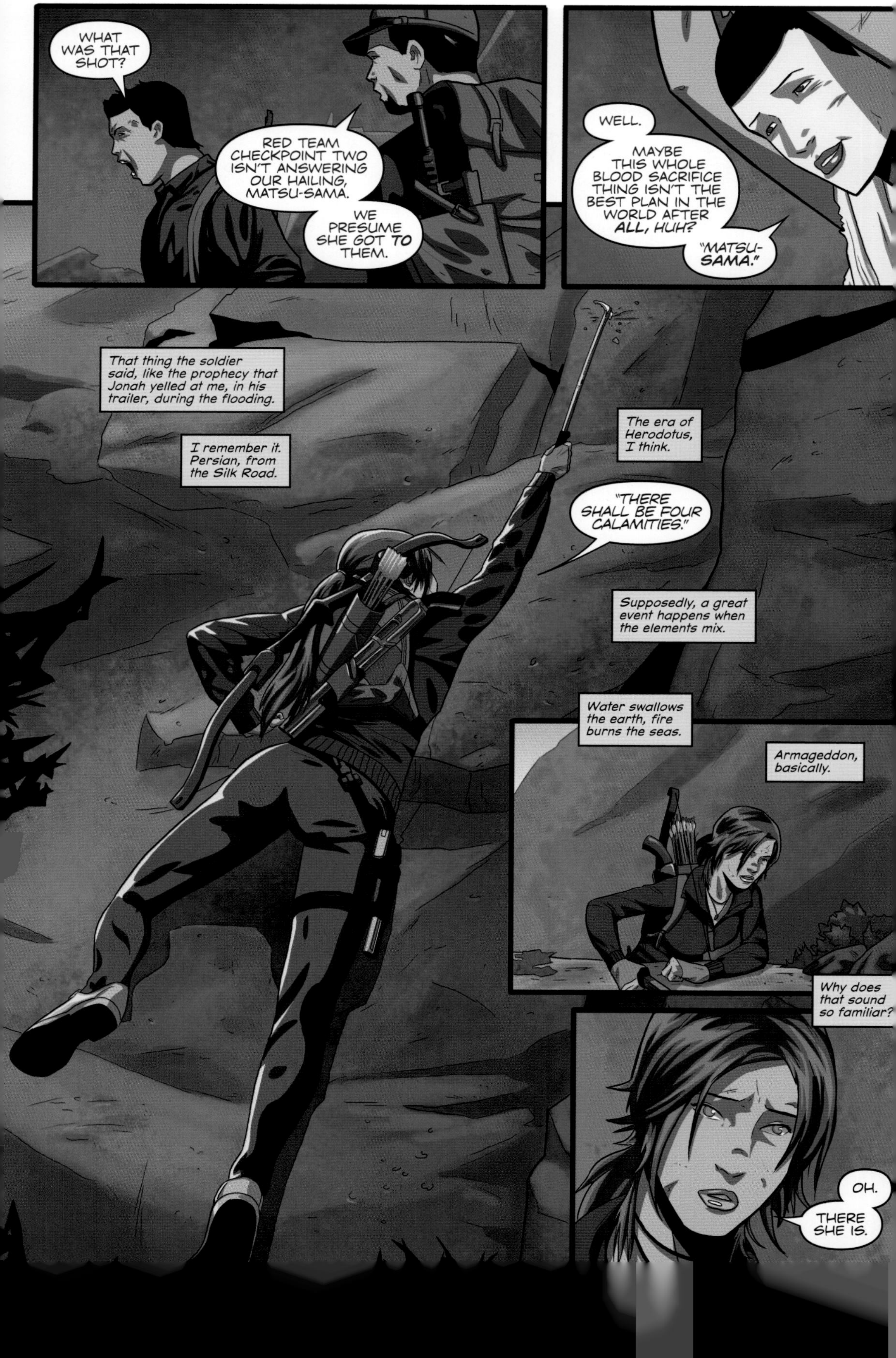
WHAT WAS THAT SHOT?
RED TEAM CHECKPOINT TWO ISN'T ANSWERING OUR HAILING, MATSU-SAMA.
WE PRESUME SHE GOT TO THEM.
WELL.
MAYBE THIS WHOLE BLOOD SACRIFICE THING ISN'T THE BEST PLAN IN THE WORLD AFTER ALL, HUH?
"MATSU-SAMA."
That thing the soldier said, like the prophecy that Jonah yelled at me, in his trailer, during the flooding.
I remember it. Persian, from the Silk Road.
The era of Herodotus, I think.
"THERE SHALL BE FOUR CALAMITIES."
Supposedly, a great event happens when the elements mix.
Water swallows the earth, fire burns the seas.
Armageddon, basically.
Why does that sound so familiar?
OH.
THERE SHE IS.

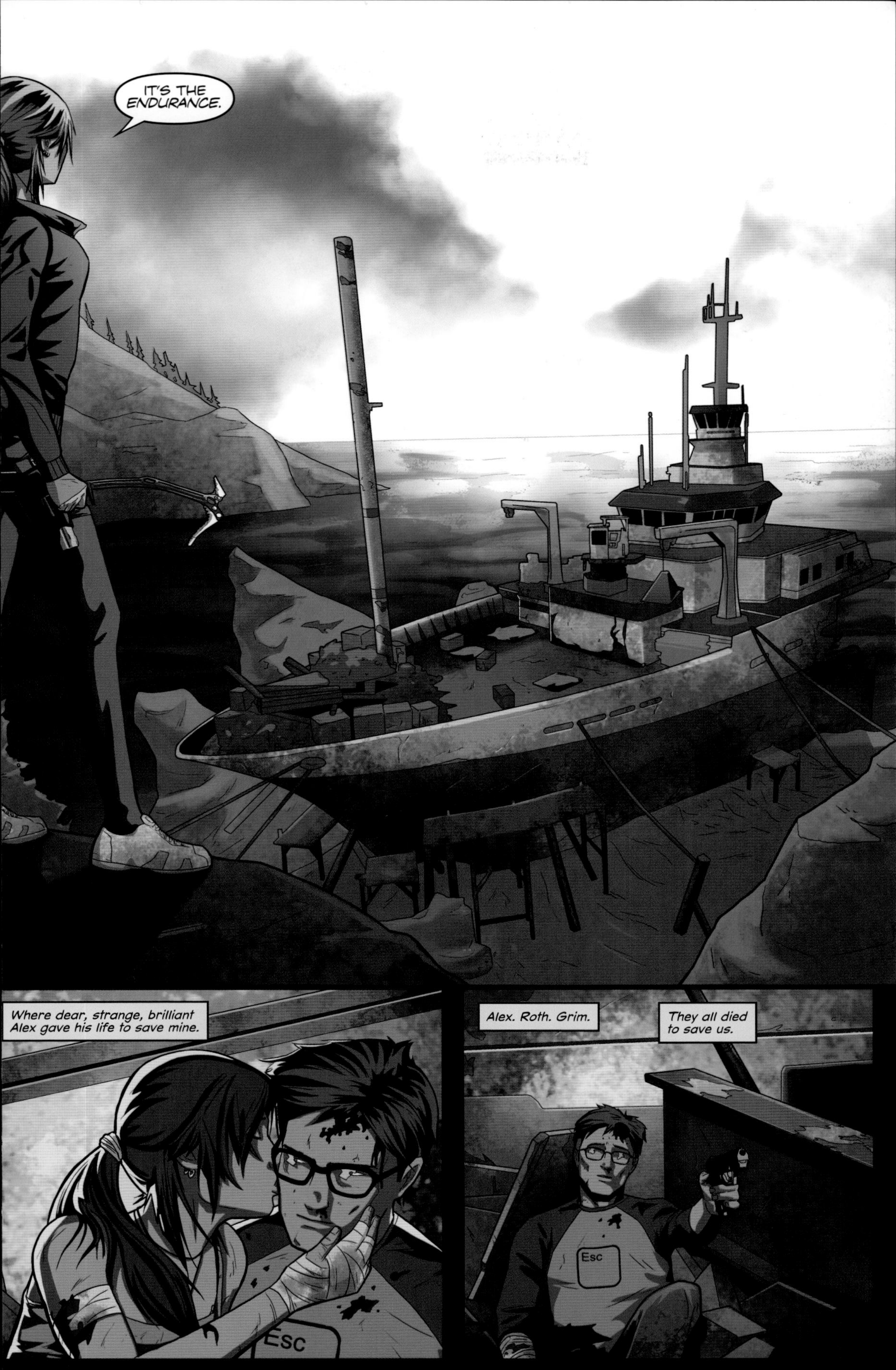
IT'S THE ENDURANCE.
Where dear, strange, brilliant Alex gave his life to save mine.
Esc
Alex. Roth. Grim.
They all died to save us.
Esc

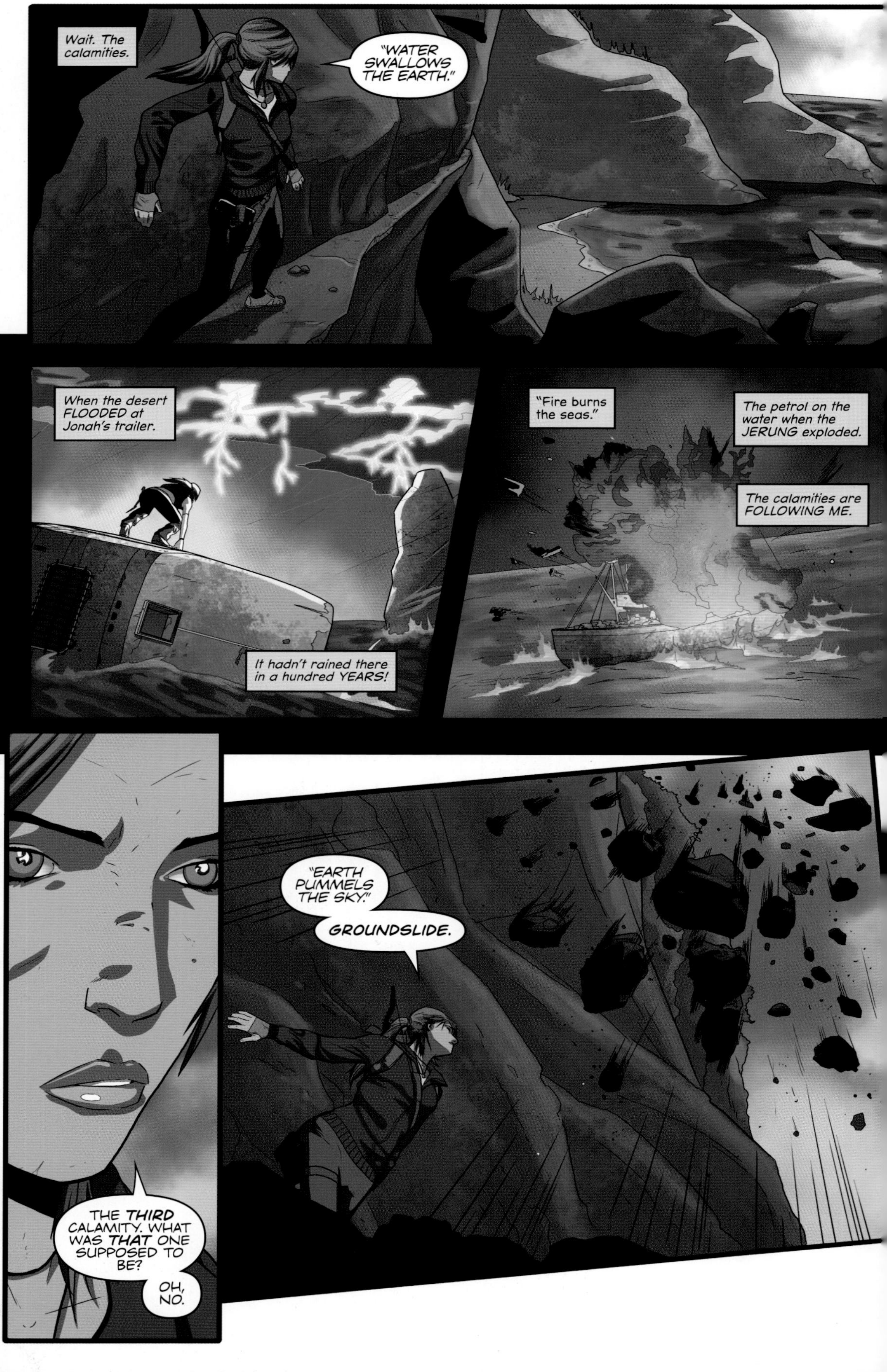

Wait. The calamities.
"WATER SWALLOWS THE EARTH."
When the desert FLOODED at Jonah's trailer.
It hadn't rained there in a hundred YEARS!
"Fire burns the seas."
The petrol on the water when the JERUNG exploded.
The calamities are FOLLOWING ME.
THE THIRD CALAMITY. WHAT WAS THAT ONE SUPPOSED TO BE?
OH, NO.
"EARTH PUMMELS THE SKY."
GROUNDSLIDE.

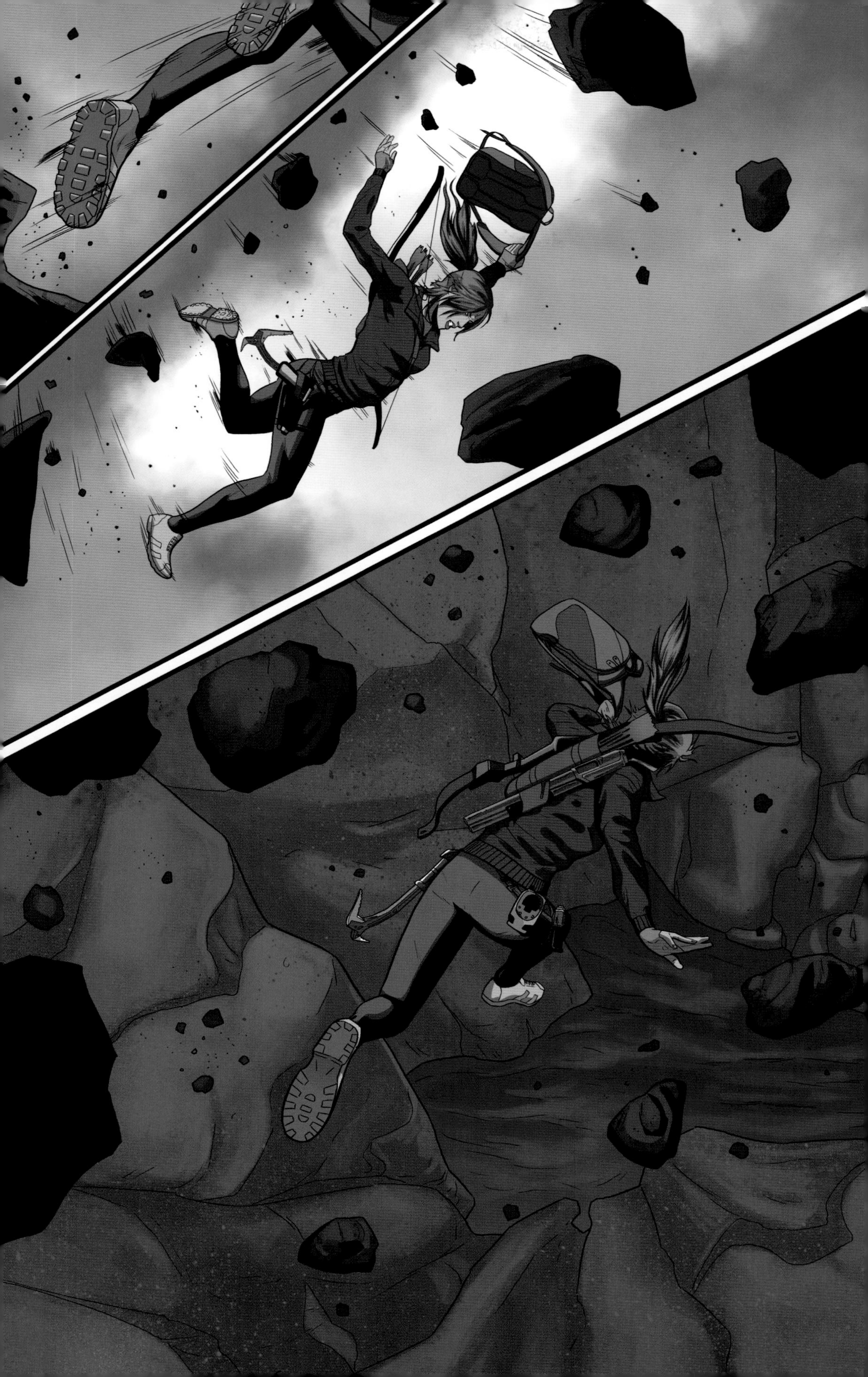

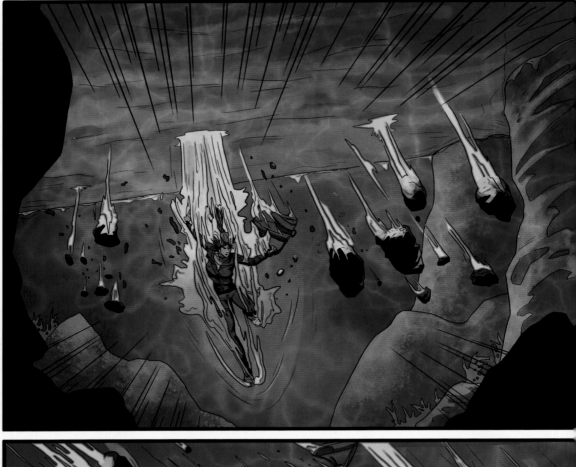

LARA.

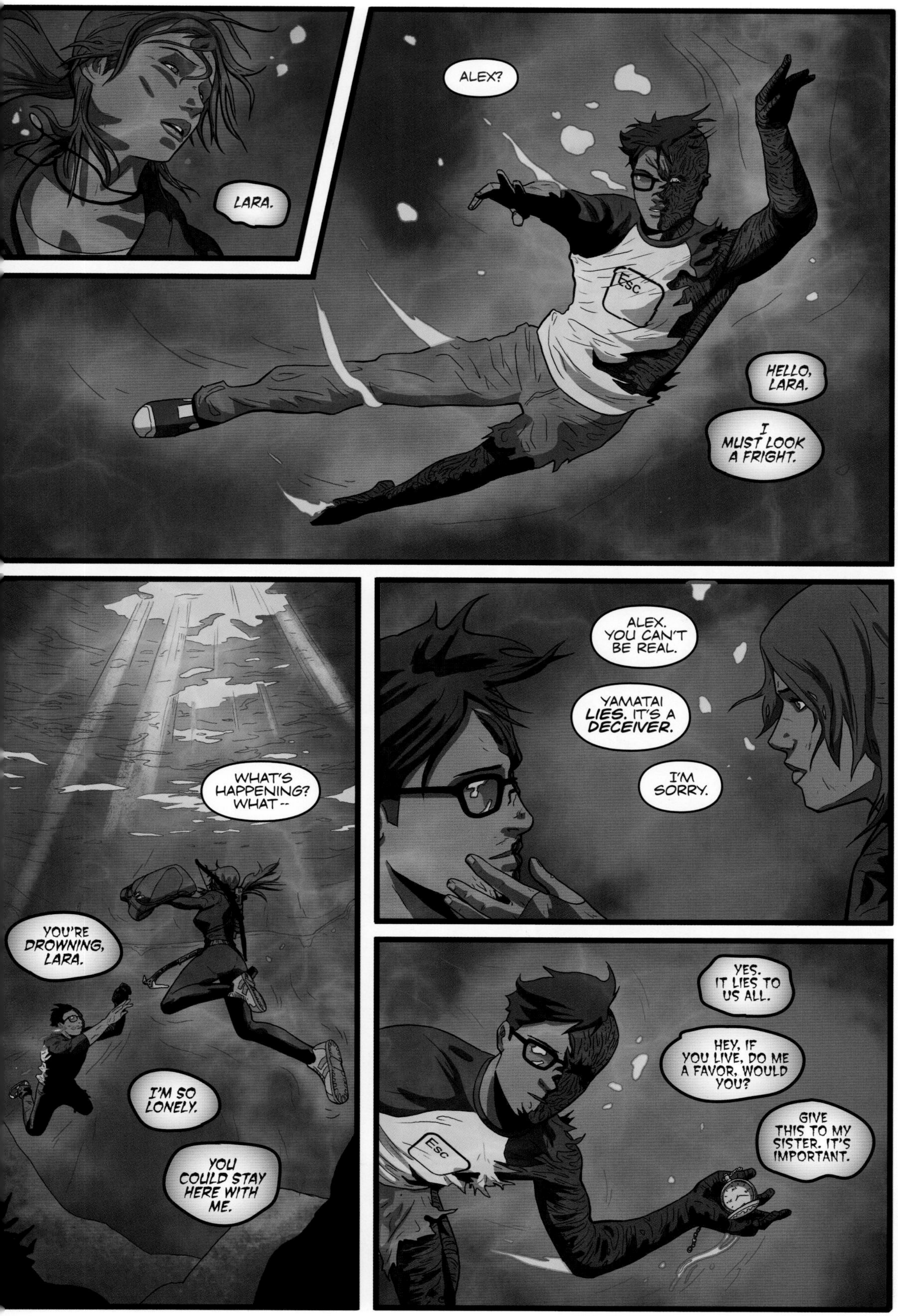
ALEX?
LARA.
HELLO, LARA.
I MUST LOOK A FRIGHT.
Esc
WHAT'S HAPPENING? WHAT --
YOU'RE DROWNING, LARA.
I'M SO LONELY.
YOU COULD STAY HERE WITH ME.
ALEX. YOU CAN'T BE REAL.
YAMATAI LIES. IT'S A DECEIVER.
I'M SORRY.
YES. IT LIES TO US ALL.
HEY, IF YOU LIVE, DO ME A FAVOR, WOULD YOU?
GIVE THIS TO MY SISTER. IT'S IMPORTANT.
Esc

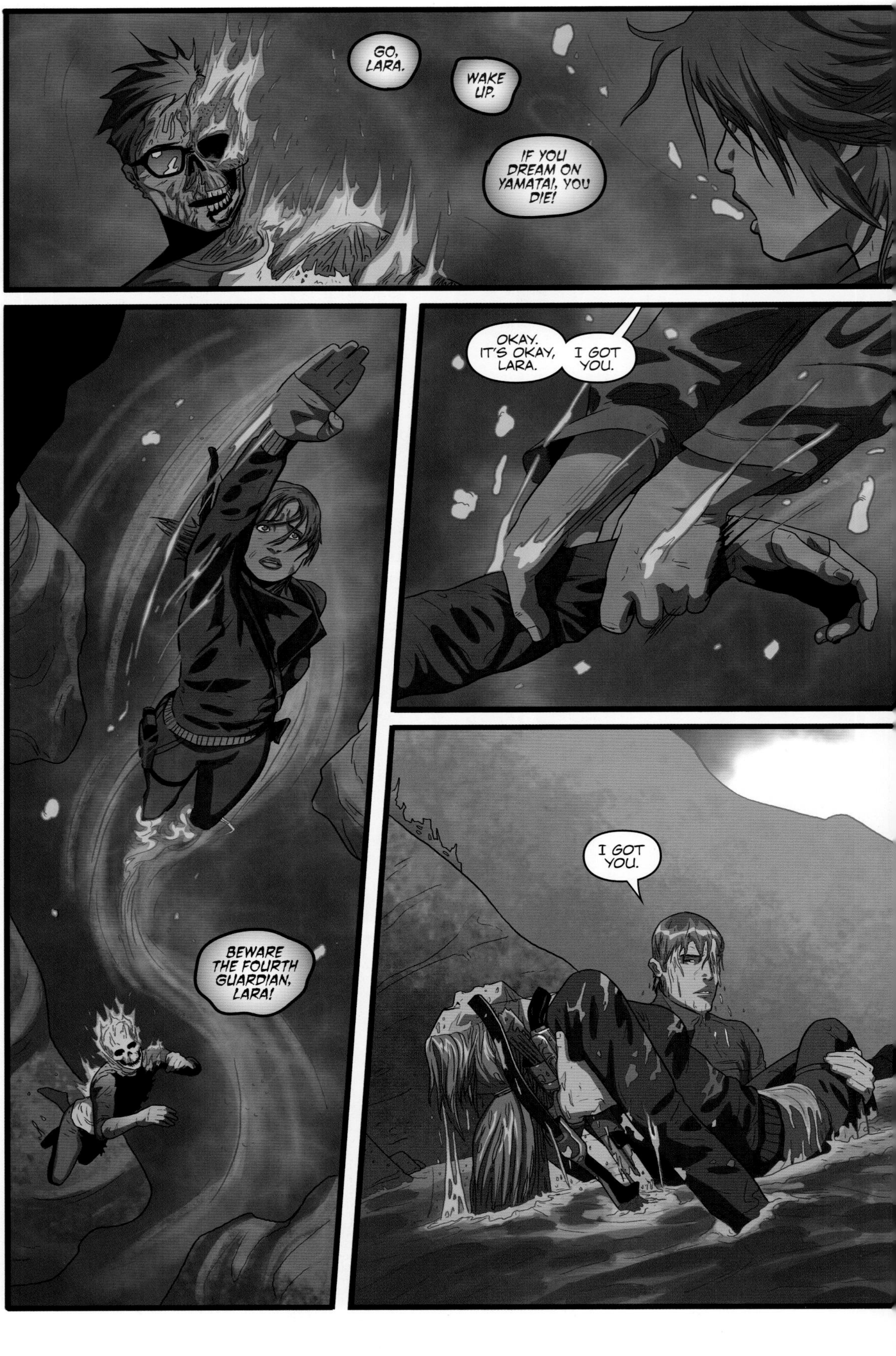
GO, LARA.
WAKE UP.
IF YOU DREAM ON YAMATAI, YOU DIE!
BEWARE THE FOURTH GUARDIAN, LARA!
OKAY. IT'S OKAY, LARA.
I GOT YOU.
I GOT YOU.

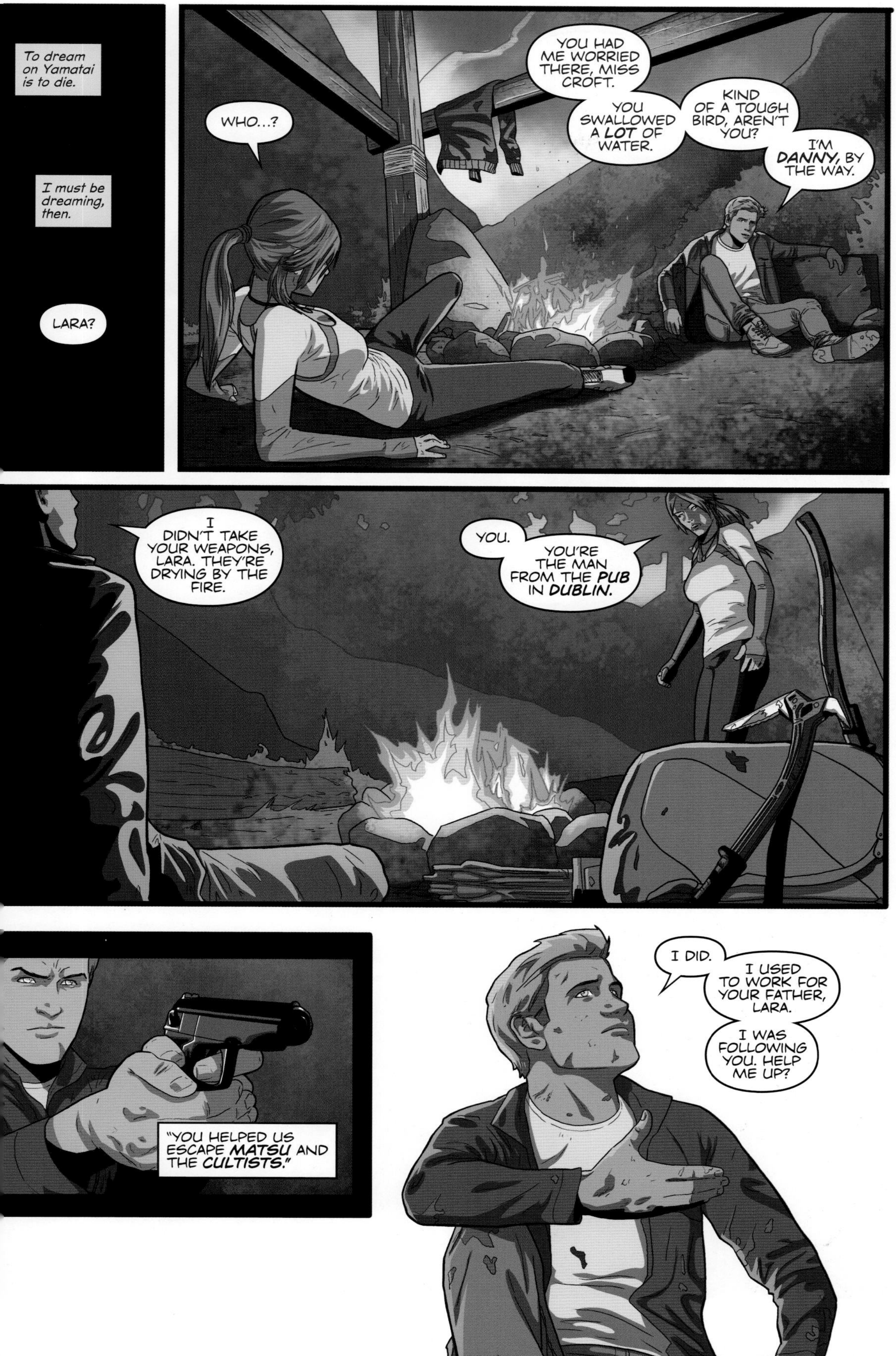
To dream on Yamatai is to die.
WHO...?
I must be dreaming, then.
LARA?
YOU HAD ME WORRIED THERE, MISS CROFT.
YOU SWALLOWED A LOT OF WATER.
KIND OF A TOUGH BIRD, AREN'T YOU?
I'M DANNY, BY THE WAY.
I DIDN'T TAKE YOUR WEAPONS, LARA. THEY'RE DRYING BY THE FIRE.
YOU.
YOU'RE THE MAN FROM THE PUB IN DUBLIN.
"YOU HELPED US ESCAPE MATSU AND THE CULTISTS."
I DID.
I USED TO WORK FOR YOUR FATHER, LARA.
I WAS FOLLOWING YOU. HELP ME UP?

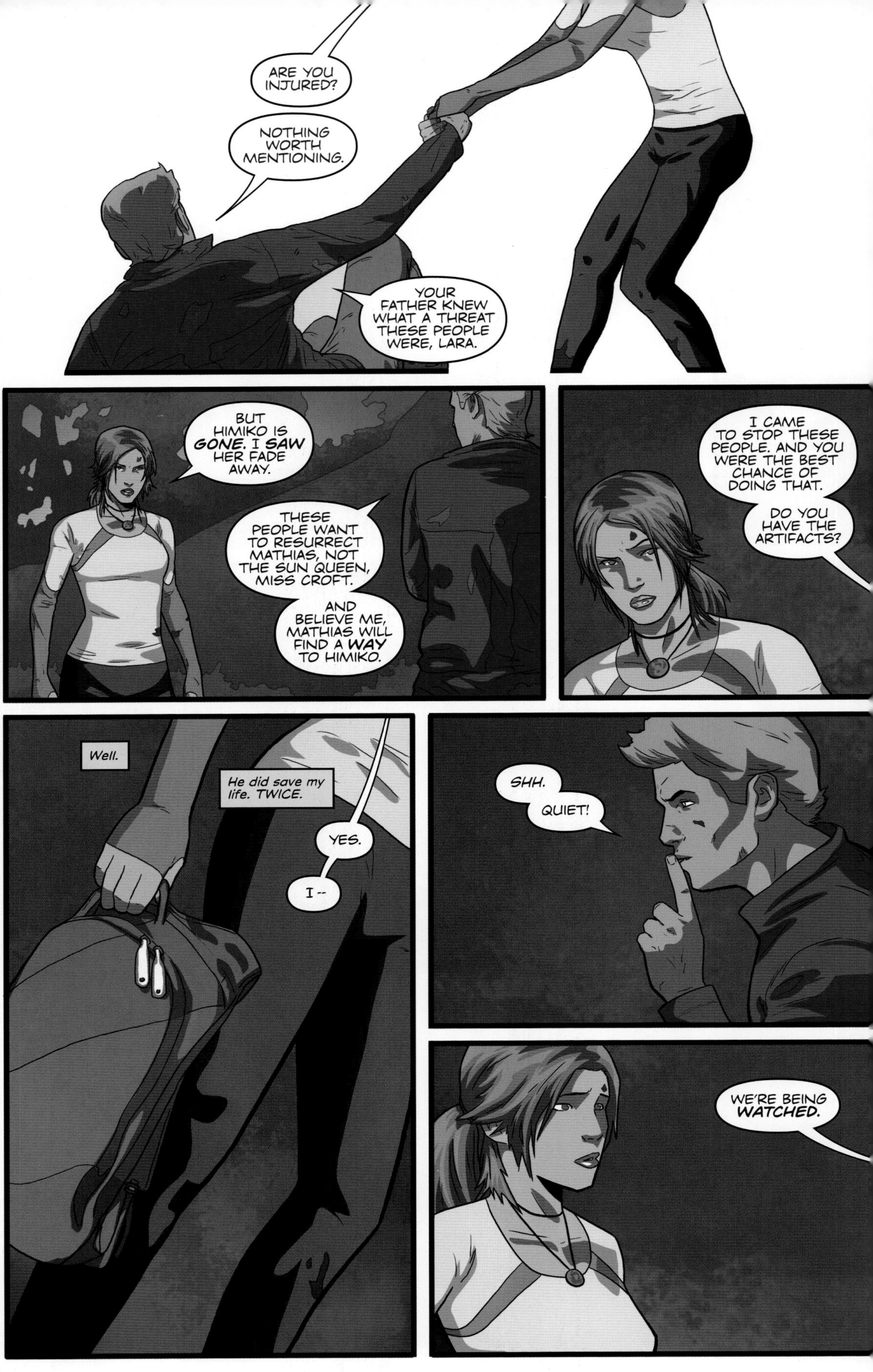

ARE YOU INJURED?
NOTHING WORTH MENTIONING.
YOUR FATHER KNEW WHAT A THREAT THESE PEOPLE WERE, LARA.
BUT HIMIKO IS **GONE.** I **SAW** HER FADE AWAY.
THESE PEOPLE WANT TO RESURRECT MATHIAS, NOT THE SUN QUEEN, MISS CROFT.
AND BELIEVE ME, MATHIAS WILL FIND A **WAY** TO HIMIKO.
I CAME TO STOP THESE PEOPLE. AND YOU WERE THE BEST CHANCE OF DOING THAT.
DO YOU HAVE THE ARTIFACTS?
Well.
He did save my life. TWICE.
YES.
I --
SHH.
QUIET!
WE'RE BEING **WATCHED.**

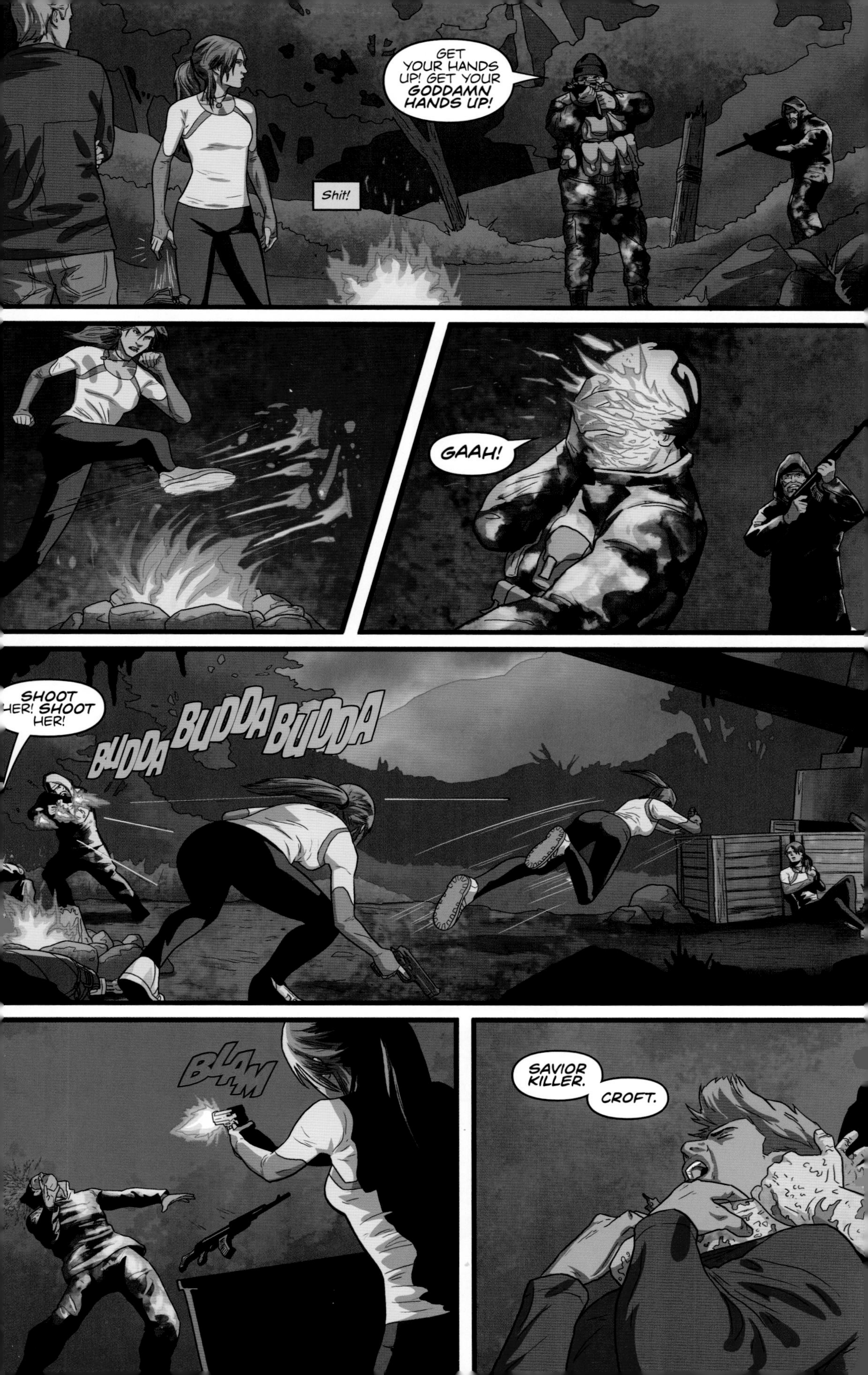
GET YOUR HANDS UP! GET YOUR GODDAMN HANDS UP!
Shit!
GAAH!
SHOOT HER! SHOOT HER!
BUDDA BUDDA BUDDA
BLAM
SAVIOR KILLER.
CROFT.

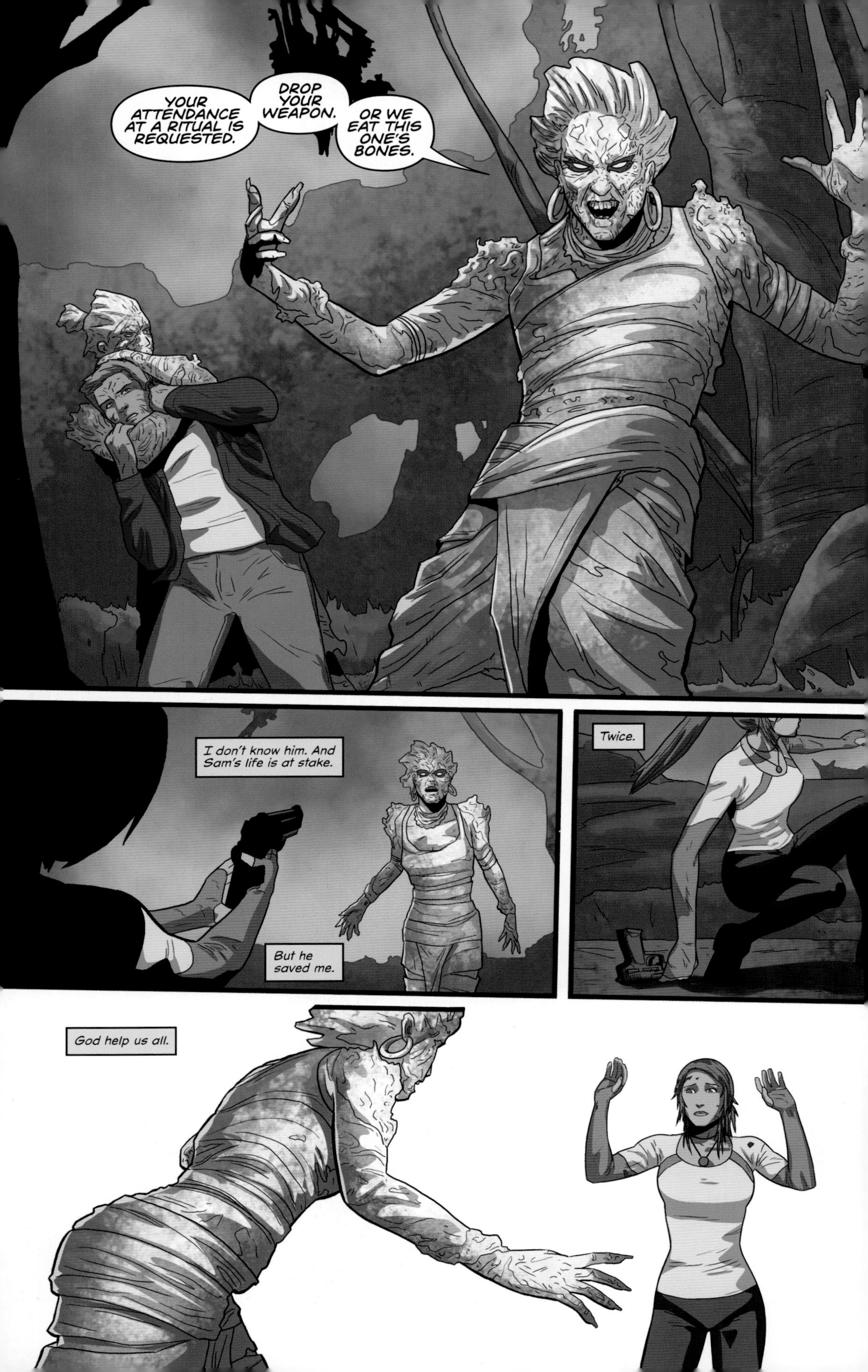
YOUR ATTENDANCE AT A RITUAL IS REQUESTED.
DROP YOUR WEAPON.
OR WE EAT THIS ONE'S BONES.
I don't know him. And Sam's life is at stake.
But he saved me.
Twice.
God help us all.

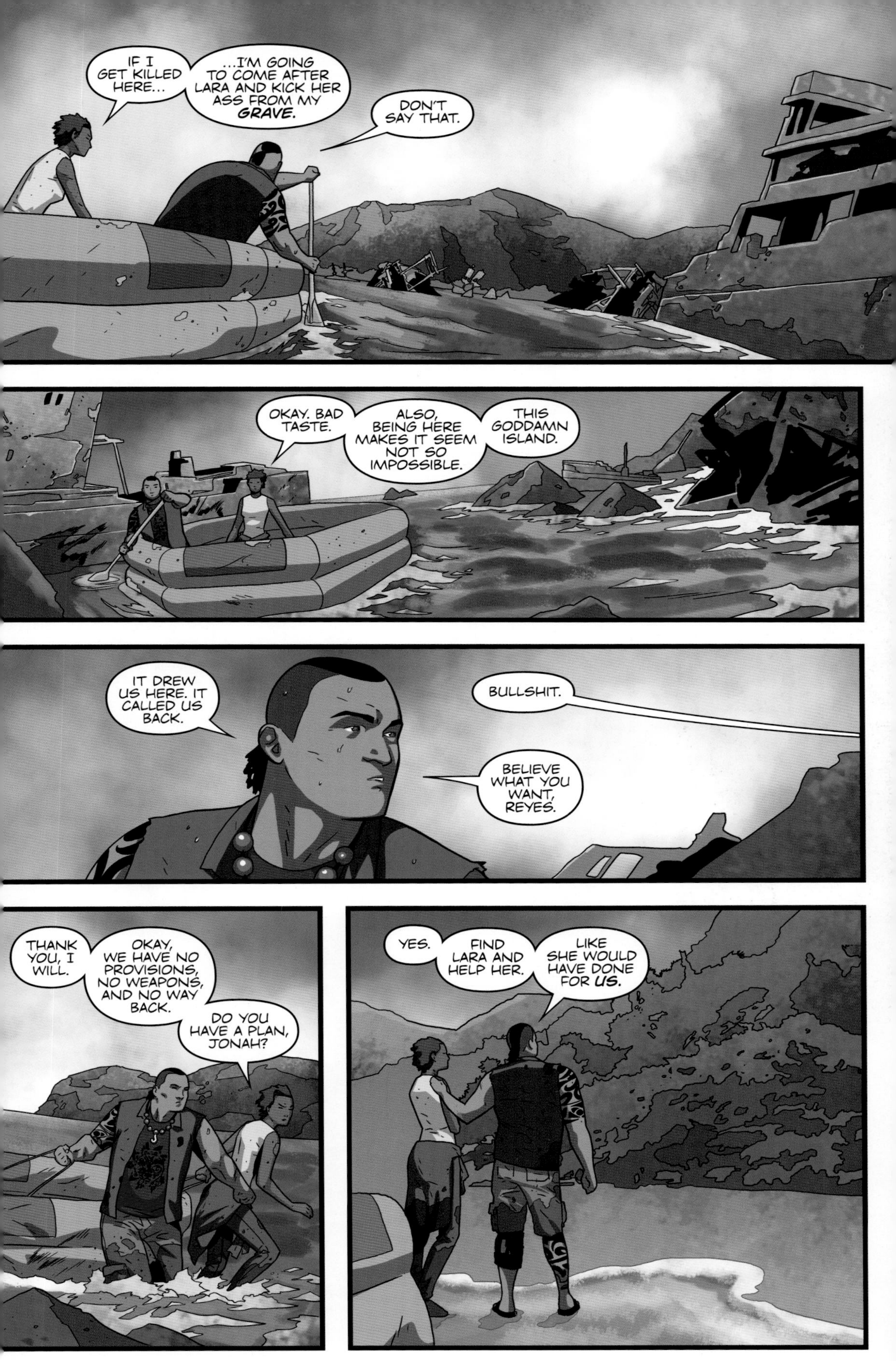
IF I GET KILLED HERE...
...I'M GOING TO COME AFTER LARA AND KICK HER ASS FROM MY **GRAVE.**
DON'T SAY THAT.
OKAY. BAD TASTE.
ALSO, BEING HERE MAKES IT SEEM NOT SO IMPOSSIBLE.
THIS GODDAMN ISLAND.
IT DREW US HERE. IT CALLED US BACK.
BULLSHIT.
BELIEVE WHAT YOU WANT, REYES.
THANK YOU, I WILL.
OKAY, WE HAVE NO PROVISIONS, NO WEAPONS, AND NO WAY BACK.
DO YOU HAVE A PLAN, JONAH?
YES.
FIND LARA AND HELP HER.
LIKE SHE WOULD HAVE DONE FOR **US.**

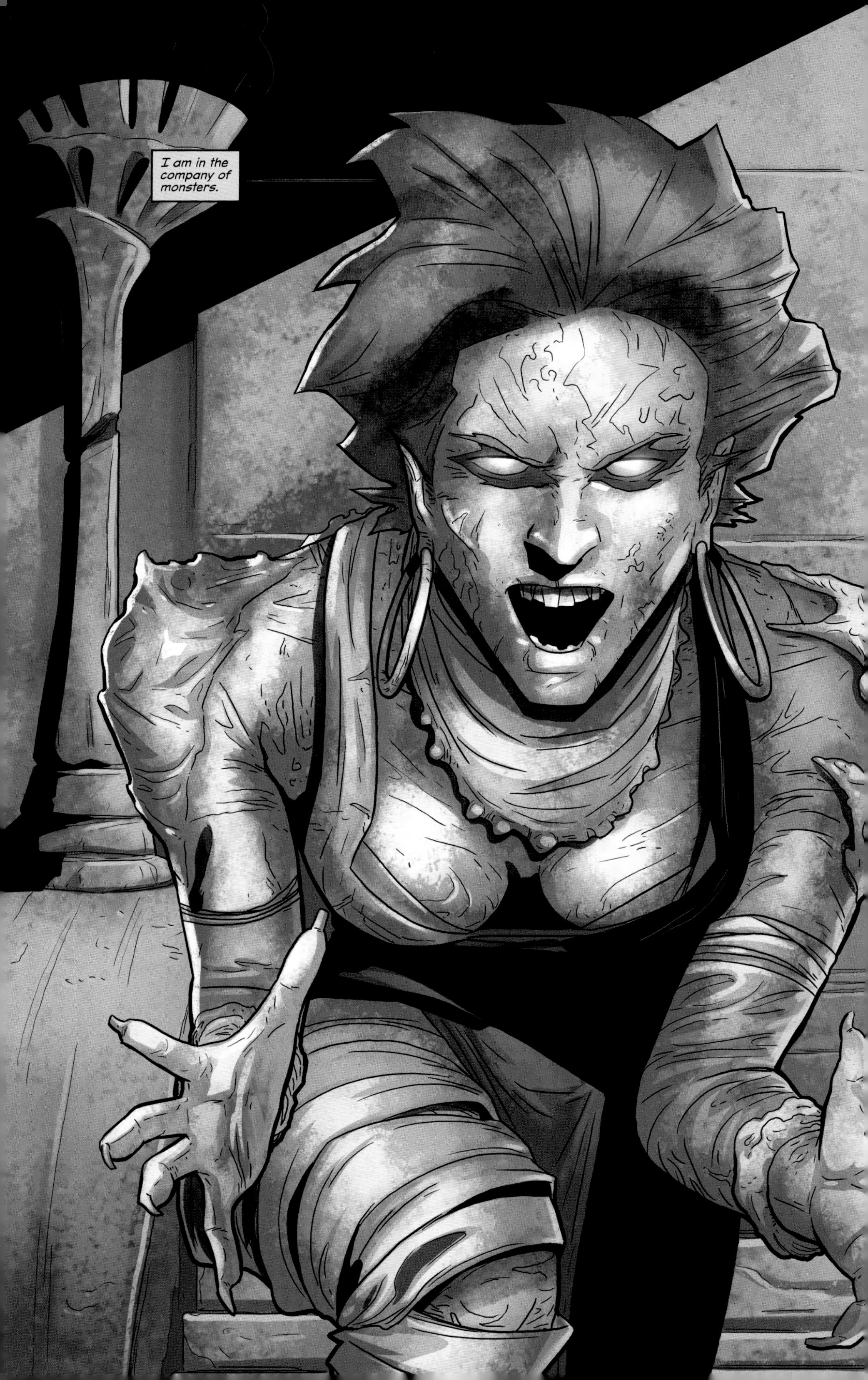
I am in the company of monsters.

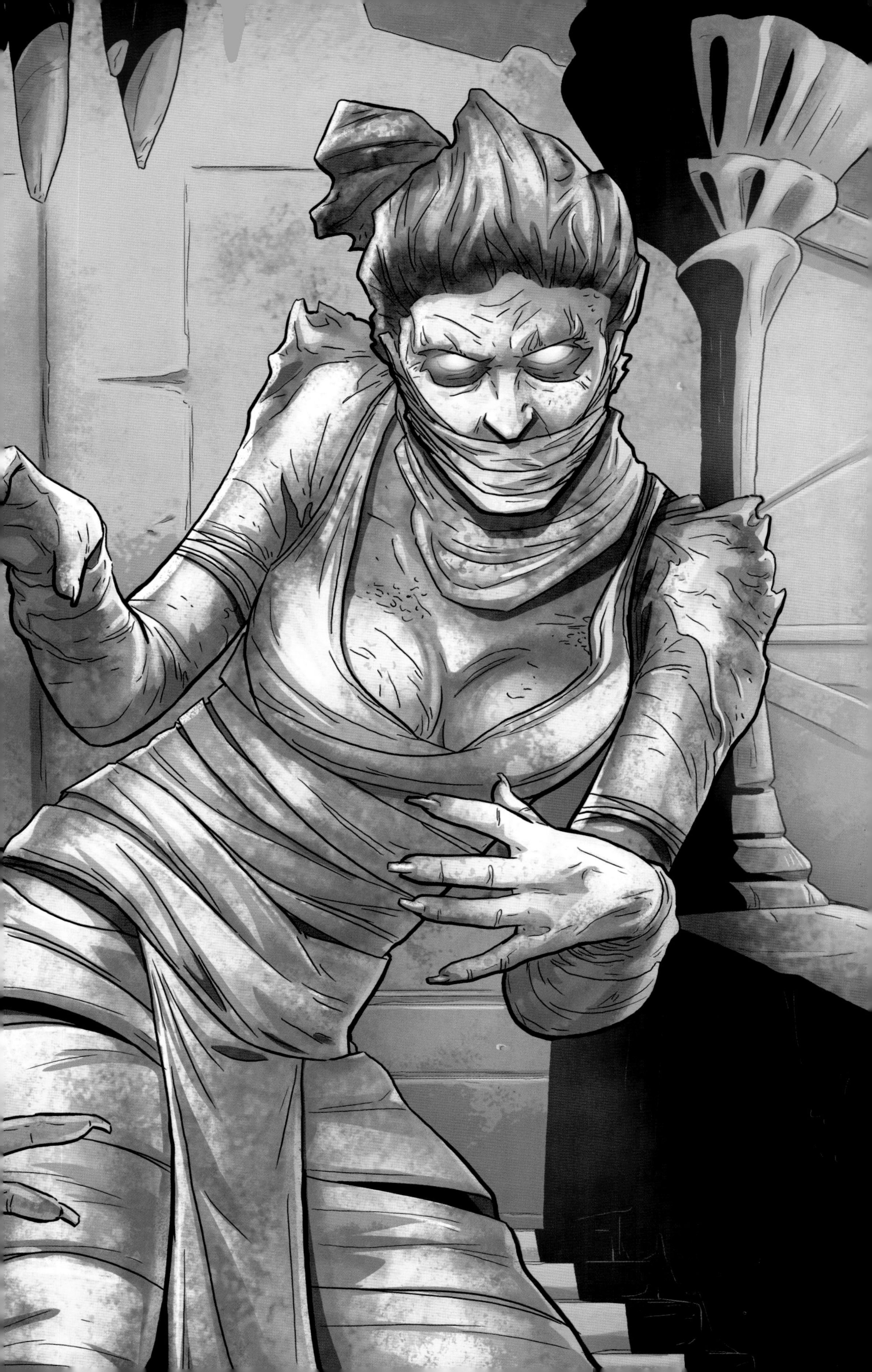

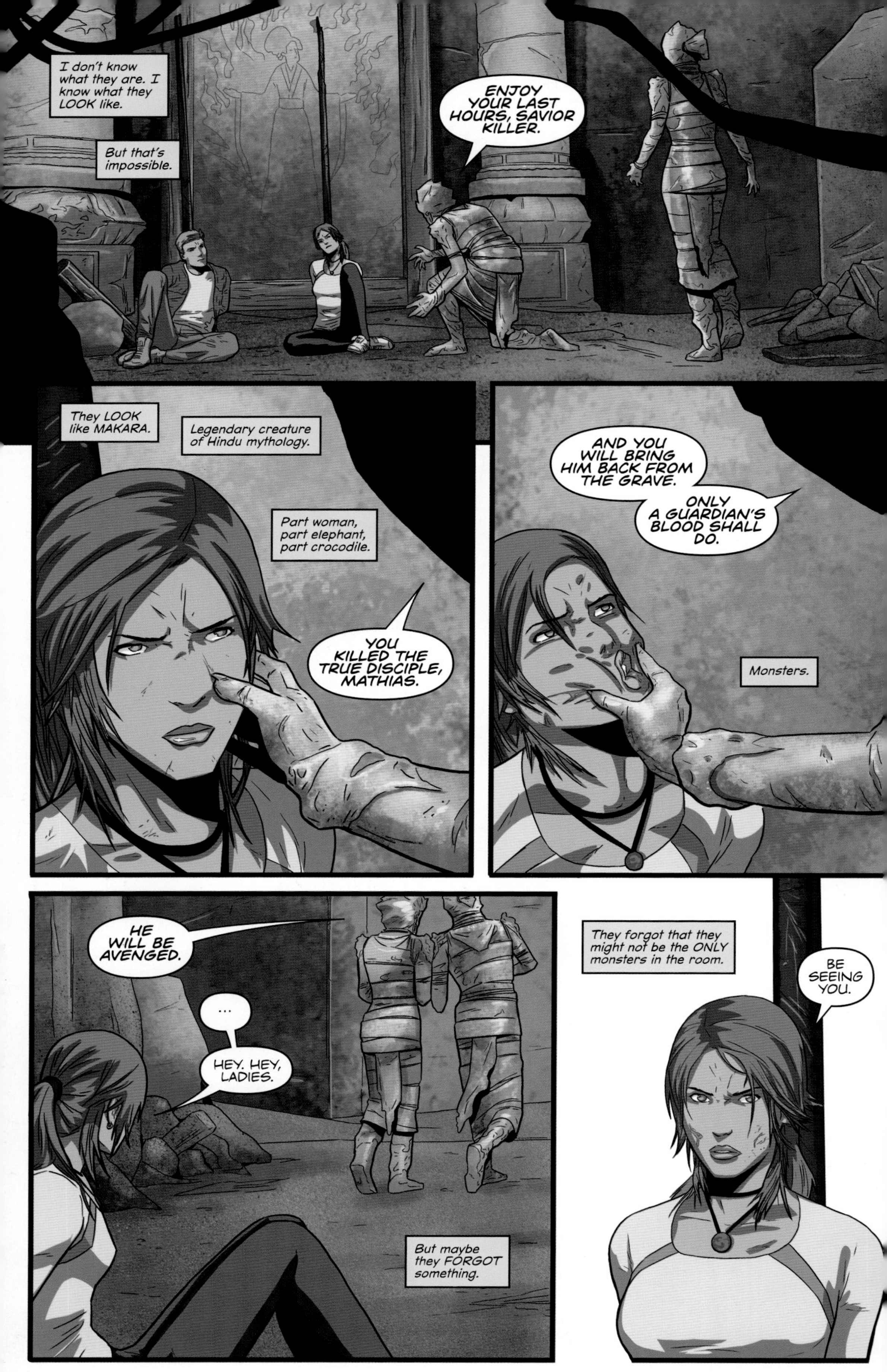
I don't know what they are. I know what they LOOK like.
But that's impossible.
ENJOY YOUR LAST HOURS, SAVIOR KILLER.
They LOOK like MAKARA.
Legendary creature of Hindu mythology.
Part woman, part elephant, part crocodile.
YOU KILLED THE TRUE DISCIPLE, MATHIAS.
AND YOU WILL BRING HIM BACK FROM THE GRAVE.
ONLY A GUARDIAN'S BLOOD SHALL DO.
Monsters.
HE WILL BE AVENGED.
...
HEY. HEY, LADIES.
But maybe they FORGOT something.
They forgot that they might not be the ONLY monsters in the room.
BE SEEING YOU.

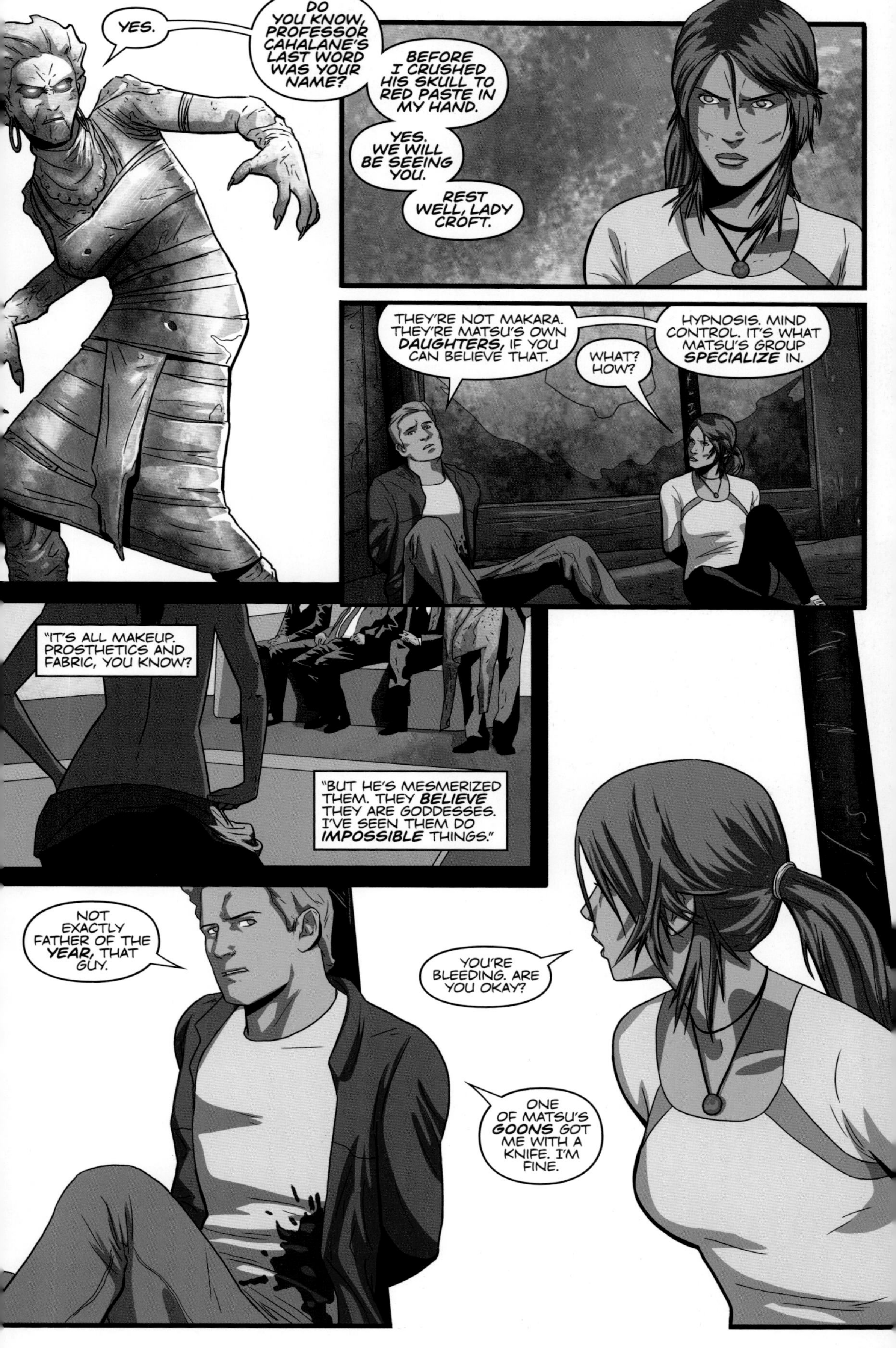
YES.
DO YOU KNOW, PROFESSOR CAHALANE'S LAST WORD WAS YOUR NAME?
BEFORE I CRUSHED HIS SKULL TO RED PASTE IN MY HAND.
YES. WE WILL BE SEEING YOU.
REST WELL, LADY CROFT.
THEY'RE NOT MAKARA. THEY'RE MATSU'S OWN DAUGHTERS, IF YOU CAN BELIEVE THAT.
WHAT? HOW?
HYPNOSIS. MIND CONTROL. IT'S WHAT MATSU'S GROUP SPECIALIZE IN.
"IT'S ALL MAKEUP. PROSTHETICS AND FABRIC, YOU KNOW?
"BUT HE'S MESMERIZED THEM. THEY BELIEVE THEY ARE GODDESSES. I'VE SEEN THEM DO IMPOSSIBLE THINGS."
NOT EXACTLY FATHER OF THE YEAR, THAT GUY.
YOU'RE BLEEDING. ARE YOU OKAY?
ONE OF MATSU'S GOONS GOT ME WITH A KNIFE. I'M FINE.

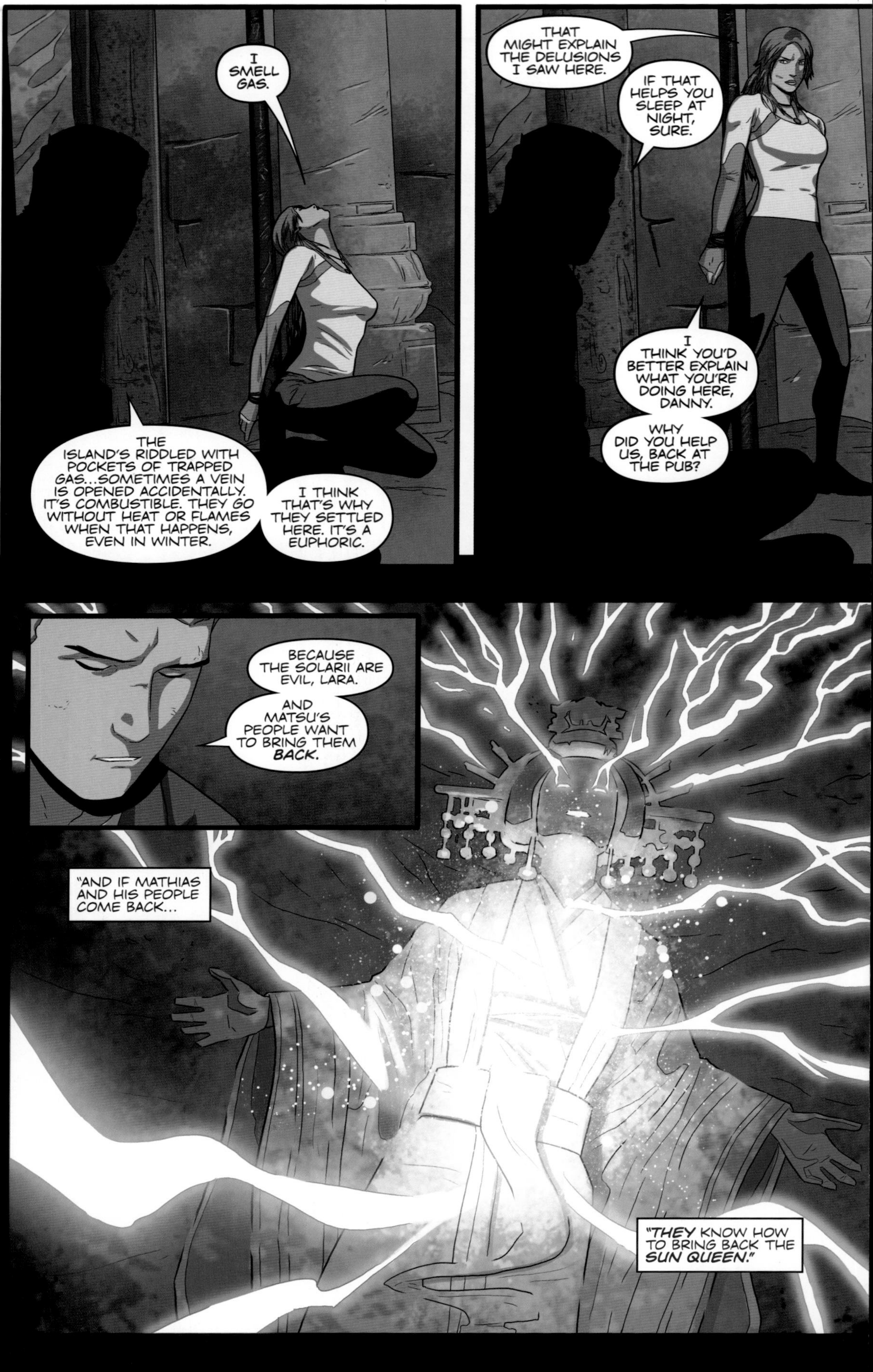
I SMELL GAS.
THE ISLAND'S RIDDLED WITH POCKETS OF TRAPPED GAS...SOMETIMES A VEIN IS OPENED ACCIDENTALLY. IT'S COMBUSTIBLE. THEY GO WITHOUT HEAT OR FLAMES WHEN THAT HAPPENS, EVEN IN WINTER.
I THINK THAT'S WHY THEY SETTLED HERE. IT'S A EUPHORIC.
THAT MIGHT EXPLAIN THE DELUSIONS I SAW HERE.
IF THAT HELPS YOU SLEEP AT NIGHT, SURE.
I THINK YOU'D BETTER EXPLAIN WHAT YOU'RE DOING HERE, DANNY.
WHY DID YOU HELP US, BACK AT THE PUB?
BECAUSE THE SOLARII ARE EVIL, LARA.
AND MATSU'S PEOPLE WANT TO BRING THEM **BACK.**
"AND IF MATHIAS AND HIS PEOPLE COME BACK...
"***THEY*** KNOW HOW TO BRING BACK THE ***SUN QUEEN.***"

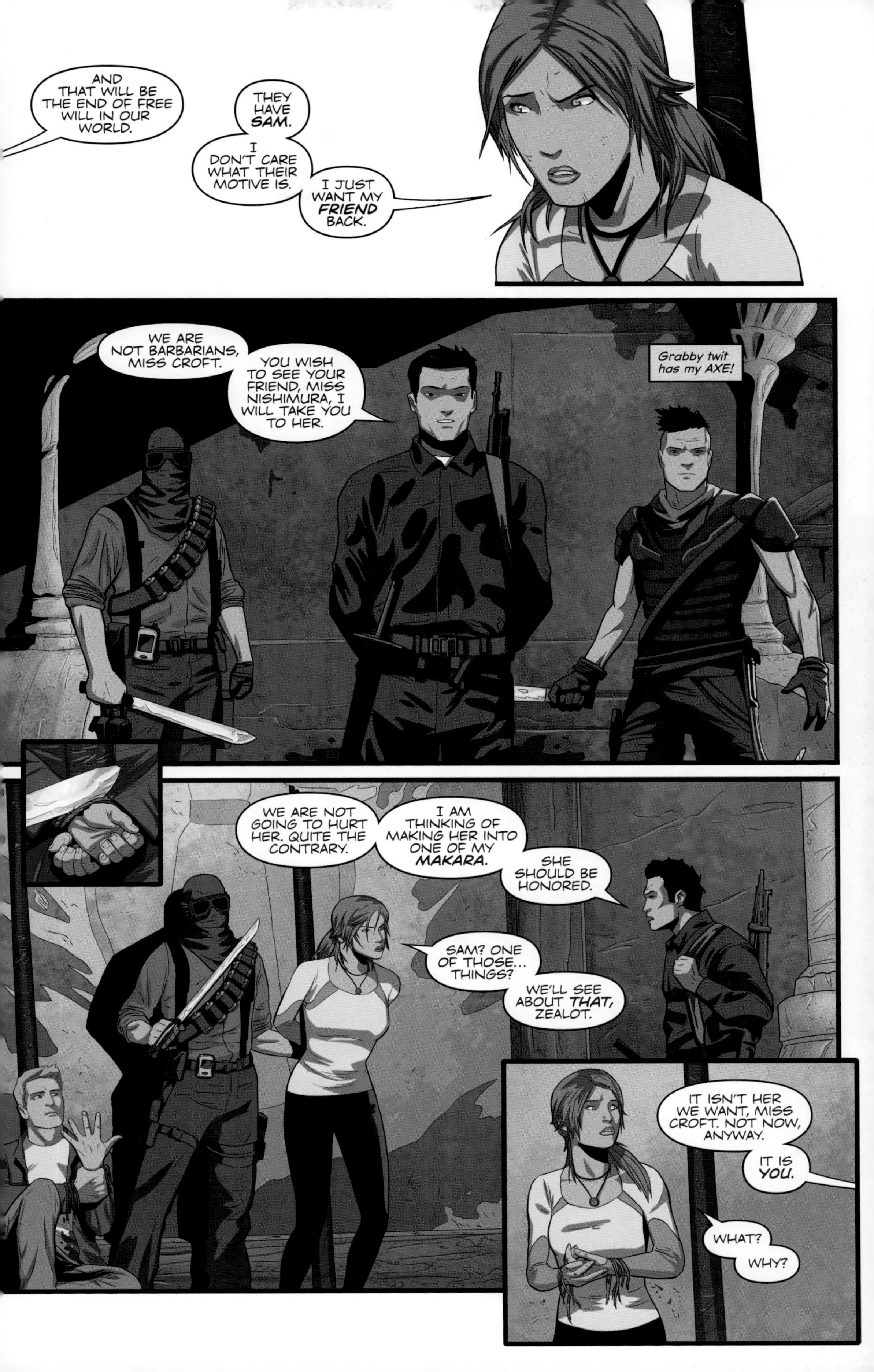

AND THAT WILL BE THE END OF FREE WILL IN OUR WORLD.
THEY HAVE SAM.
I DON'T CARE WHAT THEIR MOTIVE IS.
I JUST WANT MY FRIEND BACK.
WE ARE NOT BARBARIANS, MISS CROFT.
YOU WISH TO SEE YOUR FRIEND, MISS NISHIMURA, I WILL TAKE YOU TO HER.
Grabby twit has my AXE!
WE ARE NOT GOING TO HURT HER. QUITE THE CONTRARY.
I AM THINKING OF MAKING HER INTO ONE OF MY MAKARA.
SHE SHOULD BE HONORED.
SAM? ONE OF THOSE... THINGS?
WE'LL SEE ABOUT THAT, ZEALOT.
IT ISN'T HER WE WANT, MISS CROFT. NOT NOW, ANYWAY.
IT IS YOU.
WHAT?
WHY?

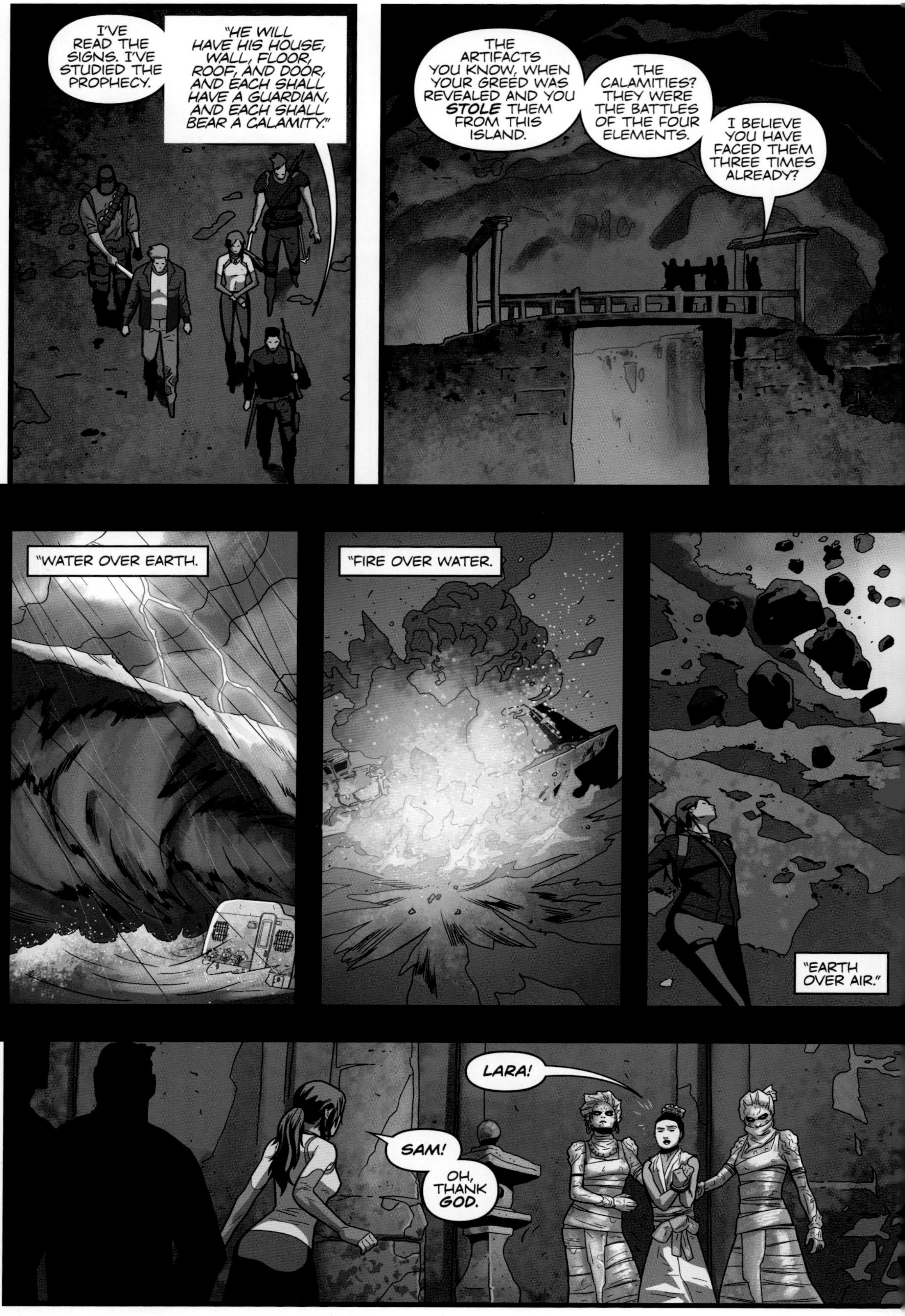
I'VE READ THE SIGNS. I'VE STUDIED THE PROPHECY.
"HE WILL HAVE HIS HOUSE, WALL, FLOOR, ROOF, AND DOOR, AND EACH SHALL HAVE A GUARDIAN, AND EACH SHALL BEAR A CALAMITY."
THE ARTIFACTS YOU KNOW, WHEN YOUR GREED WAS REVEALED AND YOU STOLE THEM FROM THIS ISLAND.
THE CALAMITIES? THEY WERE THE BATTLES OF THE FOUR ELEMENTS.
I BELIEVE YOU HAVE FACED THEM THREE TIMES ALREADY?
"WATER OVER EARTH.
"FIRE OVER WATER.
"EARTH OVER AIR."
LARA!
SAM!
OH, THANK GOD.

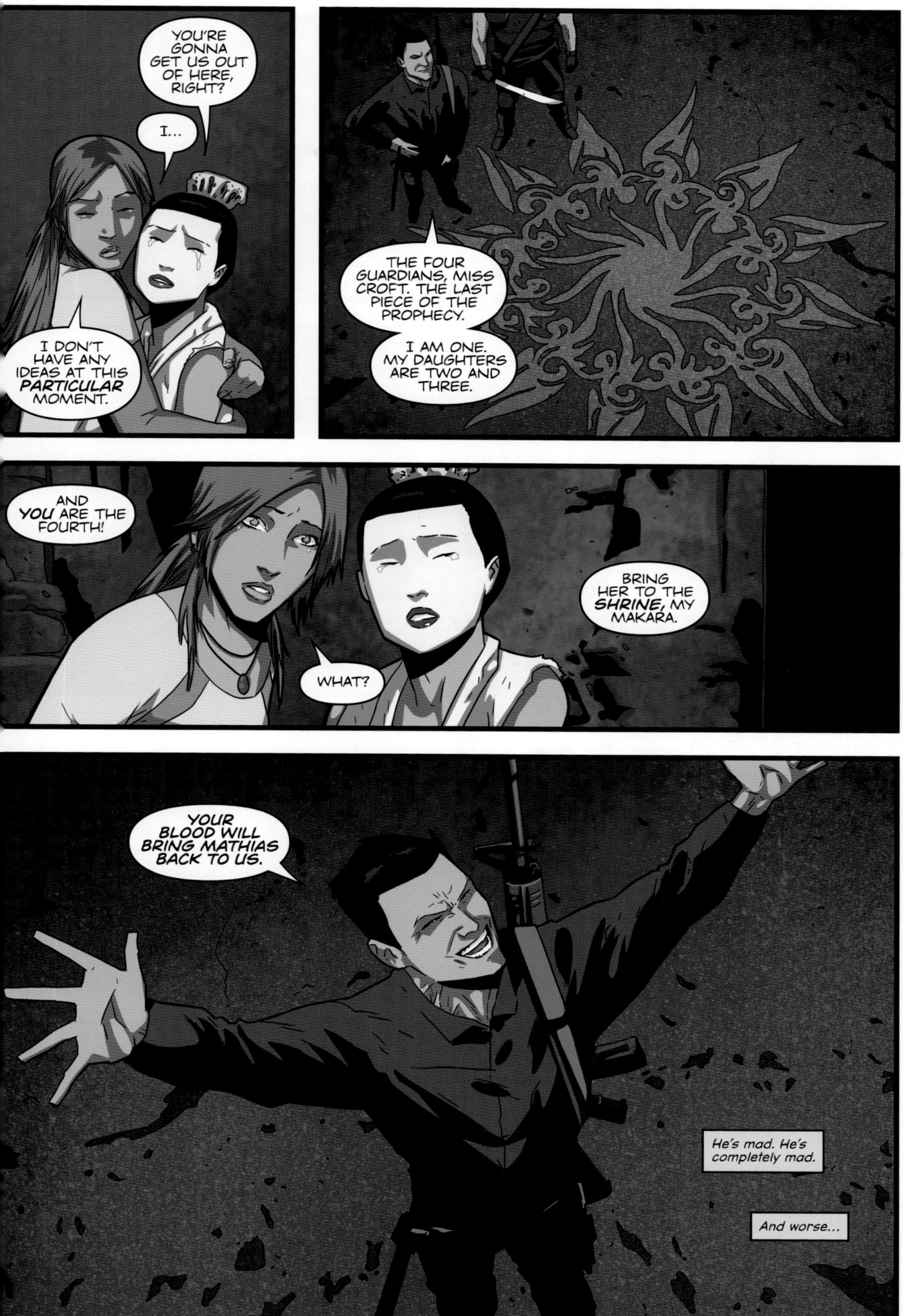
YOU'RE GONNA GET US OUT OF HERE, RIGHT?
I...
I DON'T HAVE ANY IDEAS AT THIS PARTICULAR MOMENT.
THE FOUR GUARDIANS, MISS CROFT. THE LAST PIECE OF THE PROPHECY.
I AM ONE. MY DAUGHTERS ARE TWO AND THREE.
AND YOU ARE THE FOURTH!
WHAT?
BRING HER TO THE SHRINE, MY MAKARA.
YOUR BLOOD WILL BRING MATHIAS BACK TO US.
He's mad. He's completely mad.
And worse...

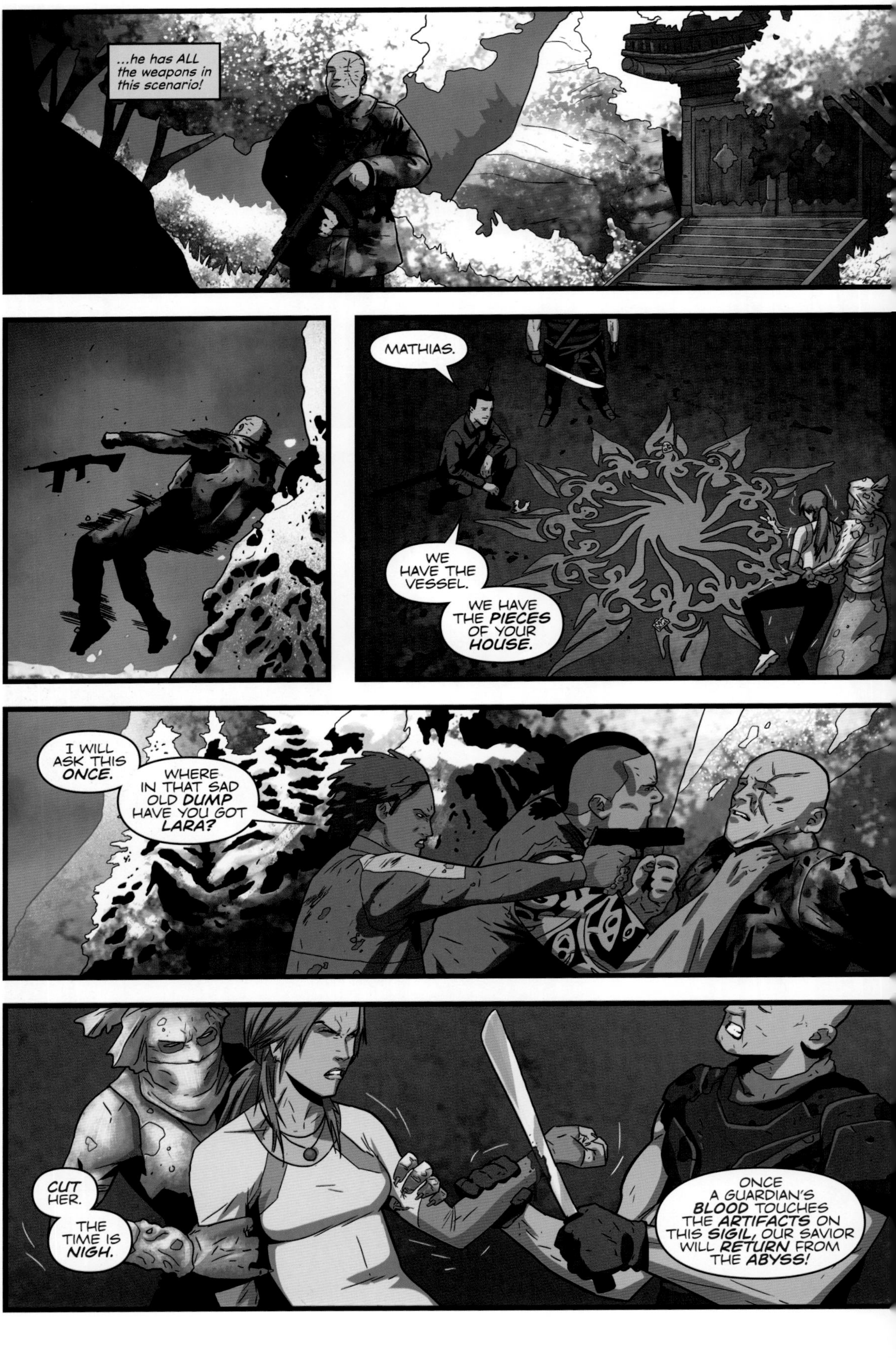
...he has ALL the weapons in this scenario!
MATHIAS.
WE HAVE THE VESSEL.
WE HAVE THE PIECES OF YOUR HOUSE.
I WILL ASK THIS ONCE.
WHERE IN THAT SAD OLD DUMP HAVE YOU GOT LARA?
CUT HER.
THE TIME IS NIGH.
ONCE A GUARDIAN'S BLOOD TOUCHES THE ARTIFACTS ON THIS SIGIL, OUR SAVIOR WILL RETURN FROM THE ABYSS!

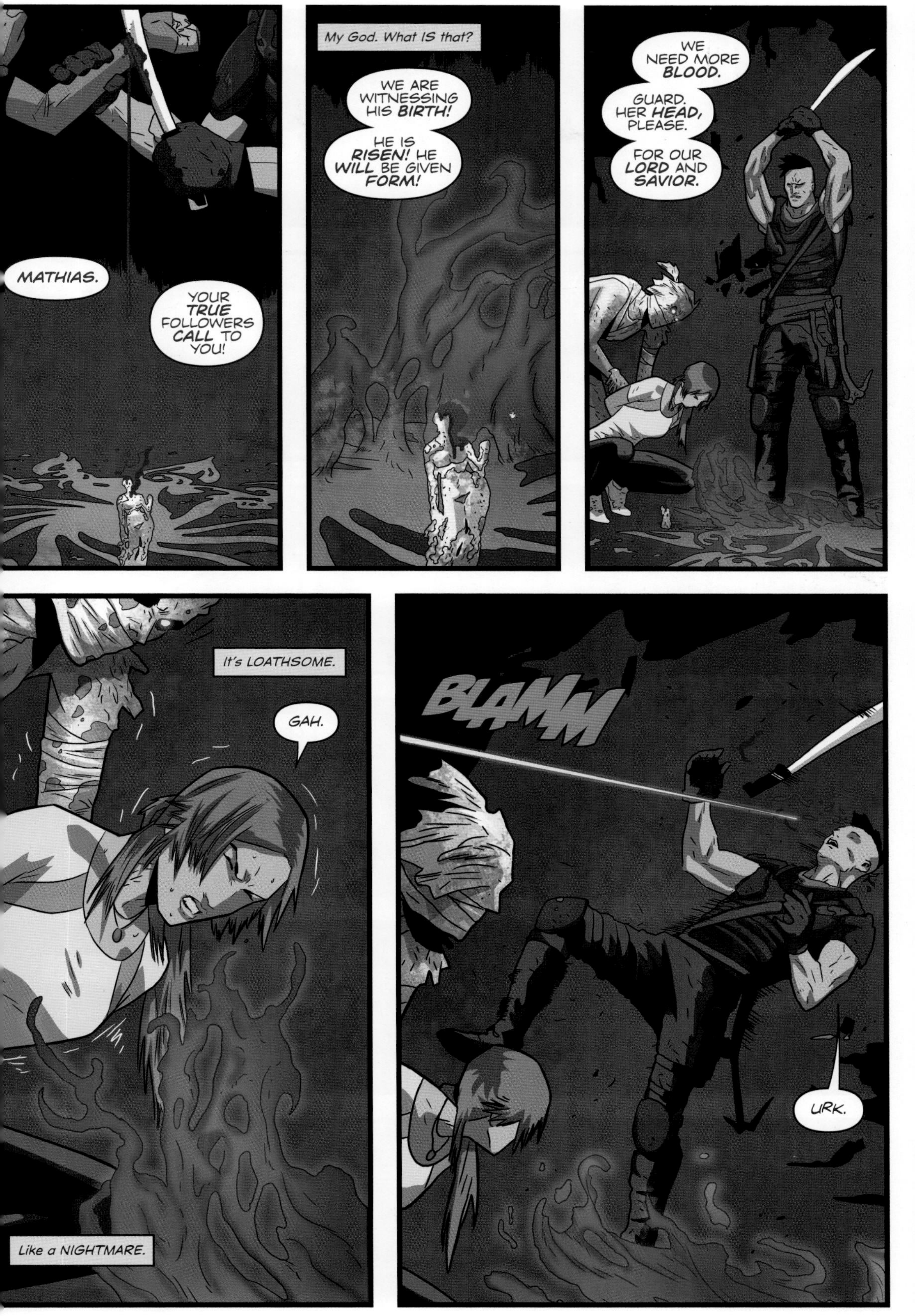
MATHIAS.
YOUR TRUE FOLLOWERS CALL TO YOU!
My God. What IS that?
WE ARE WITNESSING HIS BIRTH!
HE IS RISEN! HE WILL BE GIVEN FORM!
WE NEED MORE BLOOD.
GUARD. HER HEAD, PLEASE.
FOR OUR LORD AND SAVIOR.
It's LOATHSOME.
GAH.
Like a NIGHTMARE.
BLAMM
URK.

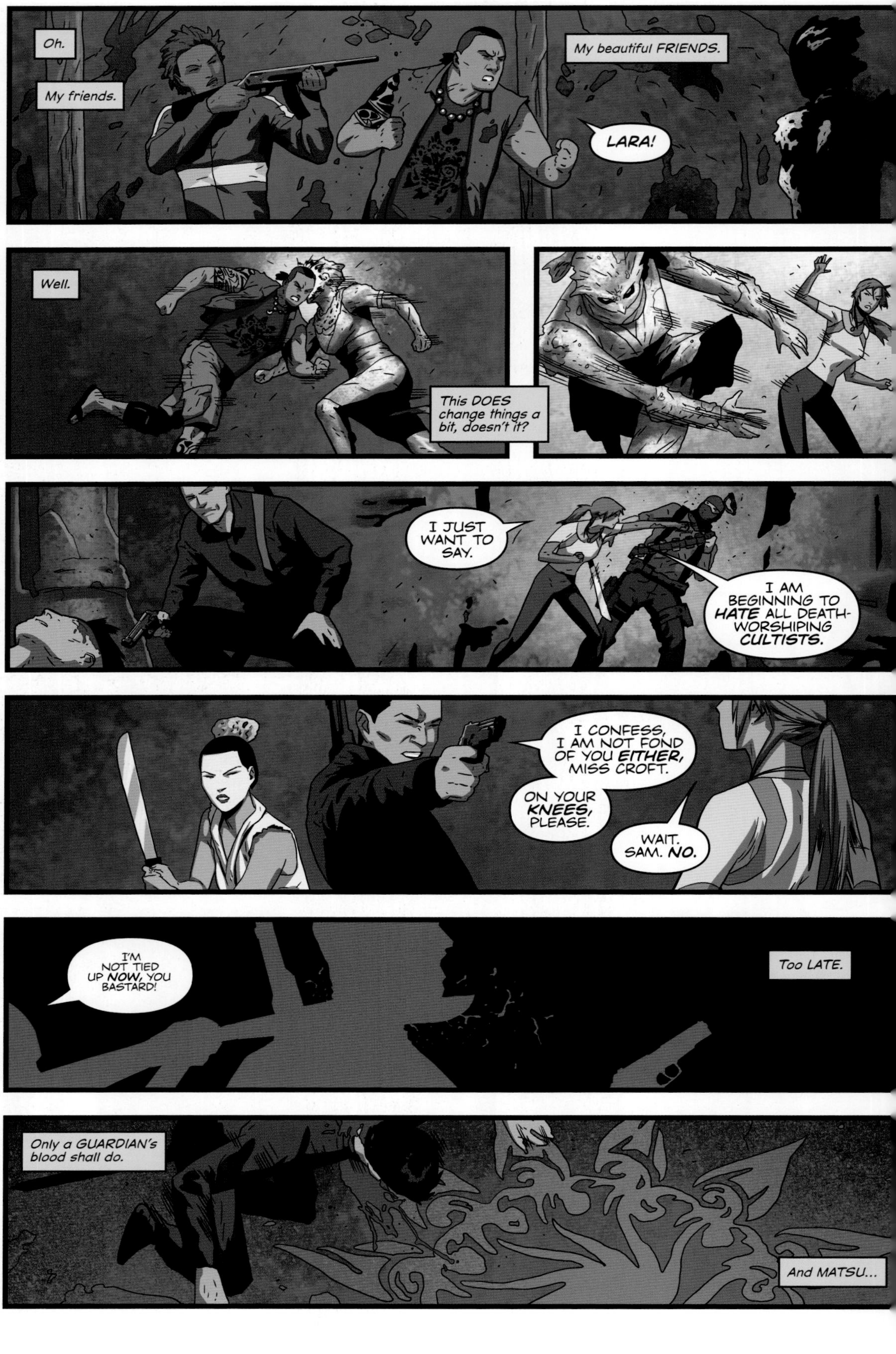
Oh.
My friends.
My beautiful FRIENDS.
LARA!
Well.
This DOES change things a bit, doesn't it?
I JUST WANT TO SAY.
I AM BEGINNING TO HATE ALL DEATH-WORSHIPING CULTISTS.
I CONFESS, I AM NOT FOND OF YOU EITHER, MISS CROFT.
ON YOUR KNEES, PLEASE.
WAIT. SAM. NO.
I'M NOT TIED UP NOW, YOU BASTARD!
Too LATE.
Only a GUARDIAN's blood shall do.
And MATSU...

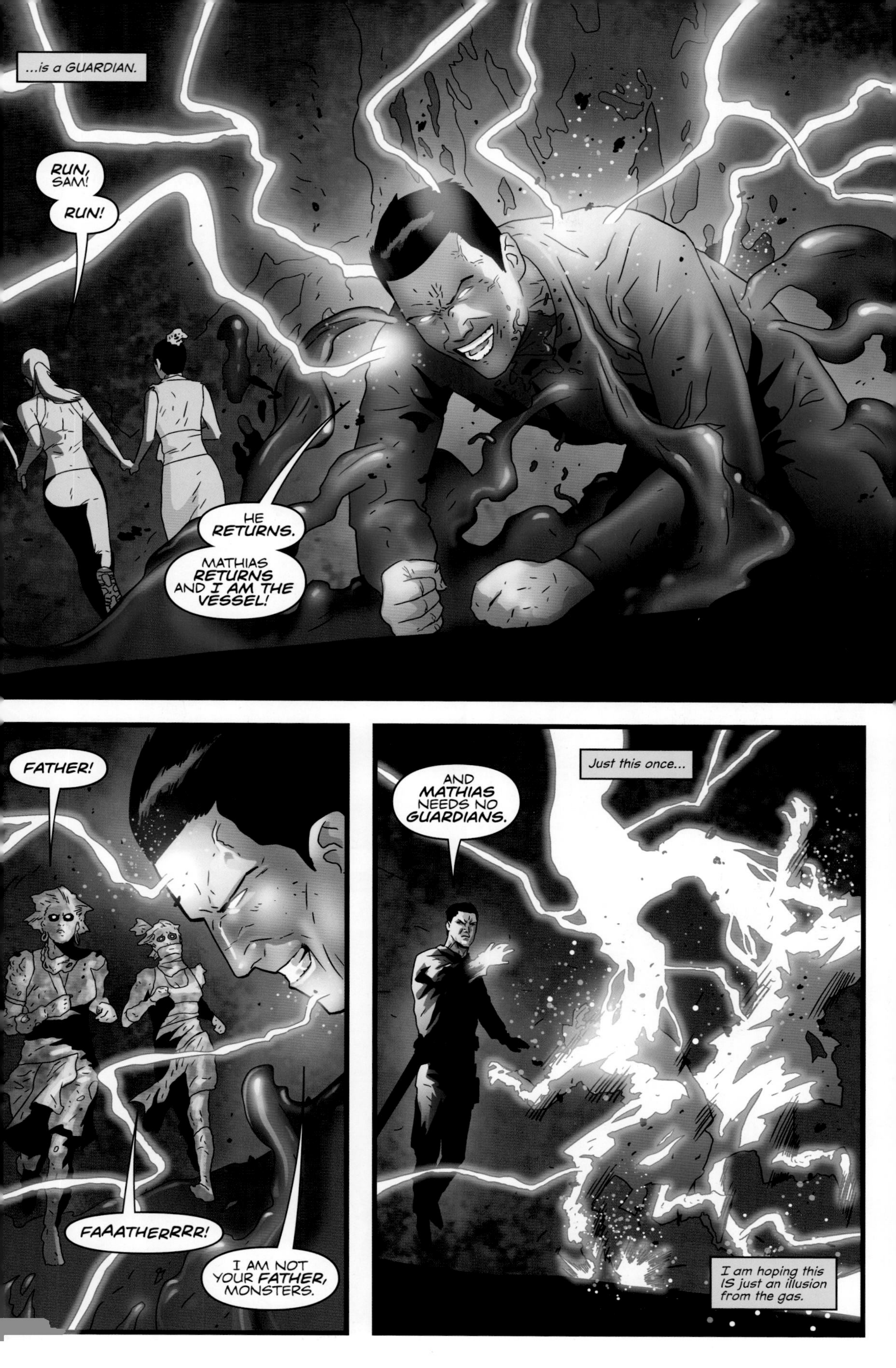
...is a GUARDIAN.
RUN, SAM!
RUN!
HE RETURNS.
MATHIAS RETURNS AND I AM THE VESSEL!
FATHER!
FAAATHERRRR!
I AM NOT YOUR FATHER, MONSTERS.
Just this once...
AND MATHIAS NEEDS NO GUARDIANS.
I am hoping this IS just an illusion from the gas.

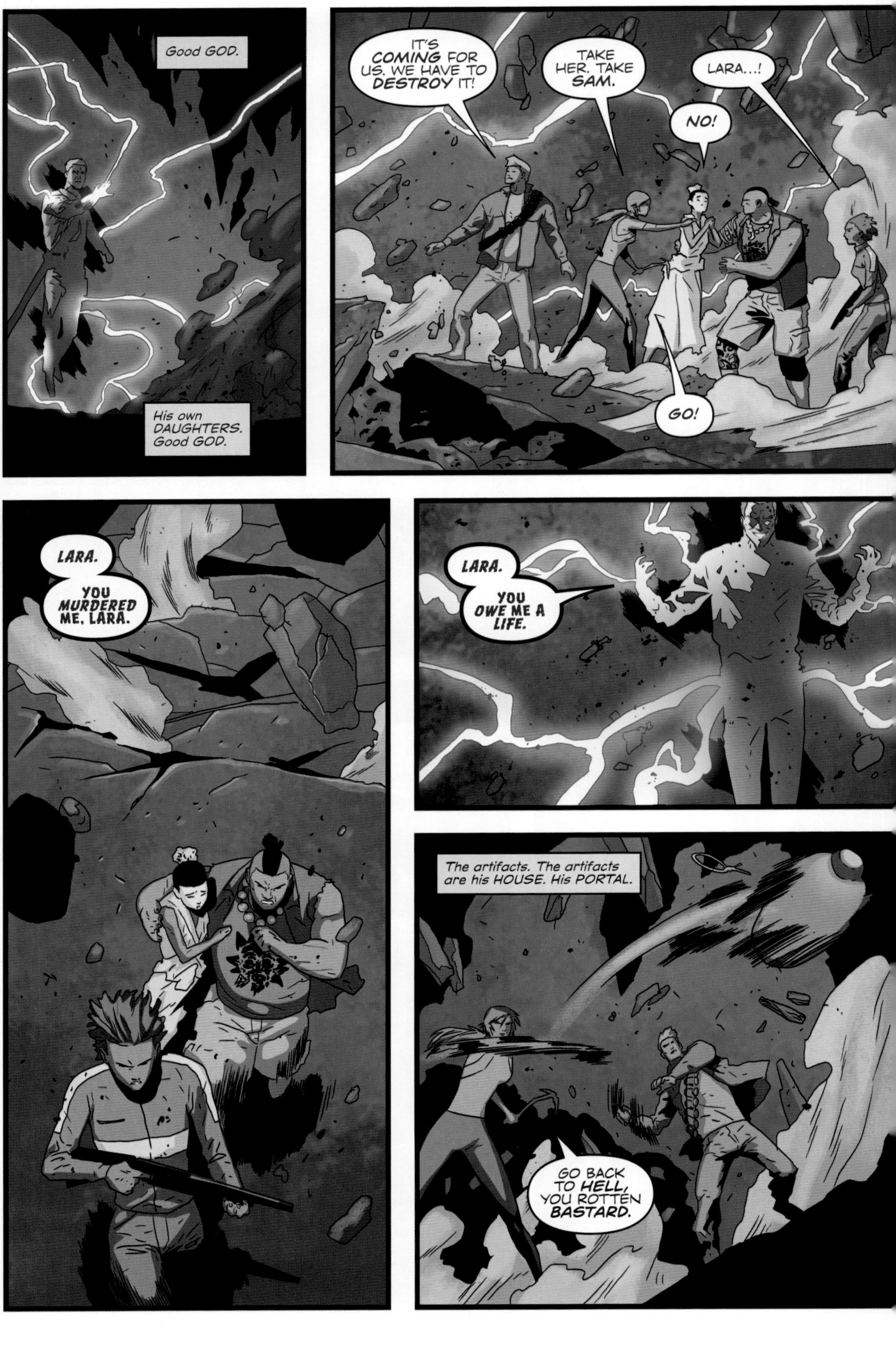
Good GOD.
His own DAUGHTERS. Good GOD.
IT'S COMING FOR US. WE HAVE TO DESTROY IT!
TAKE HER. TAKE SAM.
LARA...!
NO!
GO!
LARA.
YOU MURDERED ME, LARA.
LARA.
YOU OWE ME A LIFE.
The artifacts. The artifacts are his HOUSE. His PORTAL.
GO BACK TO HELL, YOU ROTTEN BASTARD.

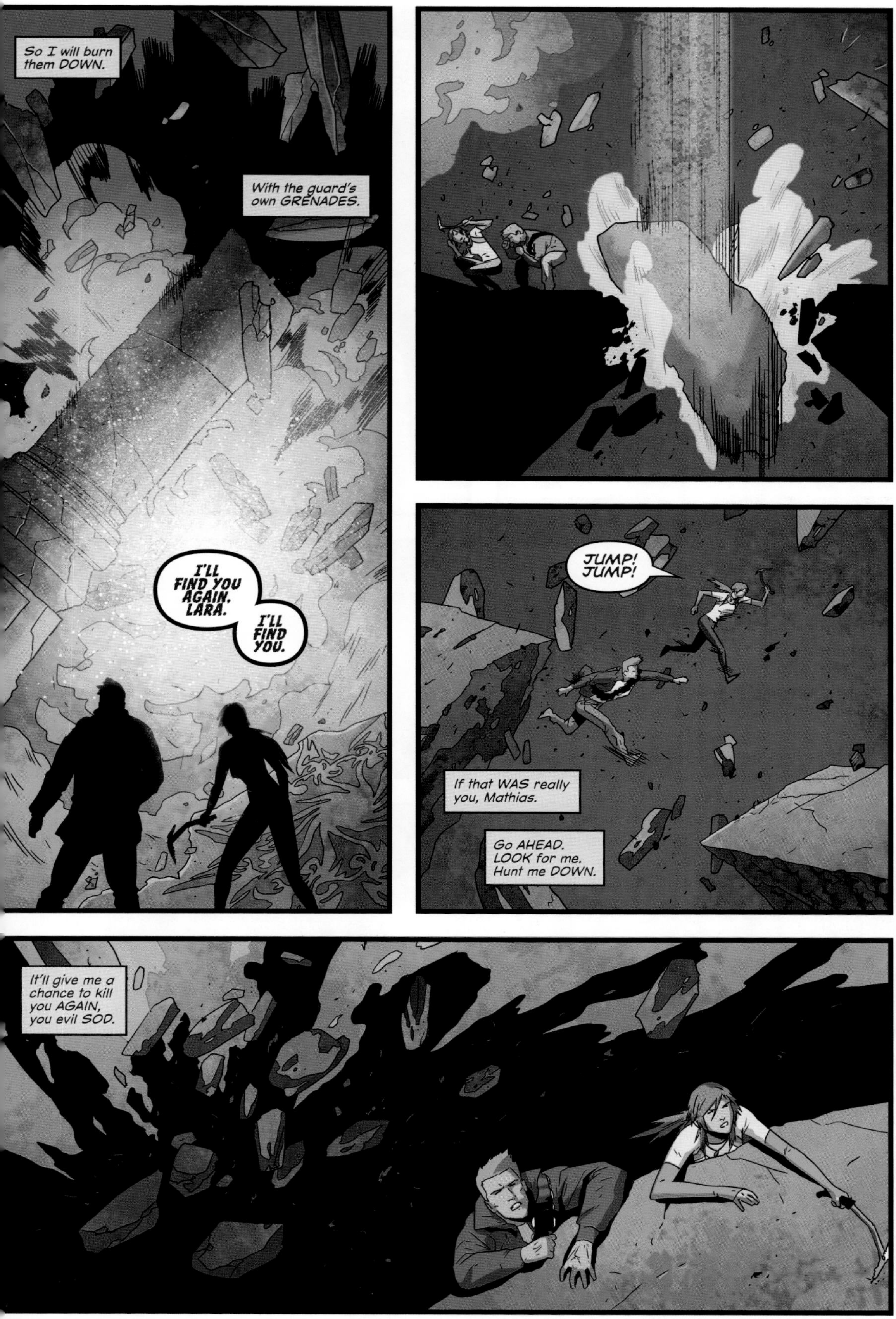
So I will burn them DOWN.
With the guard's own GRENADES.
I'LL FIND YOU AGAIN, LARA.
I'LL FIND YOU.
JUMP! JUMP!
If that WAS really you, Mathias.
Go AHEAD. LOOK for me. Hunt me DOWN.
It'll give me a chance to kill you AGAIN, you evil SOD.

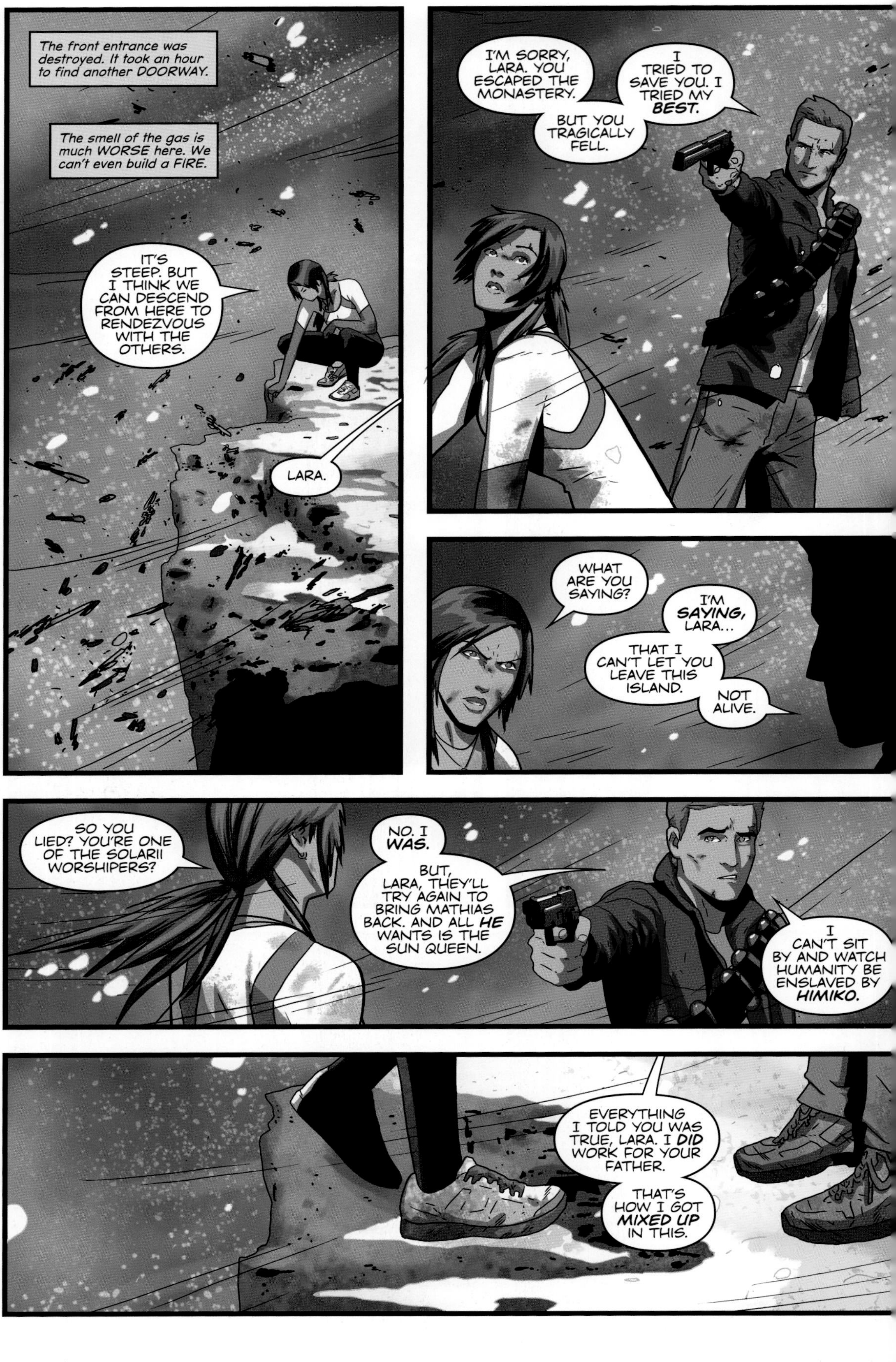
The front entrance was destroyed. It took an hour to find another DOORWAY.
The smell of the gas is much WORSE here. We can't even build a FIRE.
IT'S STEEP. BUT I THINK WE CAN DESCEND FROM HERE TO RENDEZVOUS WITH THE OTHERS.
LARA.
I'M SORRY, LARA. YOU ESCAPED THE MONASTERY.
BUT YOU TRAGICALLY FELL.
I TRIED TO SAVE YOU. I TRIED MY BEST.
WHAT ARE YOU SAYING?
I'M SAYING, LARA...
THAT I CAN'T LET YOU LEAVE THIS ISLAND.
NOT ALIVE.
SO YOU LIED? YOU'RE ONE OF THE SOLARII WORSHIPERS?
NO. I WAS.
BUT, LARA, THEY'LL TRY AGAIN TO BRING MATHIAS BACK. AND ALL HE WANTS IS THE SUN QUEEN.
I CAN'T SIT BY AND WATCH HUMANITY BE ENSLAVED BY HIMIKO.
EVERYTHING I TOLD YOU WAS TRUE, LARA. I DID WORK FOR YOUR FATHER.
THAT'S HOW I GOT MIXED UP IN THIS.

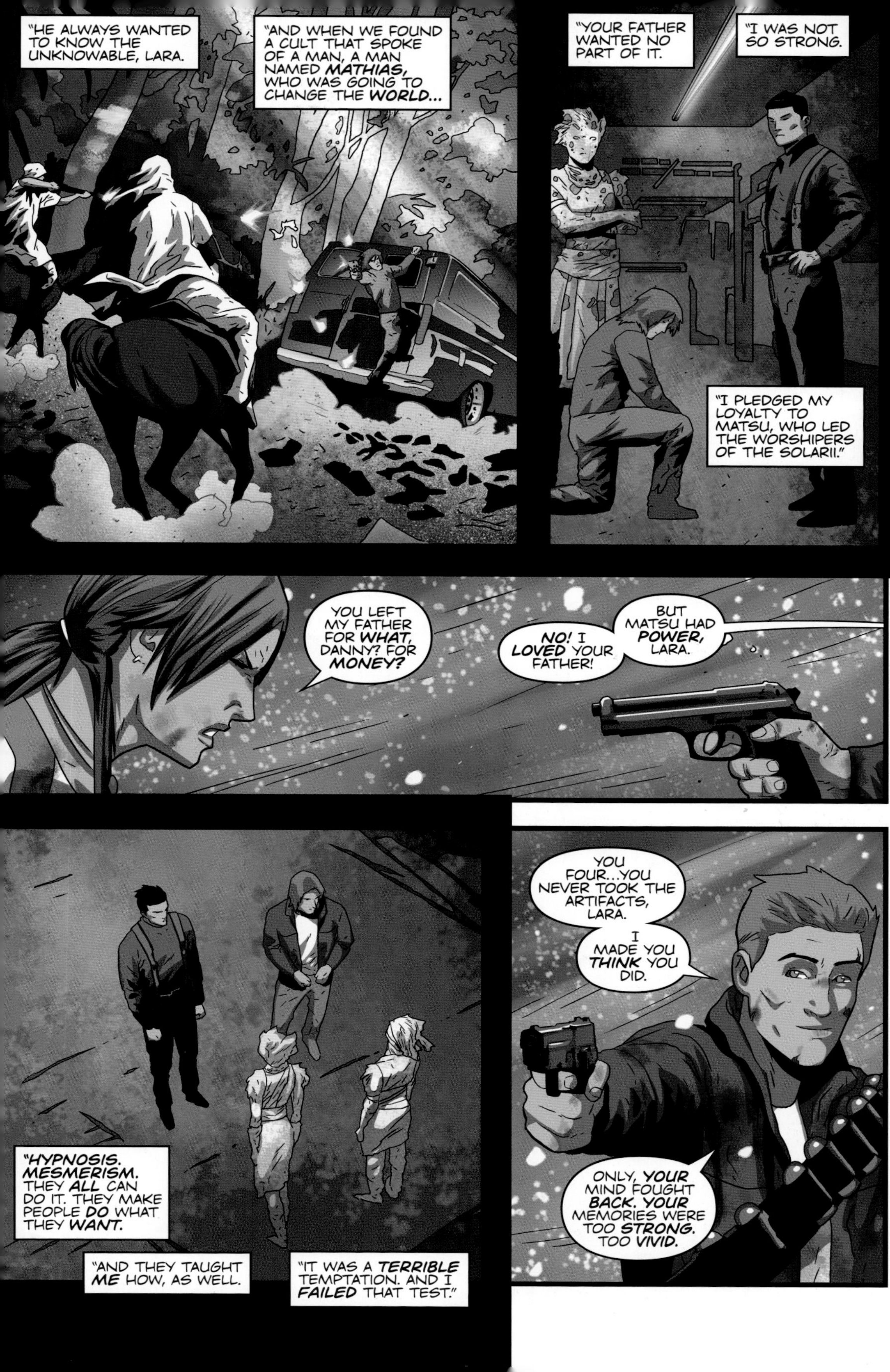
"HE ALWAYS WANTED TO KNOW THE UNKNOWABLE, LARA.
"AND WHEN WE FOUND A CULT THAT SPOKE OF A MAN, A MAN NAMED MATHIAS, WHO WAS GOING TO CHANGE THE WORLD...
"YOUR FATHER WANTED NO PART OF IT.
"I WAS NOT SO STRONG.
"I PLEDGED MY LOYALTY TO MATSU, WHO LED THE WORSHIPERS OF THE SOLARII."
YOU LEFT MY FATHER FOR WHAT, DANNY? FOR MONEY?
NO! I LOVED YOUR FATHER!
BUT MATSU HAD POWER, LARA.
"HYPNOSIS. MESMERISM. THEY ALL CAN DO IT. THEY MAKE PEOPLE DO WHAT THEY WANT.
"AND THEY TAUGHT ME HOW, AS WELL.
"IT WAS A TERRIBLE TEMPTATION. AND I FAILED THAT TEST."
YOU FOUR...YOU NEVER TOOK THE ARTIFACTS, LARA.
I MADE YOU THINK YOU DID.
ONLY, YOUR MIND FOUGHT BACK. YOUR MEMORIES WERE TOO STRONG. TOO VIVID.

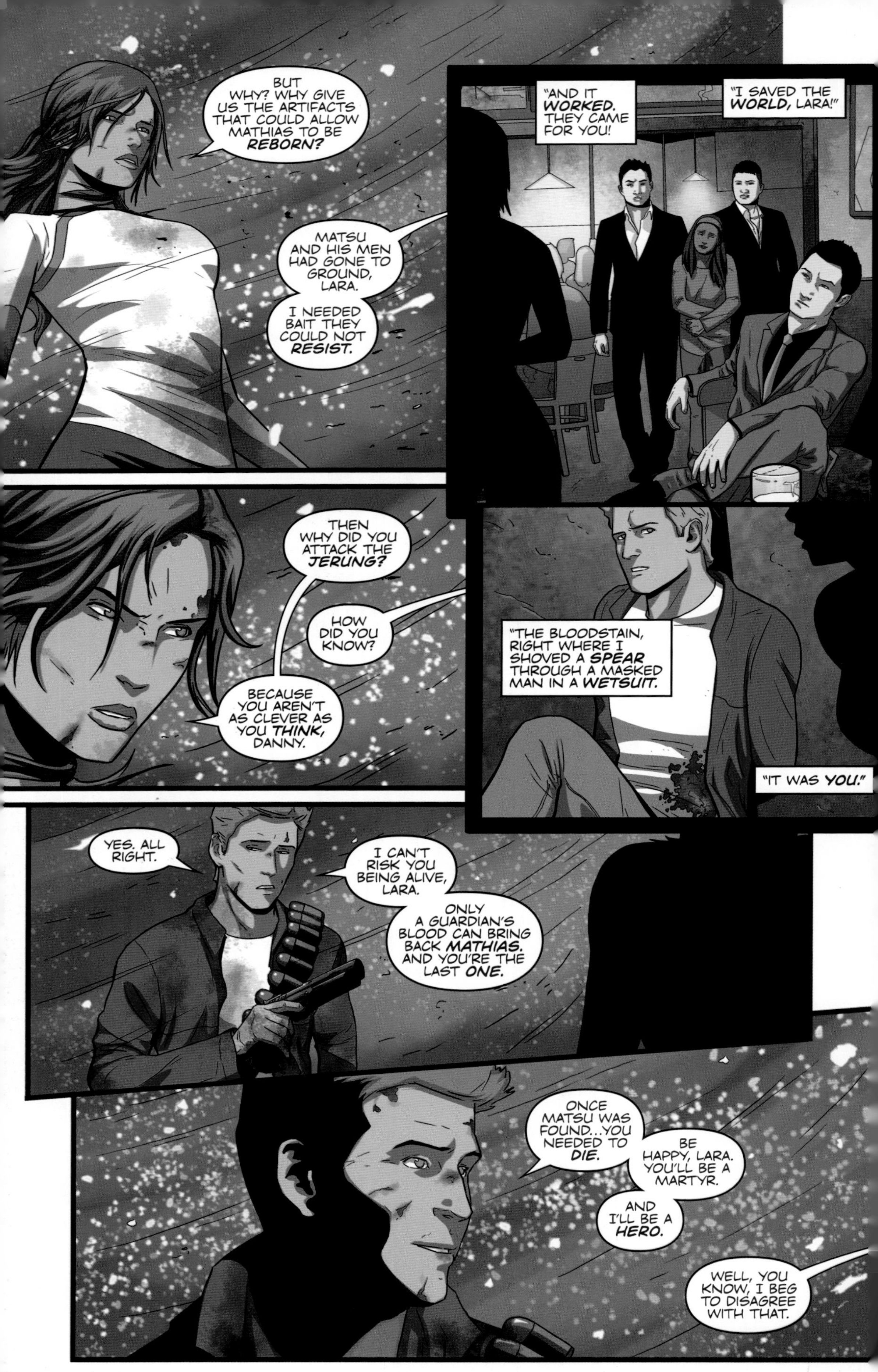
BUT WHY? WHY GIVE US THE ARTIFACTS THAT COULD ALLOW MATHIAS TO BE **REBORN?**
MATSU AND HIS MEN HAD GONE TO GROUND, LARA.
I NEEDED BAIT THEY COULD NOT **RESIST.**
"AND IT **WORKED.** THEY CAME FOR YOU!
"I SAVED THE **WORLD,** LARA!"
THEN WHY DID YOU ATTACK THE **JERUNG?**
HOW DID YOU KNOW?
BECAUSE YOU AREN'T AS CLEVER AS YOU **THINK,** DANNY.
"THE BLOODSTAIN, RIGHT WHERE I SHOVED A **SPEAR** THROUGH A MASKED MAN IN A **WETSUIT.**
"IT WAS **YOU.**"
YES. ALL RIGHT.
I CAN'T RISK YOU BEING ALIVE, LARA.
ONLY A GUARDIAN'S BLOOD CAN BRING BACK **MATHIAS.** AND YOU'RE THE LAST **ONE.**
ONCE MATSU WAS FOUND...YOU NEEDED TO **DIE.**
BE HAPPY, LARA. YOU'LL BE A MARTYR.
AND I'LL BE A **HERO.**
WELL, YOU KNOW, I BEG TO DISAGREE WITH THAT.

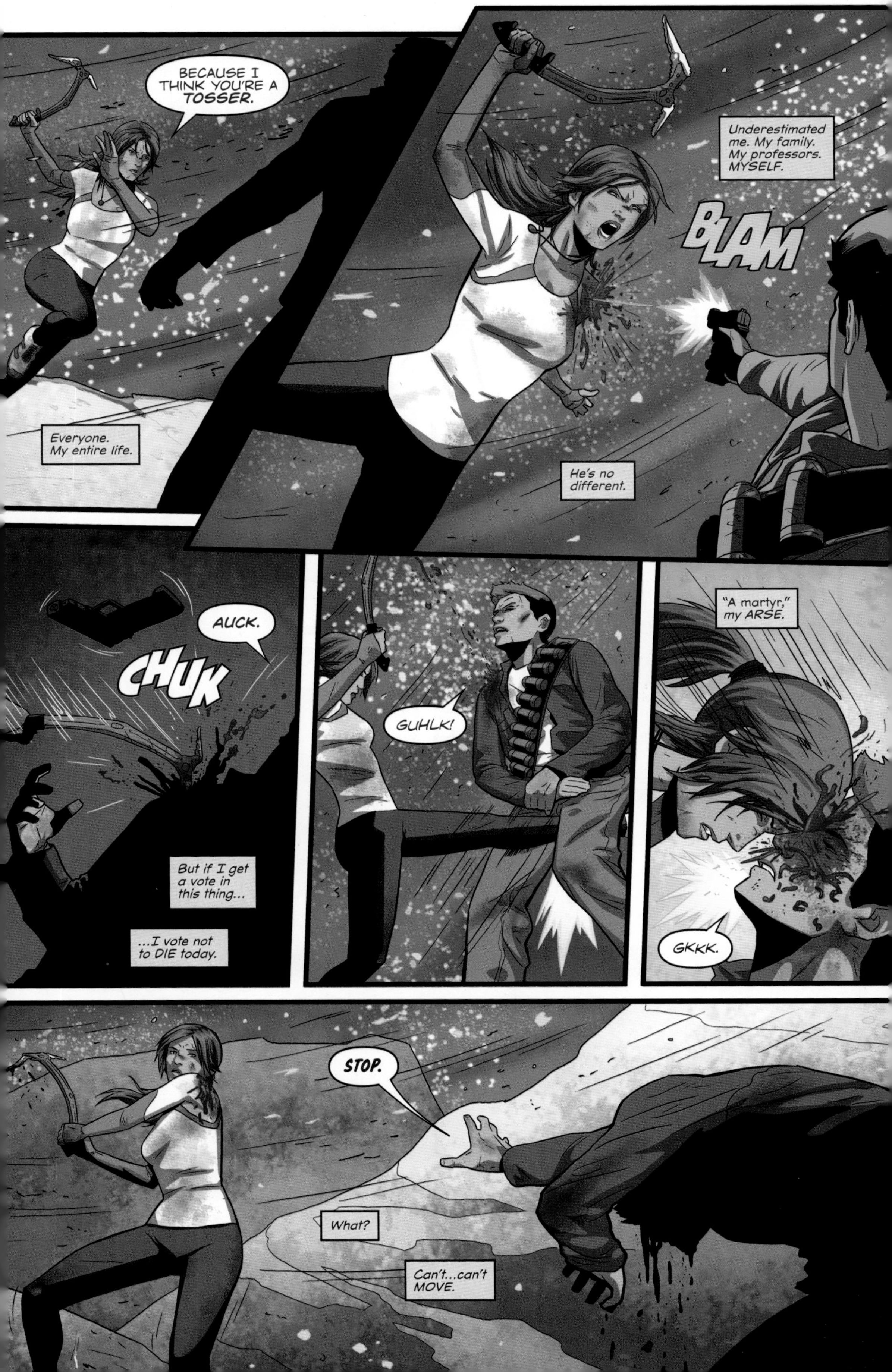
BECAUSE I THINK YOU'RE A TOSSER.
Everyone. My entire life.
Underestimated me. My family. My professors. MYSELF.
BLAM
He's no different.
AUCK.
CHUK
But if I get a vote in this thing...
...I vote not to DIE today.
GUHLK!
"A martyr," my ARSE.
GKKK.
STOP.
What?
Can't...can't MOVE.

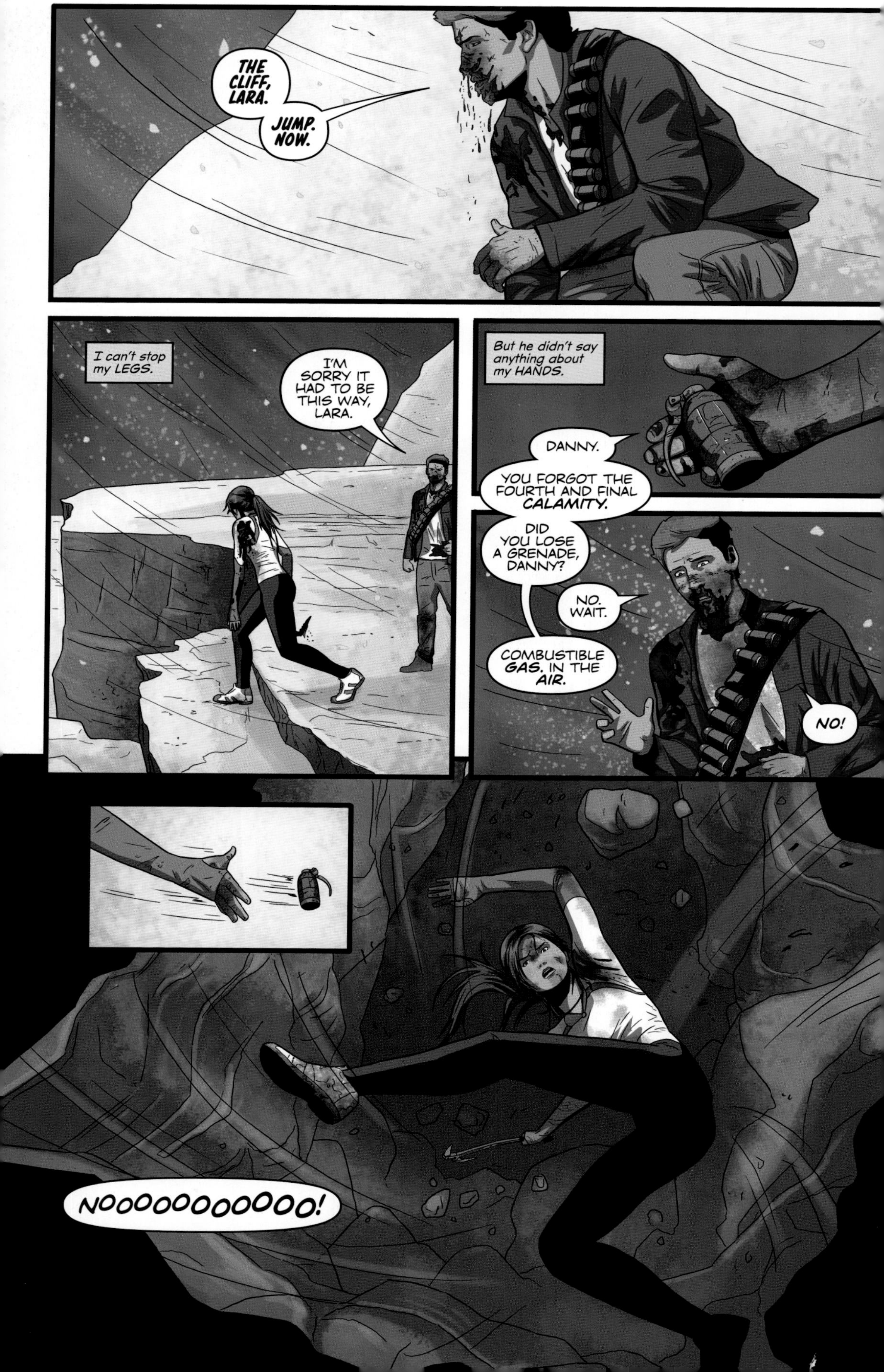
THE CLIFF, LARA.
JUMP. NOW.
I can't stop my LEGS.
I'M SORRY IT HAD TO BE THIS WAY, LARA.
But he didn't say anything about my HANDS.
DANNY.
YOU FORGOT THE FOURTH AND FINAL CALAMITY.
DID YOU LOSE A GRENADE, DANNY?
NO. WAIT.
COMBUSTIBLE GAS. IN THE AIR.
NO!
NOOOOOOOOOO!

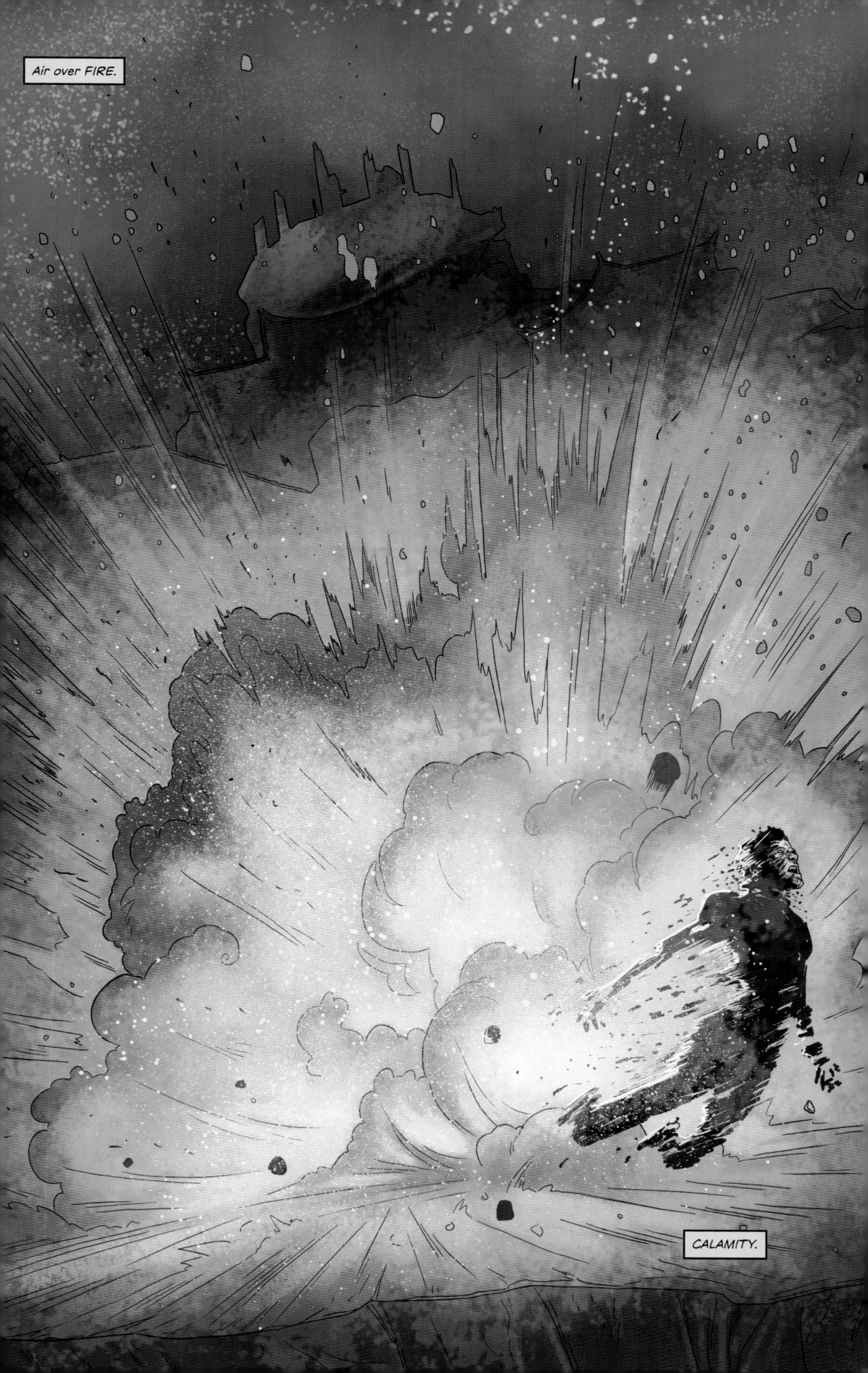
Air over FIRE.
CALAMITY.

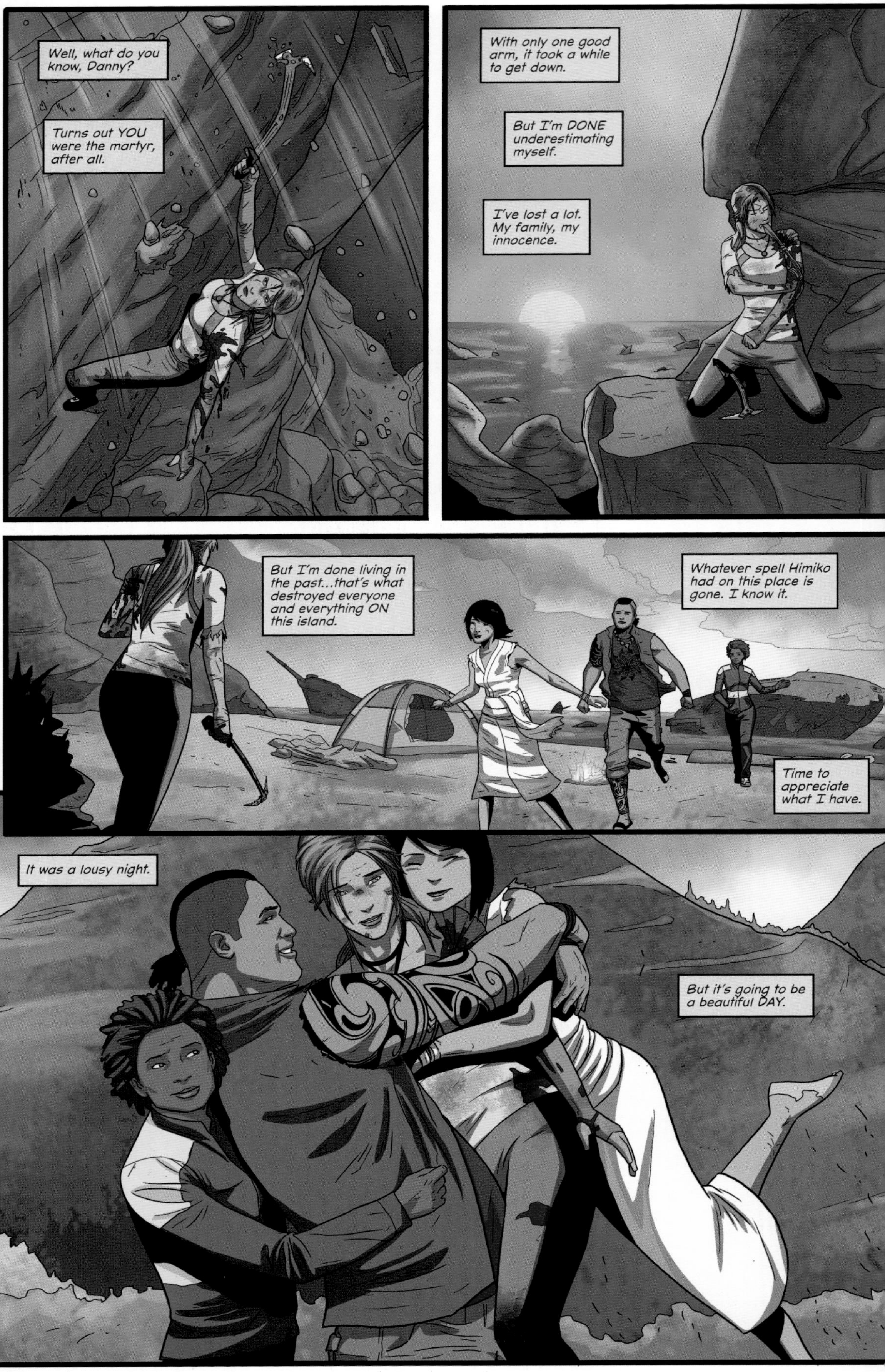
Well, what do you know, Danny?
Turns out YOU were the martyr, after all.
With only one good arm, it took a while to get down.
But I'm DONE underestimating myself.
I've lost a lot. My family, my innocence.
But I'm done living in the past...that's what destroyed everyone and everything ON this island.
Whatever spell Himiko had on this place is gone. I know it.
Time to appreciate what I have.
It was a lousy night.
But it's going to be a beautiful DAY.

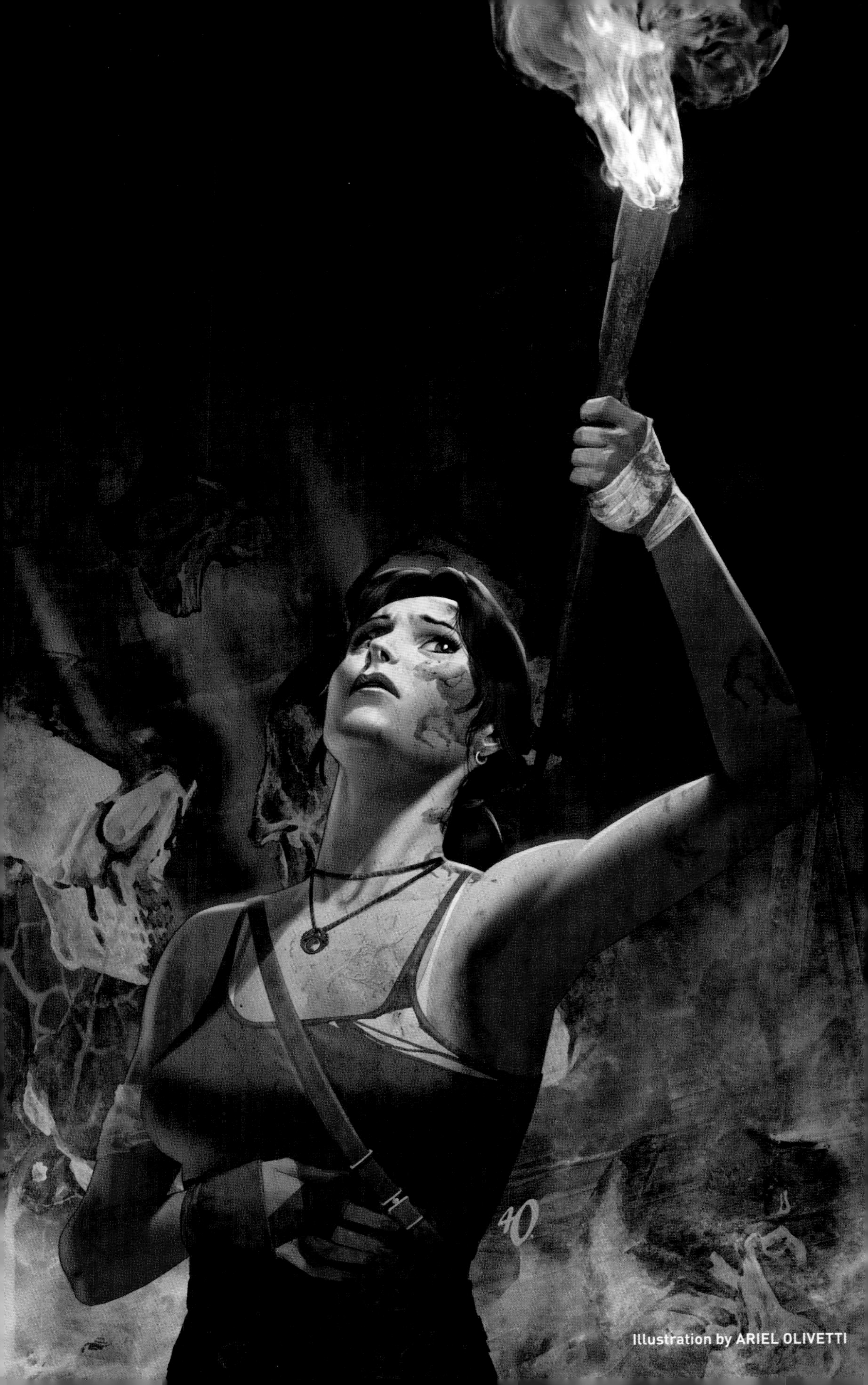

Illustration by ARIEL OLIVETTI

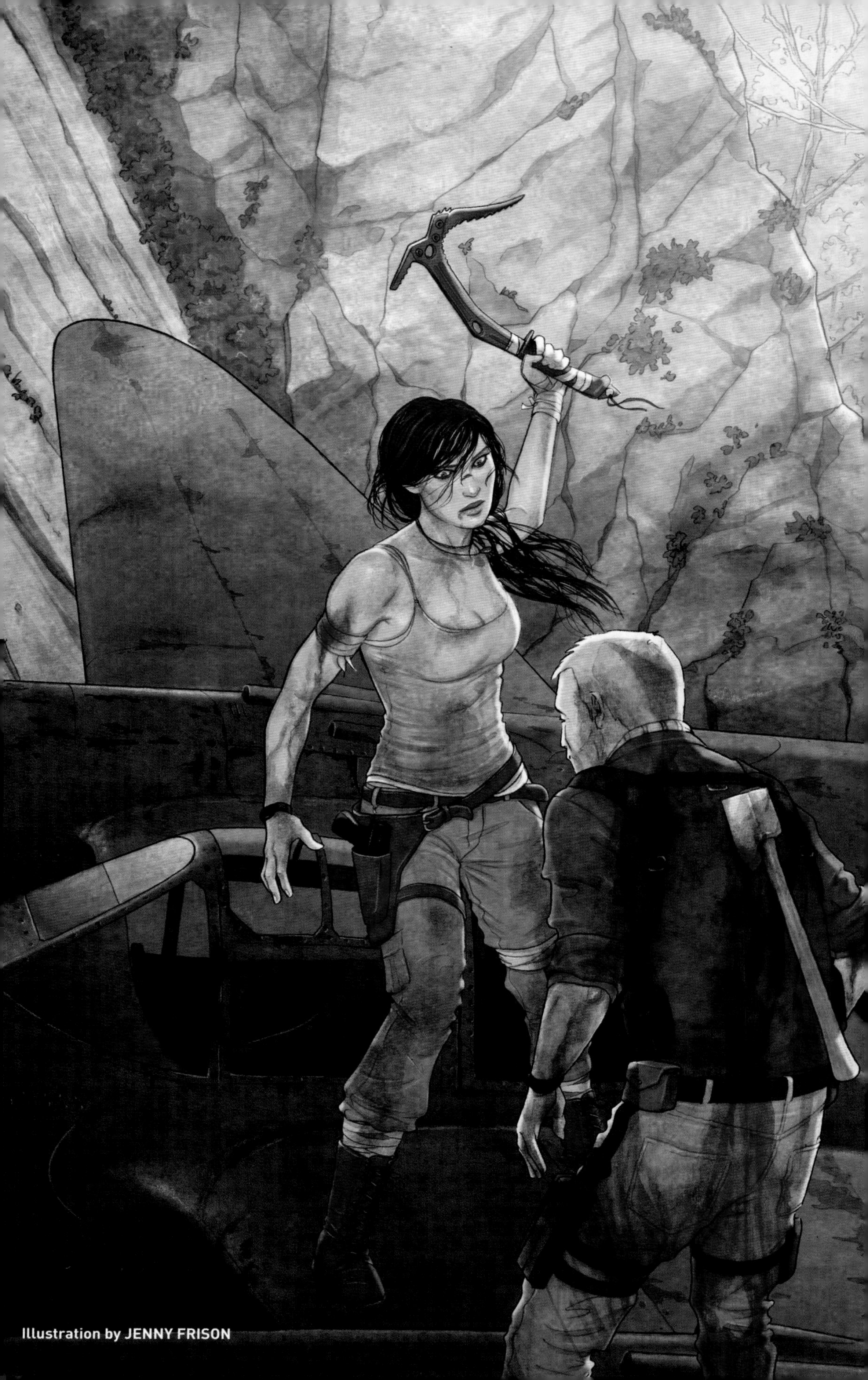

Illustration by JENNY FRISON

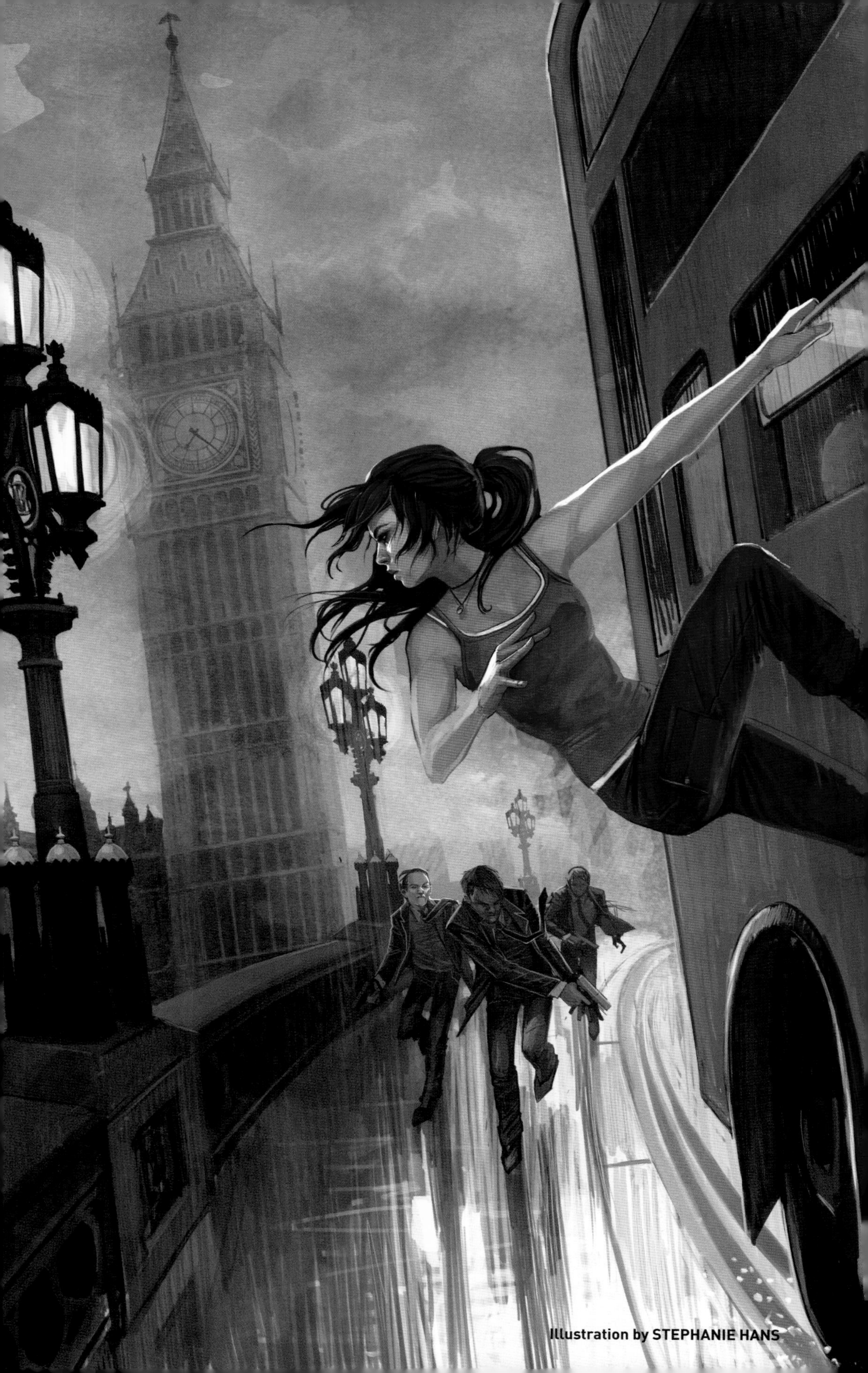

Illustration by STEPHANIE HANS

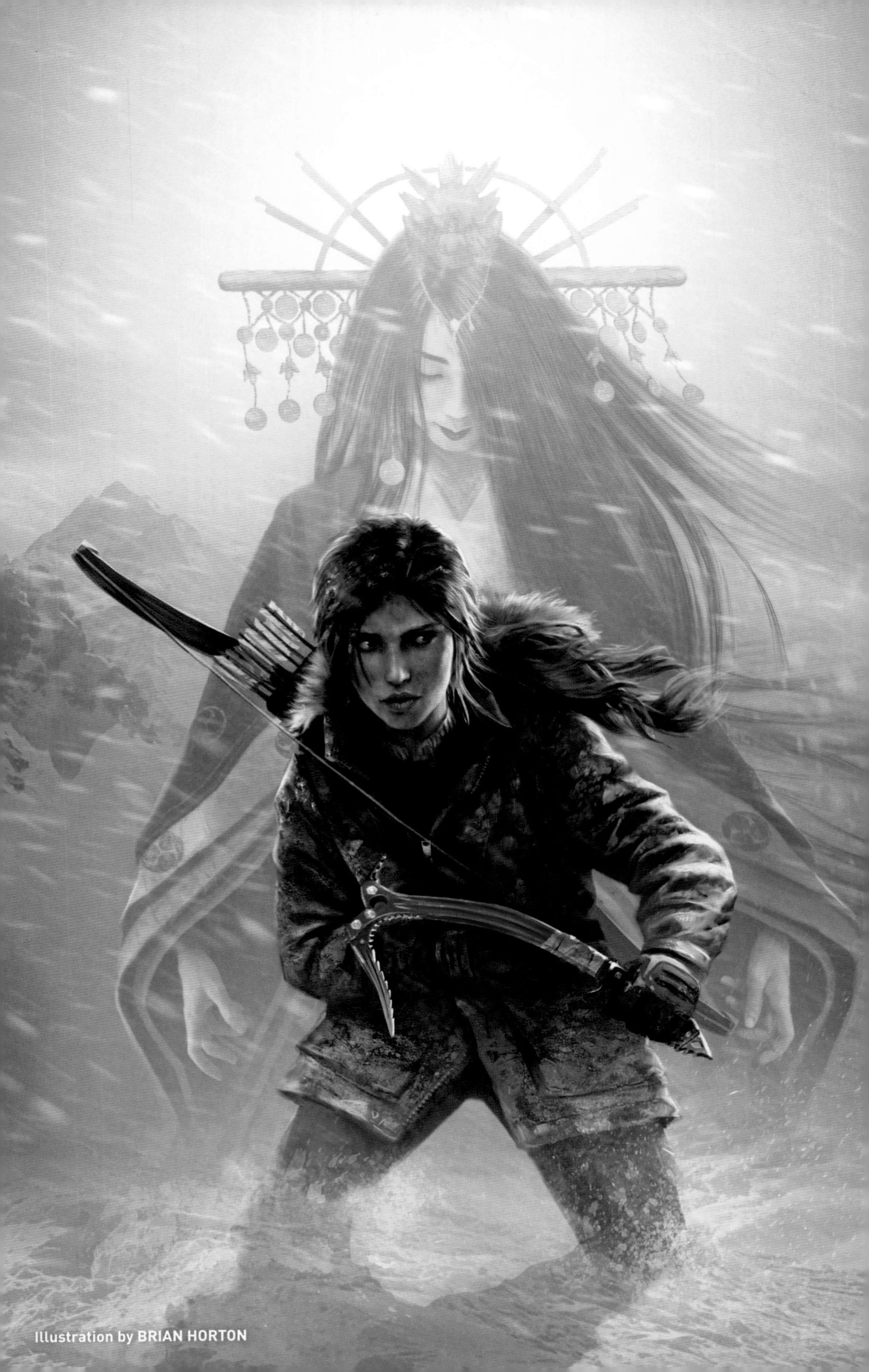

Illustration by BRIAN HORTON

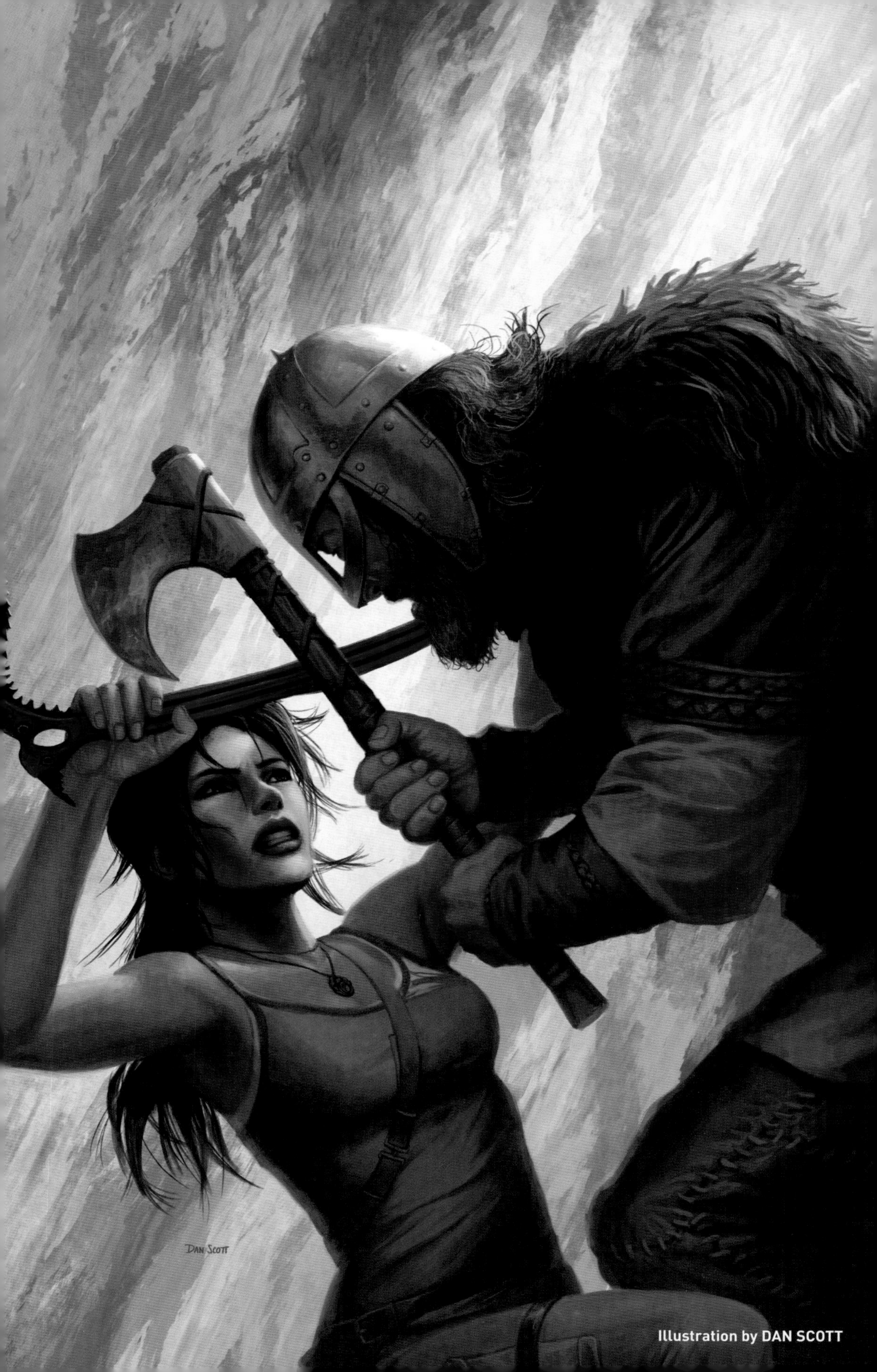
DAN SCOTT

Illustration by DAN SCOTT